THE LAUGH OF LOST MEN

by the same author

The Jerusalem Guide (with Diane Shalem and Giora Shamis)
Cork (with Eiléan Ní Chuilleanáin)
Voices from Stones (with Myrna Haugaard)
Dublin Ninety Drawings
West of West
Dublin Bay
Dublin Drawn and Quartered
The Blue Guide to Ireland
Archaeology and Biblical Interpretation (contributor)
Dublin and Ireland

print portfolios
The Jerusalem Folio
Kilkenny: City and Topography
The Myth of Icarus

THE LAUGH OF LOST MEN

An Irish Journey

BRIAN LALOR

With 16 woodcuts by the author and
photographs by Allegra Duvica Lalor

MAINSTREAM
PUBLISHING

EDINBURGH AND LONDON

First published in Great Britain in 1997 by
MAINSTREAM PUBLISHING COMPANY (EDINBURGH) LTD
7 Albany Street
Edinburgh EH1 3UG

ISBN 1 85158 858 2

A catalogue record for this book is available from the British Library

Designed by Jenny Haig
Typeset in Centaur
Printed and bound in Great Britain by Butler and Tanner Ltd, Frome

For Marco and Patricia Haugaard

'As we advance to make our bow, you will look in vain for signs of servility, or for any evidence of a desire to please. We are an arrogant and depraved body of men. We are proud as bantams and vain as peacocks. A sardonic laugh escapes us as we bow, cruel and cynical hounds that we are. It is a terrible laugh, the laugh of lost men.'

Flann O'Brien, *Blather*

'To asperse a sunset in these days is a political indiscretion; and equally so, to praise it, if there happens to be a cement factory in the foreground that ought to be praised instead. Somebody must trespass on the taboos of modern nationalism, in the interests of human reason. Business can't. Diplomacy won't. It has to be people like us.'

Robert Byron, *The Road to Oxiana*

Contents

ACKNOWLEDGEMENTS

I would like to thank all those who helped me in any way during my work on this book: Noelle Campbell-Sharpe and the staff of the Cill Rialaig Project, Ballinskelligs; Bernard and Mary Loughlin and the Tyrone Guthrie Centre, Annaghmakerrig; David Rose, director of the Oscar Wilde Autumn School; the director and staff of the National Library of Ireland, and public library staff in Bantry, Belfast, Cahirciveen, Cavan, Cork, Derry, Monaghan; Peggi Jordan; Fergus Lalor; Eve Lalor; Mary Mangan; Jack and Barbara O'Connell; Paddy O'Leary; Birgitta Saflund; David Sheehan; Lee Snodgrass; and particular thanks for his help and encouragement to Jonathan Williams; the Dublin Graphic Studio and John Verling's studio in Ballydehob, County Cork, where the woodcuts were printed; the Head of the Department of Irish Folklore, University College Dublin for permission to quote from *Seán Ó Conaill's Book* by Séamus Ó Duilearga; Harriet O'Donovan Sheehy for permission to quote from *The Little Monasteries* by Frank O'Connor; Faber and Faber for permission to quote from *In Memory of W.B. Yeats* by W.H. Auden; Jonathan Cape for permission to quote from *The Road to Oxiana* by Robert Byron; Town House Books for permission to quote from *Retrospections of Dorothea Herbert*; Evelyn O'Nolan for permission to quote from the work Flann O'Brien (Brian O'Nolan); Shane Cullen for permission to quote from *Fragments sur les institutions républicaines IV*. The author acknowledges the copyright of any quoted material which has not been mentioned above.

INTRODUCTION
D'OÙ VENONS-NOUS?

Coole Park and Tahiti make unlikely bedfellows — wide acres of eighteenth-century woods and demesne parkland in the west of Ireland, and a tropical French colonial island in the South Pacific. In 1897, both were simultaneously struck by an inspirational thunderbolt, the effect of which upon succeeding generations of artists and writers could hardly have been more significant. Coole Park, Lady Gregory's home in County Galway, was first visited by W.B. Yeats in that year, with momentous consequences for the development of theatre and poetry in Ireland over the following half-century. At the same time, Tahiti achieved its final perfection for Paul Gauguin, in a corresponding vision.

Ill, isolated and heavily in debt in the years before his death, Gauguin in 1897 painted his final artistic testament, an immense and richly coloured contemplation of life, set in the Pacific paradise which he had discovered or perhaps imagined in the archipelagos of Polynesia. Entitled on the canvas *D'où venons-nous? Que sommes-nous? Où allons-nous?*, the painting posed a sequence of universal questions: 'Where are we from? What are we? Where are we going?'

Gauguin chose not to explain the enigma of this work except in the most cursory manner, but the central concern of the great painting is the passage from birth, through life, towards death. Against a pervasive background of marine blue, the honey-coloured bodies of the islanders exude life: from, on the right, a seated group of women with a sleeping infant, through a life-embracing standing central figure, to a single contemplative darker figure with an aged woman, there is a rhythm of fruitfulness, peace, tranquillity.

The questions of the painting's title are applicable to any society. Like Gauguin, I do not intend to be drawn by such formidable conundrums, yet with the acute sense of change which pervades all aspects of Irish society today, these questions are a widespread source of speculation, as well as the cause of much conflicting opinion. The first question of the title, 'Where are we from?', seems a good point from which to begin a journey, whether physical or conceptual. Rather than attempt to deal with the great sweep of events in Irish history, I wish to look at a much narrower canvas, and to concentrate on some of the transitions which have occurred during a part of my own lifetime.

In the 1950s, half a century after Gauguin painted *D'où venons-nous?*, I daily left a comfortable middle-class home and walked or cycled to a rural primary school in the hill-country of north County Cork. Mine was a house which throbbed with the warmth of an Aga in the kitchen, the convenience of a maid in a black dress and frilly apron to wait at the table, answer the front door. Everything was sedate, conservative, old-fashioned, although not untypical of any professional or business household of the period in Ireland. At school I sat between barefoot boys in hand-me-down ragged clothes, their weathered faces already raw with experience of life. Many had their heads shaved like Masai warriors, scalp and knees marked with the port-wine stain of iodine, a treatment against ringworm. We each carried a log or turf sod to school, like hedge-scholars of the eighteenth century. The more affluent minority ferried their sods in the parental motor-car.

These boys' intellectual potential was the same as mine: some were bright, others not. The prospects of these sons of day-labourers and small farmers were grim and circumscribed: a life of poverty at home, or undignified labour on the building sites of England. Each day I journeyed, an impressionable and observant child, from the world of the ordained and protected to that of the deprived and anarchic. The children, clad in adult suit jackets tied at the waist with string, pullovers unravelling in stalactites of spiralling wool, their hands callused and wart-pocked, were evidence of hard physical work and a poor diet. The school regime was authoritarian and violent.

One of the more enduring impressions of this revealing encounter with rural poverty and deprivation concerned the spider child, a creature from the darkest recesses of a primitive society. This unfortunate and vicious boy exposed my tender soul, both to terror and to the realisation that there was no law to protect the weak. He was a large and muscular farm boy with both legs in knee-high orthopaedic braces so heavy and cumbersome that they severely inhibited his movements. His arrival in the classroom was heralded by what sounded like the clanking of a knight in medieval armour, and once he sat down he could rise only with difficulty. At breaks between lessons, the swift arms of the 'spider' reached out and grabbed some unsuspecting little boy. During this free time, the victim was tortured and crushed until the next lesson brought release. The master never intervened.

Only a moral authority inured to barbaric behaviour could have let this deeply disturbed child prey upon the weaker of his classmates. Poverty, violence, ill health, ignorance, all on a nineteenth-century scale, were commonplace in those mid-years of the twentieth century. Dickensian conditions of gross brutality, allied to medieval levels of superstition, were the norm. On a subconscious level, I became aware as a child that the Irish world of my emerging consciousness was not a homogeneous place, that the standards which prevailed in one place had no application elsewhere. Like Gulliver in Brobdingnag, once you had passed over the threshold of another consciousness, you were in its power.

The 70-odd years between the foundation of the Irish Free State in 1922 and the election of the Irish Republic's first woman President in 1991 were marked by a determined Church and State attempt to create the impression of a unified and culturally homogeneous population. Politicians frequently referred to 'the seamless garment of Irish nationalism', as though this costume represented the national folk dress, a sort of tricolour unisex sausage balloon, worn by all creeds and classes. Dissension was not encouraged; stepping out of the religiously or politically defined line was frowned upon. Navel-gazing became the approved direction for self-development, on both a personal and a national level.

The reality, as might be expected, differed greatly from the officially promoted version of the emergent Irish nation. The inhabitants of the Pale, the 'home counties' of the Dublin area, continued to administer and think for the population at large, as had been the case under British rule. Regional and county divisions with rivalries of tribal intensity still flourished. City looked down upon town, town looked down upon countryside, farmers scorned the landless, all showed contempt for the 'travelling people', Ireland's nomads. Intellectuals romanticised the reality or, disdaining it, emigrated. The homogeneity which the founders of the State had willed to the people as their restored birthright was nowhere in evidence, local interests being far closer to the people's hearts than national perspectives.

Political, social and religious policies in the Republic veered from the right to the extreme right. In the six counties of Northern Ireland things were no better: democratic unionism ruled with a diminutive 'd' and an engorged 'u', the withering intolerance of old antagonisms becoming institutionalised.

In the last years of the twentieth century, a different and more optimistic spirit prevails. My journey is an attempt to encounter something of the changed situation. While I was planning this journey, I debated with myself the various ways in which it might be made: on foot (too slow), by car (more efficient, but isolating), by bicycle (a nice idea but hazardous in a world of ill-mannered drivers). Each proposed method appeared fraught with disadvantages. I had opted for the pragmatic solution of using all methods of travel, depending on the occasion, but was still worrying over the matter when I met Kantico. In a previous life I had known him as a tree farmer in County Cork. Now in billowing saffron robes and shaven head, he had become an ordained Buddhist monk who had taken a vow of poverty.

Kantico related to me a journey which he had recently made in the depths of winter, from County Cork into Kerry, on foot and with no money, relying totally on the goodwill and hospitality of strangers to provide the permitted single daily meal, as well as shelter for the night. He neither went hungry nor slept out under the stars. People were hospitable and responded to his mission, seeing him as a *bacach* or holy beggar, a traditional species of Irish travelling man, a knight of the road, now utterly vanished from the countryside. Kantico made the preposterous idea of wandering penniless through the countryside in winter seem the most reasonable of occupations.

The image of Kantico's orange robes blending with the rusty reds of decaying bracken and the chocolate browns of cutover bog, a bright dot in a dun landscape, has in it something of the heroic as well as the comic, a conscious decision to set time aside and cast the modern world into relief by a denial of material concerns, letting people respond to his asceticism in whatever manner they pleased – rejection or acceptance. I have neither the conviction nor the desire to thus prove myself, yet I liked the image: a lone bright speck of oriental spirituality in the midst of an Irish bog.

On a crisp January afternoon I drove out of the village of Schull in West Cork, passing under the gullwing outline of Mount Gabriel. Further on it began to rain, then there was a downpour. Later I passed through townlands, villages, towns, unseeing and unseen, approaching my destination towards evening. In the enveloping mists a figure in orange at the roadside gesticulated – surely not *another* Buddhist monk on the loose in rural Ireland? It proved to be a plastic-clad county-council worker, warning of hazards ahead.

THE WELL OF THE SAINTS

Having spent the first months of the year in the south of Ireland, in March I set off for the borderlands of Ulster. I came from the lush and untrammelled coastal region of the south-west, and travelled north, via Dublin, towards more austere territory. In Dublin, the Ides of March had come, the prelude to St Patrick's Day and its parade. The event is an American import, following the manner in which the Irish of Boston and New York celebrate their ancestry. The ambience of the Dublin parade is bogus: Park Avenue attempting to smile in the face of torrential rain, drum majorettes twirling their batons, their bare thighs blue with cold.

Of some things one can be sure on St Patrick's Day – icy winds, rain, throngs of marching bands, a strong complement of Irish America walking in reverential awe, as though they had been unexpectedly transported through the pearly gates and discovered heaven to be full of Catholic Irish in knee-britches and caubeens. In New York, rabid Irish nationalists or ancient IRA worthies are favoured as Grand Marshal of the parade; at least in Dublin one is spared this embarrassment, and a soccer player was master of ceremonies.

A prelude to the day was to be the unveiling of the millennium clock – an attempt by the National Lottery to celebrate the countdown to the beginning of the twenty-first century. The significance of this event escapes me. At ten o'clock on a dark Friday night, I join a large downtown crowd gathered along the Liffey quays awaiting the launching of the clock. The word 'launching' is apt enough, since the 'timepiece' is actually submerged in the river, Anna Livia Plurabelle receiving yet more junk, along with bicycles and supermarket trolleys, into its dark waters – in this case six tons of mechanical clockwork.

From where I stand on Bachelor's Walk, the clock is invisible. On O'Connell Bridge, a ceremony of some sort is taking place, the speeches inaudible because of a strong west wind, the words carried out to sea. There are fireworks. A mother tells her complaining son that she wishes she had left him at home; the grandmother protests that *she* had wanted to remain at home but had been forced to come. 'For what, I ask you?' I decide that the millennium can wait for another day.

On the Sunday, St Patrick's Day, the parade winds its way through the city. The crowds – like children let out from school and in high spirits – cheer for anything, wind and rain a part of the experience. The Ohio State Marching Band passes by, Tennessee ditto, Irish Americans baring their buttocks to the Liffey breeze, smiling American smiles. Veterans of previous parades, they are enveloped in see-through anoraks, wise virgins. The foolish virgins follow, local bands of ill-clad teenagers from the outer suburbs of Dublin, perished and unsmiling – cold, wet and at home. The floats are uninspired; they might have been designed in the 1950s, or even the 1930s. Where I stand at Christ Church Place, my party is entertained by a commentator whose job is to inform the crowd whom they are looking at. He announces Liverpool when it is Belfast, Wyoming when it is Wormwood Scrubs. Nobody minds, except possibly the bands; the crowds wave and wave – they wave white for peace, green for Ireland and St Patrick, red and white for McDonald's.

Parades breathe on money, and the contributors with deep pockets are much in evidence: Guinness, retail businesses, utilities and national industries. Their trademarks, the name of the beast, is emblazoned on every available space. Superquinn, one of Ireland's principal supermarket chains, appears to have brought its entire staff to march in the parade. I recognise one of the cashiers from my local branch on Baggot Street, her glazed expression intent on checking the bar-codes on the foreheads of the crowd, as though she were marching through a broccoli forest; as an old broccoli head, I feel past my sell-by date and avoid her gaze. The supermarket staff should have been marching to choruses from *Aida*: 'slaves we were unto Superquinn in Dublin'. Privately, I hope that they are at least getting paid for this piece of crassness. Pharaoh's slaves are followed by more hypothermic toddlers, again from the city's furthest regions, then American college alumni and the occasional representative of other parts of the Irish diaspora – Liverpool, Birmingham (England and Alabama), Glasgow, Dubai. Clearly, the further they have come, the greater their pleasure in participating; it is some sense of homecoming. The event is analogous to travelling the world and staying in Hilton hotels, one's security resting on the premise that nothing will change. Marching in the Dublin St Patrick's Day parade is to experience Irish life, as rewritten to a Z grade Hollywood script.

Thankfully, it is not all beer and bar-codes; there is also Macnas, a beast of a different stripe. Macnas, a Galway-based street-theatre company, is one of the few actual attractions of the parade, possibly the only local attraction for many people. Here imagination, entertainment and appropriateness merge with happy consequences; there is a concerted attempt to bridge the gulf between the need to entertain and the banality of the material generally on offer.

The theme of the Macnas presentation is of course St Patrick and the legend of his having driven the snakes out of Ireland, defeated the native pagans, and introduced Christianity to the Irish. Theatre has the advantage over commerce that it is more interesting to look at. First comes a float-mounted green hill of Erin with enough snakes to scare Mowgli and Baloo. Then follow Medusa-headed stilt-walkers and monks of great size, human-sized ones too, wrestling with serpents; finally a giant snake, carried by plain-chanting cowled clerics. The opposition, a pagan priest, belabours the crowd before a mobile Croagh Patrick, the saint's holy mountain, on which stands St Patrick, or is it Santa Claus? – at any rate, a large man with a white beard. The stilt-walkers, snakes, monks and mountains are continually surrounded by weaving and circling dancers, bearing mineral water, mobile phones, first aid. The atmosphere is as tribal as anybody could have wished, the performers made up to the heights of surrealism. They are closer to the essential truth of the historic event than anything previously seen, a case of the vision versus the present-day reality. Macnas the vision, the Ohio marching bands and Pharaoh's slaves the reality.

The parade winds on.

Afterwards, I remember the millennium clock and head for the Liffey. A crowd on the bridge are gazing intently into the river as though someone were drowning. Below the surface lies what appears to be some relic of the

Titanic, a vaguely glimmering row of sad and submerged lights. Beneath the water's surface shines the clock, a row of illuminated digital symbols, clicking away the seconds like a time bomb set to explode at the first moment of the next century, 119 million seconds away. This much-heralded, discussed and praised millennium clock is like a large digital watch and, as with such timepieces, is not an ideal manner of communicating information. Confusion is all around: Japanese tourists and Dubliners, young, old and authoritative, speculating. Americans, Germans, all snapping their cameras, whirring videos, explaining the enigma to each other.

'You count from the left.'

'No! Read from the right.'

'Nein, Ulli, meine liebe, dass ist –'

'Ma ze?'

'It gives the hours, minutes and seconds.'

'Entschuldigen Sie.'

'Say, isn't that cute, what does it do?'

'It's the millennium clock; you can tell time by it.'

'Is Irish time different from Michigan?'

'Pourquoi?'

'Sweet Jesus, it's the Lu-sit-ania.'

The cameras flash. The faces, stuck through the balusters of the bridge parapet, must, from the clock's viewpoint, resemble decapitated heads. Below, in the water, the digits inexorably decline towards a fictional doomsday, a mathematical construct that has always attracted the attention of madmen, millennialists, prophets, doomsayers. The advent of the last millennium was not regarded auspiciously, or celebrated with much decorum. Will this one be any better? A girl's voice in the crowd mentions the prophecies of Nostradamus, how he had predicted the assassination of Itzhak Rabin, an outbreak of salmonella in Coventry, the end of the world in 2001. It is time for me to move on!

On Burgh Quay the nineteenth century holds sway, a fun-fair with the stock entertainments of a Victorian fairground – honky-tonks and barkers. On Sir John Rogerson's Quay there is a festival of air pollution, ozone layer busting, and espousal of more recent past times; half a dozen coal-burning steam engines are belching out enough acrid smoke to satisfy the darkest satanic mill-owner. Heath Robinson harvesting machines gurgle mysteriously, all manned by country people to whom these antiques are childhood memories. I peer into the intestines of a harvester, a mass of turning wheels and labouring belts, more complex than a microchip. Some men winnow straw, others thrash and grind husks, a woman spins yarn from the loose wool. A German barrel organ grinds out metallic tunes, danced to by a tiny girl, entranced by a gesticulating painted bandsman on the organ.

The parade had been watched by 350,000 people and 10,000 people had marched in it, so the evening's television news stated, showing clips of marching Minneapolis veterans, supermarket slaves, university alumni, puce-faced teenagers. A last clip showed one of the many vintage cars which had taken part, this one with a ten-times-life-size head of Imelda Marcos on a waving human body. Perhaps it was Queen Maeve, or St Patrick's mother?

For a national symbol acceptable to all brands of Irish Christians, Protestant to the Protestant denominations, Catholic to the Catholics, Patrick has done better than he deserved, his legend more substantial than the reality, in so far as it can be discerned. He was a Romanised Briton, did not drive out the snakes because the Ice Age had already attended to that problem, did not bring Christianity to Ireland because Palladius and others had been there already. Christianity was certainly established in the south of the island before Patrick's arrival. As for the shamrock, Patrick is more likely to have used it to garnish some venison than to explain Christian theology. Fifteen hundred years after his passing, a third of a million people watched him being honoured by hosts of grocers, brewers and electricity manufacturers, accompanied by people of Irish extraction from all over the world. With the millennium threatening, there surely must be something more real than this?

Since late January I had been in West Cork, the region of the south-western coastline which thrusts its bony promontories out into the Atlantic, staying at an isolated farmhouse between the town of Skibbereen and the village of Ballydehob. Years before, my family and I had rescued this house from oblivion and had converted it to modern use. A jagged bony ridge of rock rises behind the house, *Knock a Phuca*, the Hill of the Bad Fairy; below, in a little valley, the Leamawadra river flows, overgrown with scrubby trees and brambles, its Irish name *Léim a Mhadra*, 'the hound's leap', accurately indicating its width. Its course meanders from dour Constale Lake on the slopes of Mount Kidd, through rough fields, to enter the sea in Roaring Water Bay.

This now-thriving and scenically beautiful area of the country is historically and indelibly identified with the events of the Great Famine of the 1840s which had its epicentre in the region. The population was decimated, and the scenes of devastation were internationally publicised. The folk-memory remains a searing wound and is still a cause of bitter recriminations.

In the course of reconstructing the 70-foot-long drystone farm building in the townland of Rossard, I discovered within its fabric the original Famine-period dwelling house or 'cabin', preserved in the later building by being incorporated into it and built over, rather than being, as was more customary, demolished or used as a cowshed. Earth-floored and dry-stone-walled, the cabin measured fifteen feet by nine, and was cut into the sloping land so that it was partially submerged in the hillside. It had a single door flanked by two minute windows, an open fireplace and a 'keepie-hole' for the family's few possessions. For the period it was probably a better than average cabin, built of stone rather than sods of earth. A certain comfort could be maintained for a family and its livestock of pigs and poultry, whose only shelter it provided. The cabin became my studio.

In early February, while I am pottering in the house, a news flash interrupts some half-heard radio programme – the IRA cease-fire is over. Within an hour, a massive bomb has exploded at Canary Wharf in London: evidently the IRA are back in business. This is tragic and depressing news, but I cannot claim to be surprised. There never appeared to be much evidence that the republican movement had abandoned the intention to shoot or bomb its opponents into the IRA's own particular concept of a united Ireland – an image as unattractive as its methods.

Here in West Cork, the activities of the paramilitary organisations in Northern Ireland or Britain do not have any influence upon daily life. On the television news, the bombing might as well be happening in Cairo or Tel Aviv, except that the viewers realise that it is threateningly close.

Compared to other freedom movements, the PLO or ANC, the IRA must have proportionally a remarkably small domestic support base. Despite this drawback, they have succeeded in projecting to the world a sense of their legitimacy. This has generally been achieved by capitalising on the failure of Ulster unionists to project themselves internationally as a valid society, rather than as a catspaw of Westminster. Northern Protestants have been in Ireland as long as white Europeans have been in North America. The essential difference is that the 'Indians', the native population of Ireland, never became the minority; nor were they significantly dislodged from their tribal territories.

In North Street, Skibbereen, the rain falls in unrelenting sheets of coldness. I shelter under an archway and wait for the rain to pass, looking back towards the Catholic church at the far end of the street. Rain, cold and a scarcity of people on a February morning transform the normally colourful street into its nineteenth-century equivalent, drained of colour like a steel engraving in a Victorian travel book. I feel like a time traveller: at any moment a professional man in stovepipe hat and tailcoat might walk out of one of the substantial doorways, barefoot women in hooded cloaks pass, ragged children stand in the street and beg. Abruptly the rain ceases, the sun shines and the image fades.

Before I have time to leave Skibbereen, the rain begins again, so I dart into a small second-hand bookshop opposite the post office, which provides sympathetic shelter from the weather. My refuge is empty except for the owner, silently engaged in pricing books. I begin to browse, ever hopeful in unknown bookstores. The quiet is broken by the arrival of an American couple, middle-aged, smartly dressed in a restrained way, professional types. They declaim to the indifferent shelves:

'Oh, this is nice, nice, nice.'

'Yes, dear, nice.'

'I like this.'

'A pity we are not buying. This is nice.'

'Yes, dear, nice.'

'There is the paperback of the one we bought in DC.'

'Isn't that just nice, dear.'

'Oh, James Plunkett. One we don't have.'

'Nice. You will have to give me this one for my birthday.'

'When is your birthday, dear?'

'The day after tomorrow.'

'I thought that was your mother's birthday.'

'No, dear, my mother's birthday was yesterday.'

'How much is this please?'

(Bookshop owner exchanges pleasantries.)

'This is for my birthday. I will pretend that I don't know.'

'Yes, you do that, dear.'

They go on their way. Is this a real conversation? Do people when off-stage actually talk thus? The entire dialogue was accompanied by smiles and glances, as though book-browsing had become a team sport, with points awarded for a quality performance. I pass around the corner into the tranquillity of Field's supermarket. While I shop for groceries, I have an image of a spine seen on the shelves of the bookshop while I was being distracted by 'niceness', and again cross the street. I make my purchase for a few pounds, the Shakespeare and Company 1924 edition of Joyce's *Ulysses*, lying innocently among the Barbara Cartlands and public library rejects. Like Lord Tischendorf in the Monastery of Santa Caterina in the Sinai Desert when he discovered the barefoot monks standing for warmth in church on the *Codex Siniaticus*, the oldest known Greek manuscript of the Gospels, I wonder what sad curate might have used the comfortable bulk of *Ulysses* as a kneeler for his devotions in a bleak and wind-wracked presbytery on the Mizen Peninsula.

The road from Skibbereen to Schull is trafficless today, and the surrounding fields empty of activity as though all life had ceased. Distant plumes of smoke indicate a presence. The spring pyromania has broken out, when the small farmers of the region burn the undergrowth of rough land in order to encourage grass for their cattle. After 21 April this practice is illegal, although it continues. Today mini-Vesuvius tracks of smoke rise on every side into the far distance around the foothills of Mount Gabriel, the fire-raisers unseen.

On the right of the road, at Abbeystrowry, is a famine mass grave where 10,000 unnamed individuals were interred during the 1840s, without coffins or any record of their identity. It might be Rwanda or Bosnia, the same sinister earth barrow concealing not the burial of chieftains but the unrecorded dead of the greatest social catastrophe to occur in Europe during the nineteenth century.

In 1996, 150 years after this most destructive event in recent Irish history, a roadside sign has been erected to mark the site; previously local people were happier to forget an event which they found too distressing and shaming to wish to honour. A pretty timber and stone lych-gate has been erected over the entrance as part of a 'conservation' exercise, the irony of its inappropriateness lost to local eyes. By choosing an entirely English architectural form, redolent of Home Counties rural parishes, to commemorate the Irish famine, the well-intentioned have made their efforts ridiculous. I stop to look at the mound, in my memory an uneven and tussocky area enclosed by an iron railing. What I find is a much larger expanse of grass, as smooth as a suburban garden and as drained of emotional content as a putting green. The railings which had enclosed it are also gone, although a nineteenth-century wrought-iron monument which marked it has survived. This extraordinary piece of smithy work, erected in 1887 by a local man who had probably been in contact with survivors of the events which it commemorates, is an altogether more sinister image. The heavy iron tracery, enclosed in a series of rectangles mounting like a ziggurat, is a tortured and brutal piece of work, anarchic in its feeling. In an inarticulate manner, the smith attempted to express something of the despair of the 1840s; substitute the cross which surmounts it for a Star of David and it might be a memorial to the Holocaust.

The road winds on to approach Roaring Water Bay, and the coast becomes more visible. Below me a magical view comes into sight in the distance below the road, some of the hundred islands which dot the bay, solid indigo shapes surrounded by shimmering water, appearing and vanishing in the abrupt changes of light. The shoreline is broken by the black silhouette of Kilcoe, a fifteenth-century tower house standing on a tiny island, an empire of three little fields.

At the approach to Ballydehob, looking down on the vividly coloured twist of houses which corkscrews up out of the slob-lands of the estuary, the nineteenth-centuryness of so much of rural Ireland impresses me. Here, everything visible – railway viaduct, road and bridge, houses and churches – is a product of the period between the Act of Union of 1801 and the Wyndham Act of 1903, the century of Westminster's direct administration of Irish affairs. The only buildings of distinction are the three churches – Catholic, Church of Ireland, Methodist – spaced apart like children in a classroom who might fight if they are allowed to sit together. The houses climbing up the hill are uniform in design, variations of size or decoration on shop fronts or dwellings all corresponding to the simplest of principles. Nothing predates 1850; all evidence of the earlier village is submerged under the prosperity brought by the increased value of agricultural produce during the Napoleonic Wars.

After Ballydehob the countryside, which was previously so enclosed with small hills criss-crossed by hedgerows crowding down on the traveller, opens out unexpectedly in an expanse of brown bog. Beyond the bog Mount Gabriel, now much closer and exhibiting corrugations like a giant tortoise shell, dominates the view. The soberness of the main street suddenly evaporates, and something more primeval takes its place; on this mountainside, Bronze-Age copper-miners dug for ore. They might still recognise the view.

A mile before Schull, the road skirts the boundary wall of the ruined workhouse (burned by the IRA in 1921), where survivors of the Famine enjoyed the chilling and prurient hospitality of nineteenth-century social welfare. The welcome of the workhouse was little guarantee of survival; frequently the opposite, the casualty-rate among inmates enormous. Two minutes beyond the grim walls, the waters of Schull harbour brighten the landscape, then disappear as the main street of the village encloses the roadway. Schull, like Ballydehob and Skibbereen, preserves the same ambience of late nineteenth-century prosperity, its history, from the Neolithic to the 1790s, obscured. *The Illustrated London News* of 1 June 1846, in an article on local famine conditions, published a view of Schull's main street from precisely the same position which the visitor sees today as he enters the village. The Catholic church on the right of the wood engraving is the same building as today, although the hovels which then lined the street have been replaced by more substantial dwellings.

I am in Schull for the spring Meitheal, taking place over a February weekend. A *meitheal* was a traditional getting together of a farming community for mutual support during harvest-time or other periods when co-operative effort benefited the community. Today the word is used to denote a cultural festival bringing life to a small place in the winter, celebrating its local history and other present-day preoccupations. The Meitheal is more devoted to present life than past tragedy, but it is hardly possible to discuss history in this region of Ireland without the Famine looming large as an important topic. The Famine remains an inescapable set piece for historical recriminations and obligatory Brit-bashing: the incompetence and indifference of the Westminster administration of the day is still capable of raising the hackles of even the most unpolitical of Irish people. I wonder what meal of historical analysis or blame-laying I am about to hear.

Schull has laid out a richly varied menu for the weekend: a lecture on the Famine, another by an English woman rabbi, a major Irish poet reading his own work, the presentation of a local poetry award for the schools of the region in commemoration of a member of the community. There will be music in the pubs, concerts (barbershop and classical), talks on the environment and walks in the neighbourhood, exhibitions and a bazaar of local products. The President will attend. Accompanied by two local archaeologists, Paddy O'Leary and Lee Snodgrass, I prepare for immersion in the Meitheal.

I am apprehensive about the parish-pumpery of such gatherings, yet do not wish to underestimate the capacity of small places to articulate a valid perspective on their own present and past. I need not have worried: the principal events are the two lectures, contrasting in cultural references and geographic scope, yet united by the important and fundamental theme of human striving for survival, freedom and dignity. If a parish pump was in evidence, it belonged as much in the main square of Kishinev as on the main street of Schull. Michael O'Donovan, local farmer turned regional historian, gave a detailed and balanced analysis of the Famine, the descendants of those who survived and those who perished including the speaker and many in the audience. A combination of *laissez-faire* economics, myopia, the greed of local merchants, absentee landlords and grain and other food-crops flowing from the ports in a cornucopia of lost relief are some of the factors behind the disaster. The accounts of contemporary witnesses published in the British and international press make the tragedy as vivid as the toleration of it was obscene.

Later in the afternoon, Rabbi Julia Neuberger, local resident and chancellor of the University of Ulster, a well-known spokesperson on women's issues and on Judaism, spoke of being Jewish and of the Jewish experience. Alarmingly, echoes of the earlier topic of the Famine kept resonating through her talk. Intolerance, indifference, injustice, emigration, moving on and losing one's home, a litany of despair leading to the final horror of the Holocaust, could not but impress upon the audience that two such separate experiences of the indignities suffered by the Irish and the Jews at the hands of oppressors should create a common cause among the survivors. That this is not the case is significant. Catholic Ireland, a century after the Famine, showed the compassion of a block of granite towards those attempting to escape from Nazi Europe during the 1930s, and shows little concern today for the stateless and for refugees.

Outside Griffin's Pub, a tricolour flies from a flagpole. I wonder at its significance: some unseemly expression of nationalist joy following the recent London bombings at Canary Wharf? More acceptably, perhaps it celebrates the exploits of a local football team? As I emerge from the Bunratty Inn, I see the publican lowering the flag as the local bus pulls out of town. Then it strikes me: the President's visit, of course. Schull may be short on public buildings on which to display the national flag for an important visitor, but with public houses it is well endowed.

In the Bunratty Inn, the figures at the bar counter are those I remember from ten years before: single men aged between 30 and 70, to whom the comforts and companionship of a pub are a substitute for a private or domestic life, the myopic county-council worker, an ancient farmer in flat cap and antler-like eyebrows, some younger men. They will drink here until closing time 363 days of the year – as good as a pension scheme for the publican, a death sentence for the drinkers. I speculate on how they occupy their evenings on those two blighted days, Good Friday and Christmas Day, during which the pubs are closed.

Some days later, I am sitting on the grocery side of Slattery's spirit-grocery in the main street of Ballydehob, nursing a quiet pint of Guinness on a weekday mid-afternoon. Business on my side of the bar is static, the trade in sliced-pans or detergent at a standstill. The decor of the bar belongs to the Late Formica Age, an era when shades of brown on brown were seen as representing modernity. Anonymity and cleanliness achieved by a rub of a damp cloth were the merits of the style, the actual Victorian identity of the building emasculated beyond recognition.

Viewed from behind, the male backs ranged along the bar counter look inanimate: a set of similar caps, broad necks and backs of heads, tweed or suit jackets, anoraks, dark trousers stuck into wellingtons – they might have been mummer's dolls stuffed with straw. The backs vary in bulk and height but, perched solidly on their barstools, have the immovability of sacks of meal. The woman tending the bar moves back and forth, pulling pints of stout, dispensing half-ones of spirits, removing empty glasses. No conversation is audible, the men are faced towards the optics – the strategic arrangement of bottles, glasses and mirrors which enlivens even an empty bar. Communication has been pared to the minimum, a few words interspersed by lengthy pauses.

'That was a terrible frost.'

'It was.'

Time clearly is not of the essence. A heifer might need to be brought to the mart in Skibbereen, or a galvanised gate purchased in Bantry. Whatever, it would wait. Another pint, another short one, followed by a resumption of discourse.

'The council are very slow in laying them pipes.'

'They are.'

Silence, the occasional chink of glass, a meal sack descending from its stool and sidling to the door. Later, another enters to occupy its place; the clothing, contours and colour range of the newcomer are so similar, it might have been the original drinker returning. A clock ticks in a back room, the door rattles in a sudden squall of wind, the woman at the bar slowly polishes a glass.

Another man enters and seats himself at the end of the counter on the one vacant stool. He is identical to the other customers in appearance, although taller. A subtle movement of the head brings a drink to his end of the bar. No words are necessary – he is evidently a regular customer, like all the other drinkers. Slightly turning his ruddy cheeks to the men at the bar, he acknowledges them: Danny, Mick, Timmy, a few more. He drinks quickly and another pint is wordlessly placed before him. The desultory conversation resumes: frost, cows, gates, the council.

'Ye have no cross on ye'r church.'

This cryptic remark, delivered to the optics, or to the pub at large, is spoken by the large man without facing or addressing his neighbours. His voice is high and querulous, this pub evidently the latest in a series of visits. He repeats his statement, in the absence of a response, addressing the barwoman in a hectoring whine.

'They have no cross on their church.'

The woman ignores him, as do all the other drinkers. Further pints are consumed, but the lagging conversation has dried up – except, that is, for the large man.

'Ye have no cross on ye'r church.'

Over a period of an hour or more, this strange gnomic incantation is repeated many times. Clearly it is aimed at one of the other drinkers, but since nobody responds, I am unable to detect its target. Gradually the bar empties, as the men leave with a civil 'good luck' to those remaining. When their number is reduced to two, the large whining man and one other, the church and its lack of a cross is mentioned once more. The farmer who is being addressed, the subject of the harangue, rises from his stool and, with a cheery 'Bye, Mikey', leaves the bar.

In turning, I recognise him, a small farmer from outside the village, and the significance of the harangue becomes clear. Catholic churches are decorated with a cross externally, while Protestant ones are often without this symbol, as is the case locally. The whining farmer had emptied the bar of its customers in the course of a two-hour repetition of a single phrase, which everybody present understood, particularly the Protestant farmer to whom it was addressed. Nobody protested or replied. The Protestant farmer was the last to go, other than myself sitting in the background in mute witness. He was not going to give his neighbour the opportunity to say 'Mikey Daly drove Wesley Thornhill out of Slattery's bar with his ranting'. He could honourably leave only after everyone else had been driven into the street by the disagreeable drunk, and taken their custom elsewhere, or gone home.

To say that the large man's remarks were motivated by an interest in ecclesiastical architecture is as far from the point as to suggest that his intention was to cause a fight. He merely wished his Protestant neighbour to accept that his beliefs, church and community were not the full shilling, that they were less than their Catholic counterparts. 'Ye have no cross on ye'r church', chanted with the ritual intensity of a mantra, has the effect of elevating a stylistic mannerism of one Christian denomination to the status of major theological error. This has no real meaning, yet is symptomatic of a set of religious truisms ritually trotted out when any faith, including one's own, is mentioned. Most Irish people, of whatever denomination, except the most seriously involved, would be at a severe disadvantage if they were asked to explain the central tenets of their own faith; for them to expand accurately on the theological beliefs of others is expecting far too much.

To the liberal-minded, it does not matter tuppence what people believe

– anything is fine as long as it does not endanger the environment or frighten the au pair; the converse of this position is the stance that all other denominations are suspect, irrespective of how little one knows about them. During any period of moral or ethical controversy in Ireland, the letters pages of the newspapers are awash with lay theologians of fearsome authority, quoting Palanquin of Tours or Zachary of Aleppo, wielding Church Fathers with all the agility of kneecappers using baseball bats, denouncing heresy in ringing tones, defining subtleties of doctrine with laser-beam precision. Between these suburban archbishops and the manic Mikeys lies a world of complacent ignorance where Irish Christianity and its symbols teeter on a brink between the credible and the absurd, from genuine spiritual belief to farcical shrines and rituals where ambient or haemophiliac statues draw circus crowds with their accompanying siege train of chip vans, kitsch merchants and portable toilets.

The hot intelligence of daft religious views is an Irish commonplace, each person the bearer of a specific private vision of some eternal truth; each region the home of those sufficiently 'pure of heart' to detect heretics with all the talent of the citizens of Salem.

Lee Snodgrass phones in the afternoon with information on some holy wells near Skibbereen. When she was involved in the archaeological survey of County Cork, she had recorded them. I was in fact more interested in holy trees, but they go together, so I gratefully take the information that Shour Well is close to Lough Hyne, an isolated area of dramatic beauty where a narrow inlet connects the marine habitat of the freshwater lake with the sea. The veneration of holy trees – usually whitethorn, hawthorn, blackthorn – is a survival of pre-Christian animist religious practice and is still surprisingly widespread throughout the island. St Brigid, to whom most of the trees and wells are now dedicated, inherited the honour from pagan forebears.

Three or so miles beyond Skibbereen a road diverts to the left, and here the landscape abruptly changes from smooth fields to wooded precipices and awkward land. The afternoon sun is bright and hot. I fail to find my quarry despite precise instructions, so just drive around the byroads, absorbing the landscape, until I meet a likely-looking farmer on a tractor. He knows the location. I have already passed it. He beams down from his tractor cabin.

'Shour Well, is it? Of course I know it – a great place for cures. Wasn't a young boy cured of blindness there, some years ago? Oh, there have been powerful cures at Shour. May Eve is the pattern day, I've been there many times.'

I pronounced the word Shour as though I had come down in the last one. The farmer had an altogether richer pronunciation, doubtless a closer approximation to the Irish original.

The well shrine is on the verge of a steep byroad with a strong stream cascading down beside it. In front is a stone enclosure, a large carpet-like array of quartz pebbles, and then the shrine itself, shaped like an over-mantle, whitewashed and roughly built. A niche holds a large statue of the Virgin and many smaller ones, as well as crosses and other fragments. Behind all this is the tree, a venerable thorn-bush with wild, scraggy and unkempt branches, waving in every direction. These are festooned with devotional objects, rosary beads and religious medals, as well as an array of scraps of clothing left by pilgrims. Some of these cloth tokens are bleached by the sun, more recent offerings have quite fresh colours. A small cloth package intrigues me. Done up with ribbon like a present on a Christmas tree, it is a soft rectangle of fabric to which is sewn a little bell that tinkles in the wind. A child's possession seems obvious, a doll's mattress. A small shoe is entwined in the brambles.

I return to scrutinise the objects in the niche around the statue. They are mostly medals, fragments of statues, Dürer's praying hands in brown-painted plaster, seashells, pennies and yet more medals, all subsiding into a rich mulch of leaf mould from the overhanging trees. Some Italian coins worked into a bracelet are dated 1923. There is a plastic plectrum, 'Jim Dunlop' brand. Did the musician recover his health, his record ever reach the charts?

In the evening light the tree has a spectral look, a woody and demented Ophelia with ragged ribbons in her hair. The valley where it stands is a dark and sunless gorge; the whiteness of the lime-washed stones and the glinting of the quartz are enriched by the denseness of the deep-patterned greenery of the surrounding foliage of ferns, holly, grasses and moss. The well, a tiny depression below the niche from which the water bubbled, is clearly a Christian context, the tree and its cloth foliage a voice from the remote past. Thorntrees are invested in Irish and European folklore with formidable powers, both benign and threatening. The tree spirits which inhabit them have survived St Patrick's new broom, the Reformation, the Enlightenment, electric light and television, yet still hold a secure place in the mysterious world of hope and belief.

Suddenly it becomes very cold. Light in the declivity fails, the wind rises and the whole tree waves with a sigh, the bright fragments of cloth catching a last flash of sunlight. I retrace my way back to Lough Hyne and the open air.

The journey from Ballydehob to Bantry passes over high ground, *Bearna Gaoithe*, 'the gap of the winds', with moorland and patchwork fields around isolated farmhouses, then into the maw of one of those desperately depressing state forestry schemes which demonstrate the capacity of civil service accountants to stultify even nature. The conifers seem determined to take over the road, but then a break occurs, and the relief of open fields again. Outside Bantry the bay appears. Nothing, however, to suggest that the scale of the inlet is visible from the town.

The town square is as jam-packed with activity as in a cattle fair of the past. It is fair day, the first Friday of the month, and the clans have gathered to trade. Farmers, townspeople, itinerant dealers, Irish travellers, hippies, New-Age travellers, all throng the square, with stalls set up around its perimeter. If so much of the view were not blocked by Hi-Ace vans, it would be a picturesque scene. Every few yards represent a change of culture: Irish, English, conservative, radical, affluent, poor, paupers. Nationalist ballads, in themselves an excess of sentimentality and incitement to riot, blare from a stand, 1798, Fenians, 1916, Famine, evictions, 'My Four Green Fields', 'The Fields of Athenry', and other agricultural metaphors for 200 millennia of the Saxon jackboot. Next to such memories and comforting myopia is blindness of a different species, the hippies of the mountain, and the hippies of the plain, mostly refugees from Britain, Europe, America. They arrived in Ireland during the 1960s and are still eking out a poor, anti-capitalist living on the land. The alpine types are selling handicrafts; those of the lowlands, scrawny organic cabbages. Next are Irish travellers with a stand of 'Irish Brassware' (made in County Taiwan): 'Buy an Irish Bell, sir, good for St Patrick's Day' – the saint dismissed the reptiles by flinging his handbell down the slope of Croagh Patrick; obliging spirits returned it each time. Brass round towers, brass shamrocks, brass Celtic design on firescreens, each one was more unspeakable than the last. 'Sir, buy a lucky Irish leprechaun' – it was almost worth it to possess a brass gnome with the face of Leonid Brezhnev.

The New-Age travellers, a recent and exclusively British phenomenon, have taken over the bottom end of the antique trade today, and their wares are spread out on the street: broken ironware, burnt (literally) ceramics, a Staffordshire dog which might have survived the Blitz, cast-off children's toys, the ubiquitous tea-chest of terrier puppies – 'Mother an excellent ratter, £10'. An elderly farming couple are considering the purchase of an oil lamp with glass chimney; they must surely be among the last people in the country without electricity, inhabitants of a powerless valley, too remote even for the world's dropouts. I search enthusiastically for something to buy, but resist temptation. A bull's wool Fairisle pullover (hippies of the mountains), or a miniature brass Georgian door, its classical proportions distorted almost beyond recognition (genuine Irish travellers), fail to captivate me. I had seen a copy of C.M. Doughty's *Travels in Arabia Deserta* in the antiquarian bookshop on the main street. Arabia Felix beckons.

In the well-stocked wholefood shop, the windows are packed with 'improving literature', like the pious tracts of a Methodist street preacher offering to save the reader from a variety of factory-made Satans. If the wholefood shop is this preachy, what must the churches be like? In Bantry, the Protestant pinnacled variety is in the Market Square, the Catholic pedimented one safely distant.

I go on my way towards the hills behind the town, heading for Gougane Barra, a tiny lake in the mountains where St Finbarr established a hermitage in the sixth century and from where he travelled down the Lee Valley to evangelise Cork. Ten miles into the mountains a side road leads to the lake, with precipitous mountains rising from close to its shore, which is rimmed by little farms. On this day in late February there are a few people in the valley, the sun is shining and the air is surreally clear. Every bush and leafless tree seems precisely delineated and the waters of the lake are touched only by the most tenuous of ripples. There is a positively Pre-Raphaelite perfection about everything, somewhat undermined by discreet signs indicating car parking and toilets. At another time of year the hermitage might become a tourist trap like any other. Today, however, it is not too far removed from a separate and secret place.

The island in the lake where the saint is believed to have founded his sanctuary has been built upon and ritualised since the eighteenth century when an eccentric cleric, the Reverend Dennis O'Mahony, constructed a folly here, a make-believe hermitage, where he lived for the remainder of his life, in appropriate discomfort. The enclosure constructed by the priest, with monks' cells surrounding a courtyard, is today the focal point of the island. There is also a Celtic Revival oratory, some municipal paving and, fortunately, enough trees to soften the lines of the 'improvements'.

Signs abound, some sympathetic, others clearly written by the brother of the man appointed to lay out the *Bearna Gaoithe* forests. At the entrance to the island, an eloquent inscription relates the saint's life and declares, 'Here he communed with God. The surrounding mountains were his cloister and the lake was for him the mirror of God's grandeur.' Inside the gates, a tidied-up holy well is marked by a sign in pure underlined civil-service-ese: 'No money in <u>holy well</u> please. Box in <u>pillar</u> for same.' Traditionally, pilgrims attending the pattern day of the saint, 25 September, would throw coins in the well as a good-luck offering. To a desk-bound official, confined between his in- and out-trays, such profligacy must seem anathema.

Standing now in the centre of the mock cloister is a smooth timber cross, a recent replacement of an older one. Snuffling among the shrubberies along the shoreline, I find the demoted cross, which, if it were on display in an ecclesiastical museum, would be among the most curious and popular exhibits. Now rotting and propped beneath a holly tree, this tortured pilgrim cross has the surface of an armadillo, the coinage of the British realm and the Irish realm too having been violently hammered into its surface until there was not room for another coin. I inspect the coins in this penitential relic, which on appearance looks as if it might belong to a self-flagellating sect of zealots, lately returned from the Wilderness of Zin. The earliest coin is dated 1970, the latest from the 1990s. Contemporary coins indicate contemporary practice. The ritual may be an entirely recent one, another layer in the commemoration of St Finbarr, like the folly of 1700, the oratory of 1930. As stylistic development, it augurs poorly for popular sensibilities. Box in pillar for same.

Lured by the *leithreas* sign, I discover the saint's most recent memorial, a treasure well hidden from view: the most magnificent (or ridiculous?) public loo in Ireland. In a corner by the roadside, screened by a thorn thicket, is a large, circular, thatched and domed building which, a sign declared, 'won the silver medal in the 1993 loo-of-the-year competition'. Well it might. A Bronze-Age inhabitant of the valley would have no difficulty with this building, its form derived from pre-history. What demented architect, trawling through his album of historical styles for the new Ireland, concocted such an absurdity? Whimsy is inimical to the rugged natural beauty of Gougane Barra and its lake valley – wood, stone, earth, bark and leaves are its signature. It is now threatened by state-sponsored lepre-gnomes.

Back in Bantry, I stop beyond the town and climb a hill to look at another early Christian site, this one unmolested by Church or State. On the brow of a bare hill overlooking the deep sweep of Bantry Bay is a ninth-century monastic remnant, the Kilnaruane Pillar Stone. Surrounded by a trace of the earthen ring which once enclosed it is an upright stone carved on two faces with low reliefs, a bishop, two saints breaking bread, a fully manned currach sailing vertically up the shaft of the pillar. This last is considered to represent St Brendan the Navigator who, according to medieval legend, discovered

North America centuries before either Leif Erickson or Columbus; in 1971, the maritime explorer Tim Severin sailed from the west coast of Ireland to Newfoundland in a hide currach based on the Kilnaruane model, demonstrating that the legend was at least plausible, and might be based upon fact. Brendan's *Navigatio* was among the most popular of medieval texts.

On the road back home to Rossard, there are an abundance of people hitching. They are not hitchhikers but local people going a mile or so in some direction. I pick up and deposit, as needed. My last fare is a young man wearing round spectacles and carrying a tin whistle: English, fresh blood in the west, of sorts. I question him about his music and unleash a lengthy monologue.

'I like to play as I walk along the road, one note at a time. The notes have nothing to do with each other, you see. When I have played two notes which I like, I might play them all day, or for days at a time, until I find some other notes.'

I quietly sit through all this rigmarole and sigh with relief that I do not share a house with this person, an unconscious adept of Chinese torture.

'Music, you see, is like conversation; two people are talking, but what they are saying has nothing to do with each other, like two notes, separate.'

I vehemently protest at this analogy. Surely only an obsessive monologist could imagine *this* to be conversation? There is a long silence, so I question him further. Would he consider performing in public? He reacts with horror.

'I play only for myself.'

I suggest a tape recorder, but this too is greeted with dismay.

'I couldn't do that. I would find the tape recorder too intimidating, intrusive. I could not play.'

Attempting to extract myself from this one-note-samba quagmire, I ask about his musical tastes. He contemplates this issue for a long time before responding.

'I never listen to other people's music – only to my own.'

His turning arrives and he departs, giving me that look perfected by generations of hitchhikers who consider they have just been given a lift by a sex-crazed axe-murderer, and are glad to escape with their lives.

I drive on and turn in the track to Rossard. I resolve not to emerge for a week. Meeting people can damage one's mental health.

Some days later I needed to travel to Cork, and decided to go via Gougane Barra, from there continuing to the city, as Finbarr had done, down through the Lee Valley. Having made the decision, I neglected to inform the weather gods. On the day before my departure it had rained heavily.

Irish weather being unpredictable, the optimist always expects it to improve. It got worse.

Having decided on Gougane, that is what it had to be, come hell or high water – and there was much of the latter. Between Ballydehob and Bantry the road is frequently waterlogged, sometimes perilously, as flash floods sweep down on the roadway's convenient channel. Driving a light and low-slung car is not exactly being best equipped for the situation. In the enveloping wetness of the day, the colours of the landscape are accentuated. The walls of the whitewashed farmhouses seem to be lit from within by an eerie glow. A bright lemon-coloured bungalow looks good enough to eat, a peeling orange farmhouse nestling under wet trees suggests Tuscany. The rust red of battered sweeps of bracken shines more brightly for being backed by the blackness of soaked hills and forestry plantations, yellow dead grasses by the roadside reflect an unseen light, somewhere above the rain.

Bantry came and went, all under a shower of vertical spears of punishing rain, the streets of the town flooded, hardly a soul to be seen, dark shapes scurrying from doorways, a demented individual directing non-existent traffic in the market square, his arms flailing like windmills. The statue of St Brendan in his small bronze coracle rides over the waves of water as fearlessly as he had crossed the Atlantic in a hide currach 1,500 years before.

I approach the valley of the Lee through the Pass of Keimaneigh. Here the scarps of the pass burn red and orange with dead vegetation, all overhung by dripping willows, scrub oak and rowan. No life, no human, animal, car or beast travels this road today. So heavy is the rain now that I drive past the small turn-off to Gougane, although it is marked by a hideous assemblage of plaster saints, a monstrous white pietà which should have dissolved into a puddle in the prevailing atmosphere.

In the valley itself I am impressed by the savage majesty of the surrounding hills, now dimly seen through the rain; their outlines hang as dark shapes in the sky. Once I have left the protection of the car and am standing again on the island, my eyes become adjusted to the hills, each black expanse of rock seared and scored by torrents cutting down from the barely visible summits towards the lake. This is exactly as the nineteenth-century romantics had painted St Finbarr's hermitage: nature at its most overawing, an absolute proof of the power of the Divinity. I expected Landseer's *Monarch of the Glen* to trot nobly into the car park and pose for a photo opportunity at the Bronze-Age loo.

In the graveyard overlooking the island are buried friends of my grandfather, who, in the 1900s, was involved in the establishment of the Arts and Crafts movement in Ireland. He and his family used to come to nearby Ballingeary in the summers of the early years of the century, when such Gaeltacht areas were important oases for those engaged in the cultural revival movements of the time. The names and places of the area form part of my childhood memories, although I have no personal connection with either people or place. In Seán O'Faolain's autobiography *Vive Moi!*, he describes coming to *Tuirín Dubh*, the same house where my grandfather's family stayed; it was here that the writer ceased to be John Wheelan, and was reborn as Seán O'Faolain.

Already soaked and cold, I ascend into the graveyard to write down the inscriptions on some of the tombstones of the *Tuirín Dubh* families. My pad is wet in an instant and the biro refuses to work. A trip back to the car for a pencil only makes me wetter. The paper declines to respond even to the pencil and I have to resort to inscribing the names and dates from the tombstones on the inside of my waxed jacket with a feltpen, where a dry space takes the information. I cannot resist adding that of Tadgh Ó Buacalla, *An Táilliúir*, 'the tailor'. His epitaph, remarkably, is in English: 'A star danced and under that was I born.' Ó Buacalla, an Irish-speaking local tailor and noted conversationalist, is buried here with Ansty, his wife. He is the subject of Eric Cross's book of ribald folktales, *The Tailor and Ansty*, published in 1942. The local curate forced the tailor to burn copies of his book, an offence against the high moral tone of Catholic propriety.

Down by the lakeshore, I realise that however pretty the valley may be in sunny weather, this cannot compare with the grandeur of the scene in the midst of monsoon-season downpours. If you were seeking spiritual experiences in the wildness of Celtic Ireland, this was the place; it still is, on a sodden March day when nature has beaten back the day-trippers and seekers after miracles and holiday photographs, and left the valley for you and the Saint.

Now, imagining that I am wracked by tuberculosis, pulmonary pneumonia, whooping cough and incipient meningitis, I continue on my journey to Cork. In order to check if the outside world is still intact, I turn on the car radio. Danoli, the bright hope of thousands of Irish punters, has romped home fourth at Cheltenham. The going was wet. I switch off the radio and head for Cork.

In Macroom, the same conditions prevail as in Bantry — sheets of wet greyness clouding the view, the streets empty except for tractors, cars and buses, all thrown into confusion by minimal visibility. When I have gone ten miles on the road to Killarney I manage to read a road sign, and for the second time that day reverse into a farm gate and head back.

In Cork, Henchy's Pub at St Luke's Cross is surprisingly dry, busy and able to provide a few life-saving hot whiskeys. Finbarr, evidently, was made of sterner stuff. A bore at the bar is explaining to a group of glum losers exactly why Danoli had failed to oblige.

'The going.'

BORDERLANDS

Borderlands are where the familiar and the anarchic collide, where the real and the surreal threaten to merge into a destabilising mirage.

The main street of Newbliss is as wide as Piccadilly, three or four times the breadth of the country roads leading to it; like the ruins of the Roman forum, something is clearly missing, possibly almost everything – a plan which failed to shift from the paper to the ground, somehow abandoned in the making. On one side a stillborn classical arrangement of market house flanked by faded Georgian townhouses composed as part of a scheme for creating a dignified square. Opposite are cottages and council houses which look as if they are sinking into the ground, geological slippage the only satisfactory explanation for the seeming abandonment of the architectural principles of the far side. Like the children's game of matching halves of different faces, the combination fails to result in a satisfactory persona. Even on the Georgian side there are ominous gaps, where nothing has been built or replaced in a century or more, perhaps never built at all. The two churches – Church of Ireland outside the village at one end, Presbyterian at the other

— look used and cared for; a Masonic Hall, dated 1927, states the obvious: the border with the North excluded this community which, having once been central to itself, in the stroke of a geographer's pen was placed beyond the periphery of its own natural hinterland.

The filling-station owner opens with a direct statement, 'You'll be staying at Annaghmakerrig, of course,' my person as obvious as though I had been wearing tin-foil wings and a laurel wreath. (I am now staying at the Tyrone Guthrie Centre at Annaghmakerrig, an artists' and writers' residence, a few miles outside Newbliss in County Monaghan.)

'Yes, indeed.'

'And what are you doing there? Writing, I suppose?'

'That's correct.'

'And what would it be about then, something to do with Ireland?'

'Actually, yes.'

'Then you should write about the followers of the Reverend Ian Paisley's Free Presbyterian Church, who live south of the border, and about Protestants who are not Orangemen, and Protestants who are not unionists, aye, you should write about all that.' He is evidently referring to himself and his immediate community. The conversation turns to my ailing car.

'You say you have a wee problem, and I ask you, how are we to know, is it the fuse or not the fuse which is causing the difficulty? Knowing is the issue. Now, if you knew that the problem lay there, then you could answer it, I suppose. How are we to know? That is the real question.'

He might be discussing the difficulty of interpreting Galatians 2:16, or a fine point in one of the Reverend Ian's sermons. I regret that my mechanic seems more concerned with the spiritual well-being of my spark-plugs than actually opening the bonnet. Eventually the car is examined, and I am sent on my way to consult a senior theologian in a neighbouring town. On the road to Cootehill some deft hand has painted out the name Drum from a road sign, leaving only the Irish version, *Droim*. I puzzle over this. A point is being made — linguistic, political, sectarian?

In Cootehill, as I walk into the garage forecourt, an unknown mechanic responds with, 'You have a problem with your lights, a fuse maybe?' Word had travelled before me — bonfires on the hilltops perhaps — and after the ritual interrogation as to my identity, residence and occupation, the job is attended to without reference to Proverbs 15:1, or the *I Ching*. Shortly after, I am back in the main street of Cootehill, where a voice hails me from a parked car. It is my Newbliss sage.

'He had the part, then, and it was not the fuse, I gather. Knowing is all.'

Cootehill manages better than Newbliss to get its formal plan off the eighteenth-century surveyor's map and transformed into living architecture. Market Street is broad, its vista ended by a Church of Ireland needle spire, a landlord-inspired scheme which merges the archetypal Irish country town main street and the concept of a classical avenue into a coherent whole. The Big House, Bellamont Forest, built by a Bellamont earl, lingers behind the street in its demesne, a Palladian toy villa inspired by the Villa Malcontenta in the Veneto, pure geometry in limestone and red brick. I walk up the muddy avenue towards the house but become depressed by the encroaching conifers and retrace my steps to the town. Market Street, by comparison, is cheerful and bustling, a typical assemblage of ticky-tackery, the thriving and the defunct.

In a café, having lunch, I am joined by the waifs and strays of the town, the rank odour of poverty wafting around the cold and totally undecorated room as though we are sitting in a soup kitchen. An old man with a very grimy face orders roast beef. He is served round scoops of mashed potato floating on the surface of brown gravy. I order soup and tea.

'Will you be having the soup?'

'Yes.'

'And who is having the tea, then?' The idea that a customer should order two items simultaneously appeared novel to the waitress. I enter into the spirit of the moment.

'The tea is for his Lordship.'

Tea and soup are delivered to my table and placed on opposite sides, the soup for myself, the tea for the absent earl; I duly consume my portion, and his. As I rise to pay, the waitress remarks:

'His Lordship didn't have his tea.'

'Most probably his car, you know – a problem with the fuses.'

'Och ay, them wee fuses can be a terrible bother. It's knowing what is the problem, now that's the difficulty, knowing. My brother Wully . . .'

Another Presbyterian Zen Buddhist philosopher. Time to move on.

Outside on the street, a little boy passes me with an open brown paper bag full of marshmallow biscuits. He puts in his hand and withdraws one, smiling, crumbs and mallow on his cheeks. I envy him his pleasure and unphilosophical good humour. On the far side of the street a shop called Blessings – which I assume, unlike Adams, Boyle, Rice and Rutherford, is not a family name – is selling Catholic religious kitsch, invitations to be saved, go on pilgrimage or hear words of spiritual benefit, regulations for a retreat on Lough Derg: 'over 16 and in good health' – the requirements for the Foreign Legion. Blessings' stock in trade hovers perilously close to the 'indulgences for sale' Christianity to which the Reformation was a response. In Cootehill, with Reformation churches on every hand, this point has not yet been taken. Around the corner Argue Meats trades behind drawn blinds – another family name, not a contentious butcher. Later, I consult the phone directory. It appears that Blessings is a common local name – a rather unconvincing coincidence.

In the empty Catholic church, a banner states threateningly BE STILL AND KNOW THAT I AM GOD. Among the pamphlets and improving literature at the back of the church is a leaflet about local priests working in the grim circumstances of the prisons of Lagos, in which is included a half-literate message from Kaduna Joe, a former inmate, thanking the citizens of Cootehill for help given, blessings rendered: 'Those whose body could have rot are now still living, smiling with hopes to continue to live.' It might have been some half-literate Irish tenant farmer's desperate letter of the 1840s, begging for aid.

In a book on the Irish Blueshirts, a home-grown Fascist movement of the 1930s which dressed in pseudo-Nazi attire and sent a brigade to fight for Franco in the Spanish Civil War, I saw a photograph of Blueshirts on parade, carrying a Newbliss banner, giving the Fascist salute. Why Newbliss? It does not look like the sort of village to produce such right-wing politics; it is a quiet, timid-looking, anonymous place. My question is answered in Monaghan County Museum. In the display, large as life, appears General Eóin O'Duffy, a contemporary portrait of the Blueshirt leader, in blue shirt and Fascist insignia. He was, of course, a local boy and remains a local hero. O'Duffy graduated from local republicanism during the Anglo-Irish war to become Police Chief in the Free State. His enthusiasm for Axis politics lost him his job, and he subsequently led an Irish brigade to fight for Franco in Spain. After the Spanish adventure he died a disappointed man.

Outside Monaghan town, on the road to the North, Irish Army patrols and Garda roadblocks are positioned to intercept a UVF terrorist strike against the South. Their intelligence is presumably accurate, and the South may yet suffer what the North has had to endure for a quarter of a century. In the town the Sinn Féin office is closed owing to the 90th anniversary of the party's founding. I must return and see what sort of Hizbullah personnel staff it, or kindly silver-haired old ladies, lamenting a nephew, 'wee Hughie, in the H Block'. I return on numerous occasions, always to find the office closed, the staff no doubt on 'active service'.

In St Macartan's Cathedral, the Vatican II demolition crews have been busy filling rubbish skips with the ecclesiastical lumber of the latter half of the nineteenth century, the great age of Catholic church-building in Ireland.

The shiny white marble altarpieces, with forests of crockets, finials and ogee curves, have unceremoniously been smashed, to be replaced by altar furniture as elemental as a Brancusi. The altar table, font and lectern breathe a fresh and unencumbered spirit. In a side aisle is a stone beehive hut, a confessional, close cousin of the Bronze-Age loo in Gougane Barra. Somewhere along the way, one, or both, of these designers got his imagery in a muddle.

I approach with some trepidation Monaghan's other museum, the St Louis Convent Heritage Centre, devoted to the history of a religious teaching order. A recorded voice rings out over an extraordinary display of historical artefacts and documentation, telling me this and that about the piety, inspiration and dedication of Mother Genevieve and Sister Claire, an impressive chronicle of Irish Catholic education over a 150-year period. Behind me as I move, a nun in mufti hovers, spectre-like. She indicates with a wordless nod or gesture if I should look right or left, her presence so close, noiseless and weightless that she might have been an ectoplasmic manifestation hovering six inches above the floor. Only a nun, or an Eastern ascetic, trained in a life of bodiless existence, could achieve such a degree of non-being. When the commentary has concluded, I talk to her. She is respectful, palely quiet. I find the experience of talking to her unnerving – a survival of the manners of a dead age, unseen since the nineteenth century, when servants waited at table, aware of one's every wish, yet without either opinions or presence, the table conversation 'unheard'. She mentions her superior, Mother X, in a low voice, as though to say 'her Ladyship will esteem your concern'. I return to my phaeton and bid the coachman drive hard for Annaghmakerrig where my host, Lord Guthrie of the Lakes, is organising a rout.

The border between the Irish Republic and Northern Ireland runs more or less along the county boundaries of the six counties of the North, defining not the historical Ulster but a portion of it, the area which has remained an integral part of the United Kingdom since 1922. In Northern Ireland this area of the Irish landmass is generally indicated on maps as a small island with no near neighbours, or as one appended to Britain; southern Ireland, like Atlantis, has apparently fallen into the sea. In the Republic things are seen differently, all maps indicating the entire island of Ireland, the territory of Northern Ireland distinguished by a graphic on the map, a line, no more. Nowhere in the Republic will you see a map showing the actual national territory, with the offending British part excised. This would pose too serious an affront to nationalist sensibilities and be in conflict with the Irish

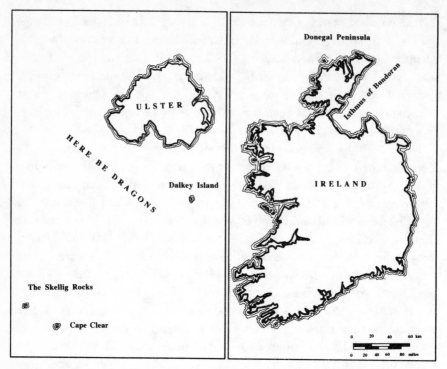

Altered States: The island of Ulster and the actual Republic

constitutional claim to 'ownership of the entire island of Ireland'. For citizens of the South it would probably be salutary, if disturbing, for a map of the actual national territory to be generally available, although widespread bereavement counselling might be needed. In the 70-year existence of the Irish Free State/Irish Republic, this map has yet to put in an appearance. The un-kosher version would consist of a three-province Republic, the entire top portion of the country missing, with Donegal poised on its tippy-toes, attempting to retain a foothold on the squat remains of the island.

Both complementary versions of the island of Ireland and its parts are statements of political conviction, structuralist answers to social and political realities. The misfortune of the border is not solely in its reluctant inclusion of those who wished to be part of a nationalist republic, or its effect in atrophying the democratic instincts of its unionist and loyalist population, but also the exclusion of those who live on its rim. The border, which encloses a viable if tiny territory, orphans those placed outside it as effectively as though a door had been slammed in their faces. And then there are drumlins.

The drumlin belt, a sequence of little glacially contoured hills scattered like chocolate buttons across the landscape, sweeps down in a great curve from Belfast Lough on the east coast, below Lough Erne and across the upper reaches of the Shannon, meeting the sea at Donegal Bay on the Atlantic. The land between the hills is pitted by myriad small lakes, fens and bogland, augmented by Iron-Age earthworks, the Black Pig's Dyke and the Dane's Cast, a territory difficult for armies to negotiate, a safeguard for the historical North against unwelcome incursions. Along the drumlin belt are scattered the small towns of the borderlands, in most respects typical of Irish towns in any part of the country, in others atypical, a transitional territory between North and South.

The most ubiquitous of all things Irish is the country town, its main street an interchangeable sequence whatever the region: central plain or northern coastline, Cahirciveen in the South, Aughnacloy in the North. The concerns of rural life are organised and structured by life on main street. In the South, the two main churches, Catholic and Church of Ireland, stand at a discreet distance from each other, with a diminutive Methodist chapel in a side street. In Ulster, both above and below the border, the denominational balance changes, with Presbyterian and Church of Ireland vying for prime place, Methodist and Catholic around the corner, many others in obscure backstreets. At some spot in the street, a patriotic monument, to 1690, 1798, 1914, 1916, a saint, a cleric of local fame, a hanged hero, more occasionally – and never without some irony – a landlord, 'from a grateful tenantry'. The monument will often occupy the square, if there is one, or, in Ulster, the 'Diamond', a flag of convenience for any urban open space. The most imposing building will be the courthouse, Georgian or Victorian cut stone or red brick, a symbol of, depending on your perspective, security or repression. Otherwise, trade and drink jostle for space on the narrow pavements, the number of pubs generally defying what might be reasonably expected bearing in mind the local population. Some are hardly bigger than a small bedroom, others lush saloons of deep carpets and fake antique bar mirrors. To order a drink in one of the small bars is to have the sense of invading some private ritual, as though the drink is being served in someone's parlour, the few customers, invariably male, solitary, silent.

Late nineteenth-century photographs of Irish country towns indicate that little has changed in the intervening century. Their appearance had evolved in their current guise in the years after the Famine of the 1840s; since then nothing much seems to have invaded their sedate calm. In Northern Ireland terrorist bombs have blown the hearts out of some, riots and marches frequently occupy their streets, military presence has made life intolerable, inhospitable conditions and erratic tax systems have driven business away for ever, yet the essentials remain: a street, an open space, churches, a monument.

Like the philosopher Bishop Berkeley, who was translated from Cloyne to Derry, I have been translated from sea-wracked West Cork to the claustrophobic web-like closeness of the border region of Monaghan. Visually there is a decline, the absence of a sea coast the most fundamental change, but this is not really the question. Something else is missing, an openness; this is the territory of the sidelong glance, of quiet watchfulness. The road from Cavan town through country roads to County Monaghan is flanked by abandoned estates, the demesne walls teetering or collapsed, the parkland fallen victim to conifer plantations. A tall, classical column by the roadside is about to be consumed by trees, rather than being conserved. This could happen anywhere; more to the point are the gate lodges, estate houses, associated dwellings – all are abandoned and derelict. Architecture which elsewhere in the country would have become estate agent's *bijoux* residences is here allowed to decline into cowsheds and ruins.

In Rockcorry, the main street has derelict houses in its most prominent positions. People must be leaving here, certainly not moving in; it is conceivable that they do not care for strangers. Who would intentionally move into a border area on the southern side? Probably only some solid republican of evil intent. First impressions have not been favourable, although I have been here before, years ago. The actual physical landscape does not help, the little hills everywhere and small, reed-fringed lakes uniformly grey in March. It is just difficult to be excited by such terrain, neither ugly nor beautiful. It is possibly the epitome of middle Ireland: run-down villages, prosperous farms, full churches.

A man on the main street, supervising the laying of pavement slabs, observes me with suspicion; later, after I have walked the streets and failed to buy postcards in the post office or two grocery shops, he made it his business to know mine. I am reminded of my fellow traveller, Bishop Berkeley; some years before in his village of Cloyne in County Cork, the postmistress informed me that 'there is no call on postcards'. In Rockcorry demand is equally slack – a telling sign. No tourists come here, there is no *Meitheal* or local festival to enliven winter days. A fine row of eighteenth-century houses on a corner of the street stand abandoned, charming stone warehouses lie scattered about, pleading for reuse, a row of labourers' cottages decline down a hill, their windows blank, doors gaping, empty. Oh *bijou*, where is thy residence in this uninspired place?

My man is closing on me all the while. Returning up past the sad cottages, he places himself on the opposite pavement and, with studied nonchalance, checks the dimensions of the kerb with a steel tape-measure, crossing the street in time to catch my eye. He is friendly, informative and impassioned about his village, and before I have an opportunity to ask a single question he reiterates the familiar dreary tale of county-council misdeeds, absence of vision among the townsfolk, absentee landlords. This last demands a question. I imagine the current earl of Bellamont, living it up in Monte Carlo. 'Oh, that man doesn't care; he inherited two farms, and lives away in Cavan town.' Not the iniquities of Lord Noblename which I had expected. Of the other local culprits, the Forestry Department must represent the nadir of ecological and environmental awareness, planting Christmas trees on the parkland of the earl's demesne. These same gentlemen are the authority empowered to abandon Gothic and Classical gate lodges, now sinking into the mire. Spick and span at the entrance to Rockcorry are the Destitute Widows apartments.

The byroads of Monaghan are strafed with potholes, craters, landslides — suitable for tractor travel, not otherwise. I bounce from Annaghmakerrig to Newbliss, the roads improving at the approach to larger towns. In Newbliss, the Gothic railway station, after the withdrawal of the train service, became a jam factory. This failed to jell.

After days of walking the byroads of the area, I have slowly begun to appreciate the character of its landscape, the drumlins draped with fine hedgerows as though a net had been cast over the rises in the land; the thorn-bushes which in West Cork are allowed to wander at will, each one a potential holy tree, are here trimmed to a topiary neatness, their tops as smooth as a soldier's haircut.

In Clones, I head for Clones Abbey. It is formidably defended against tourists by a heavily chained gate. The medieval round tower stands in a graveyard nearby. Its closed gateway bears a sign announcing opening hours, now violated by a padlock. Not willing to be diverted by mere padlocks, I skirt the churchyard wall, looking for somewhere to climb over. At the rear I find a path leading into the enclosure, unsignposted, accessible only to the tenacious. The most interesting item in this old graveyard is an early pitch-roofed house tomb, similar in style to medieval Christian reliquaries. Of which bishop or saint I know not; there is nothing to enlighten the passer-by. To the round tower, as to the abbey, access is defiantly barred.

In a side street I see a sign pointing under an archway: 'Clones Fort'. That sounds more promising — an invitation to view. A path, identical in style to the surreptitious one, leads up the hillside behind the street, between gardens and vacant lots. I follow obediently. At the summit a mound appears, covered on its top by a tonsure of thick thorn-bushes: the fort, obviously a

once-fine Norman motte. Something has happened here; a bison stampede
or a re-enactment of the Battle of the Boyne could conceivably have been
responsible for its current state. No blade of grass survives on what should
have been a grassy mound; the earth has been wrought into a savage fondue
of mud and cowshit, rucked with deep hoof-prints and furrows by heaving
livestock. Nowhere in Ireland have I seen a historic site so abused (this one
with a sign actually inviting attention), the 800-year-old Norman
earthworks reduced to desolation. Overstocked cattle being wintered out of
doors and seeking shelter have shredded the binding grassy cover of the
motte. Without cover to contain it, in a few bad winters it will flow down
upon the town, the indifferent Clones consumed like Pompeii under an
avalanche of mud.

In the newsagent's I look for postcards and find the anodyne John Hinde's
garishly tinted 1950s' version of an Ireland of golden-thatched cottages
under Mediterranean blue skies, but nothing real or even local. The girl
behind the counter scrutinises my choice. 'That's a sweet wee card,' she says,
indicating one of a farmer with dog and donkey, posing in front of a
whitewashed cottage. Donkeys are as much an endangered species in rural
Ireland as postcards appear to be.

County Monaghan is indelibly associated with the name of Patrick
Kavanagh, one of the major poets writing in Ireland in the mid-years of the
century. Local place-names form the bedrock of his work, and his
homeground is the subject of both his affection and his bitterness. With
Greek, Bulgarian and English admirers of his writing, I set off from
Annaghmakerrig to visit Inniskeen, where he was born and is buried, the
focus of much of his early work and now the centre of 'Kavanagh Country'
in both the truest and the worst senses of the phrase. Inniskeen is a small,
rural community which has latched on to the fame of its most notable son
and developed an industry around his life and works, a son whom they in life
regarded with suspicion, and who reciprocated their disdain. The former
Catholic church is devoted to Kavanagh's legend, a hagiography of the poet
of rustic poverty, spiritual and sexual deprivation, and the redeeming power
of nature.

The journey from Annaghmakerrig is fraught with difficulties. The fact
that I set off towards Galway, west rather than east, was an inauspicious
beginning. Whenever in doubt, I stop on the road and ask the nearest person
for directions: a dawdling schoolboy, an apoplectic and obese farmer with a
beetroot complexion; on each occasion the respective person looks half-
witted, but I put my faith in local knowledge to get us to our destination and

each unerringly gives the correct information. In Greece, I am informed, these 'peasants' would not have been trusted to tell us the truth, and might have deliberately lured us into some lonely spot with robbery or murder in mind. My Greek companion continually recommends the police whenever in doubt, but try finding a policeman in rural Ireland, even on the border, when you need one. In a passing downpour, a local savant informs us that 'Ireland is the bucket of the world'.

At the 'Patrick Kavanagh Rural and Literary Resource Centre', a local actor presents a performance of the poet's work, the audience a school group and my multinational carload. We follow with a visit to the poet's grave and then tour the lanes and byways of the neighbourhood, looking for the holy places of the legend: Billy Brennan's barn, the triangular field, Cassidy's hanging hill or Shancoduff townland. Eventually our halting path brings us to the Kavanagh family home, the Haworth Parsonage or Thoor Ballylee of this sad industry.

The last is the revelation needed: the reality of the poet's background, the place so mean and deprived, so utterly lacking in a sense of heart to it, that any conceivable spiritual poverty seems believable. External impressions certainly, yet there is in the raggedness of the immediate landscape, the sheer greyness of the cement-rendered farmhouse, something despairing. In the front garden of the house, as though one grave were not enough, lies a second Kavanagh resting place (the original one, transported from the graveyard), complete with dates, cross and quotation – the dreaded bilocation of poets. As a substitute for flowerbeds, the auxiliary burial place leaves much to be desired. The long-running controversy concerning Shakespeare's last resting place should be sufficient to deter these excesses.

It is probably easier, and preferable, to reconstruct the Brontë family home from imagination, contemporary records and memorabilia than it is to recreate satisfactorily the life of a recently dead individual (1967). In Kavanagh's case there is a credibility gap. A soured countryman who bore his neighbours no love is received into their bosoms with half a heart, and emerges on the other side, transmuted into our chief of men. The commerce of the matter is the key. The idea is admirable: that an important literary figure from a rural community might be commemorated in his birthplace, that such a location can be both the origin and the subject of great art. After that, something dies.

The sights of Kavanagh Country, a series of ruins and mean derelicts, transform the imaginative and spiritual into the mundane, the mud and clay of Kavanagh's verse exchanged for the actuality. There is too much of the

'Queen Elizabeth Slept Here' about the entire enterprise, too much of the clay and too little of the poetry. The physical beauty lies where it always did in Kavanagh's time, in the hedgerows and fields of the landscape which have qualities to inspire. Only this survives in Kavanagh Country. To the Shancoduff farm we went down a track of indescribable muddiness, some simulacrum of the conditions when the poet drove his few cows, the Strawberry and the Black, on the road before him. The smallness, tightness and former poverty of the place makes Kavanagh's emergence from it all the more improbable, his achievement the more durable. A placard in a ditch announces PRUNTY PEAT. How fortuitous that the Reverend Patrick Brontë 'improved' his family name.

In Carrickmacross we stop for drinks at 'The Mean Fiddler', a vast cave of muzak-supported drinking space, its cavernousness emphasised by its centrepiece, a life-sized roadside finger post bearing all the road signs now vanished from the countryside, with a bogus one saying '*leithreas*'. The banality of this talking point is enough to drive one screaming into the street, to seek a saner drinking place. The television news declares that the border with the North was closely guarded by Army, Garda and customs officials, equipped with helicopters and heat-seeking night-vision equipment. The UVF coming south, the IRA going north? No — cow-terrorism this time, Northern farmers attempting to smuggle cattle into the Republic in order to evade an EU ban on British beef cattle, allegedly contaminated by feeding the herbivore cattle with offal from the brains of politicians. A Northern politician is interviewed, one most assured of his Britishness. He demonstrates an impressive doublethink on the issue, declaring, 'The Protestant people of Ulster are British to the core — but their cows are Irish!'

Divergence of views on Kavanagh emerges with the first pint. I unwisely remark on the Resource Centre's failure to mention the generation of writers of whom Kavanagh was a part, and the poet's lack of generosity and unwillingness to acknowledge the merits of his Irish contemporaries, Austin Clarke or Louis MacNeice. My Greek lady is offended. 'I broke bread with this man. He only drank because he had to do so, was driven to it by his genius; he was pure love, a lamb.' This is such a distortion of the irascible, contentious, drunken and awkward Monaghan small farmer that I wonder where I have spent the day: was it in Lewis Carroll Country, or the Edward Lear Dong with the Luminous Nose Museum? If hagiography at home can be expanded to hero worship abroad, there is little chance for the actual life to survive. At least the poetry will endure, undimmed by transformation into the works of the gentle, mild-mannered Patrick Lambkins, the little pet.

The road signs of 'The Mean Fiddler' are again needed on the return journey. On the far side of Carrickmacross, absorbed in the ongoing argument, I inadvertently take a wrong turning. A man with a bicycle approaches unsteadily and I stop to question him. He hovers by the bicycle for a while, trying to frame an appropriate reply, the living embodiment of the bucket of the world, 90 per cent proof. Without the bicycle he can't stand; holding on to it he is unable to gesture – a dilemma. Taking a chance he lets go of the bicycle – which falls on the road – and lurches towards the car, giving eloquent and effusive directions:

'When the road turns, that's this road, the one you are on now, turn, but turn right, on a bend like, do you follow me, turn?'

He lifts his arms off the car to demonstrate and collapses heavily on the bicycle. We drive on, callously leaving the wreckage of bucket and bicycle in the middle of the road.

Neither policemen nor Kavanagh are further mentioned, as we pass through villages and hamlets, past churches and more churches – Baptist and Methodist, Presbyterian and Catholic, Church of Ireland, Christian Fellowship, Gospel Hall, Wayside Pulpit, Elim and Bible Hall, each a source of unshakable conviction, acting like magnets, drawing around them a wagon-circle of believers, believing the truths of their own faith, unbelieving of each other's, each congregation in possession of the white-hot flame of a different truth, all compromised by their failure to bear witness; the Protestant churches' failure to seek social justice, the Catholic Church's failure to take a stand against murder and terrorism.

A casual remark from a resident in Annaghmakerrig elucidated the Drum/*Droim* conflict. Drum is the location of the Republic's only chapel of Ian Paisley's Free Presbyterian Church. The graffito could be read as linguistic, sectarian *and* political.

Colonel Edward Roden Cottingham survived the Indian Mutiny and campaigns in Egypt and Bechuanaland, and in 1887 dedicated a lectern to the memory of an earlier Cottingham – 'an ancestor was Rector there' – of 1745. The Colonel's son, Captain Charles Scarborough Cottingham, saw service in the Sudan and died at Abu Haras on the Blue Nile in 1898. Archetypal honorifics for an Anglo-Irish family, soldiers and clergymen. Similar inscriptions can be found among the brass and marble memorials of almost any Church of Ireland parish church in any part of Ireland. These, in Cavan town, are followed by tablets of World War I and II. Then the commemorations cease.

This Protestant parish church of 1810 is as grey and pinnacled as can be expected. It has a taller spire and a larger nave than its rural counterparts, but the principle is constant. In the language of Irish architecture, there are few building forms as appropriate as Anglican parish churches, instantly recognisable, reserved yet confidently stating the presence of ecclesiastical tradition and social status. Kavanagh's image of the domineering mother from his long poem 'The Great Hunger', 'tall hard as a Protestant spire', emphasises the ubiquity of the image. In a choir loft, high up above the back of the nave, I come upon stacks of dusty, framed photographs of past clergy, archaic in buttoned gaiters and Canterbury caps. Beside them on the floor, a mountain of church plates, not plate, stamped with the parish insignia, numerous enough to feed a regiment. In the nave, embroidered hassocks are a small concession to human comfort.

Across the street from the Protestant parish church is the Catholic Cathedral, completed over a century later in 1942, and as redolent of empire as its neighbour, in this instance Fascist Italy rather than Victorian Britain.

Cavan is in all respects a typical Irish country town of the border counties, with long meandering streets of huckstery, pubs, betting shops, hairdressers, undertakers and grocery shops. There are the requisite number of churches, the County Court House, some Georgian, many Victorian, buildings, and modern urban sprawl at the edges, graduating from supermarkets and filling stations to the usual bungalow bliss on the outskirts. It is suburbia indistinguishable from Dublin or Cardiff, and in the midst of it is the cathedral.

Cavan Cathedral looks as if it has descended from outer space – or Salt Lake City, fully formed: the massed regiments of the Legio Decime Fretensis sounding trumpets and marching with their insignia and trophies, the bloody head of Captain Charles Cottingham from the Blue Nile carried on a pike by captive Cavan Protestants; this is surely the architecture of triumphalism writ large. While the cathedral was being built, General O'Duffy and his Blueshirts were marching about the county, proclaiming the dawn of a new era. The scale and style of the cathedral makes this abundantly clear. In the foyer a brass tablet exclaims with all the dignity of a Roman monumental inscription: ECCLESIA CATHEDRALIS SS PATRITII FEDLIMINI DIOCESIS KILMORENSIS D.O.M. Facing this piece of the imperium is one in the vulgar tongue which states: 'Awaiting the Resurrection the mortal remains of the following Bishops of Kilmore rest here beneath this Narthex.' I experience a twinge of apprehension at the thought that my visit might by mischance coincide with the last trump, and I should find myself alone in the echoing narthex with six bishops in full regalia.

The interior of this aircraft-hangar-sized nave is as cold as a tomb, and about as personal. The style of the building, the second cathedral to be built in post-independence Ireland, is an extraordinary confusion of Roman and Renaissance classicism, grafted on to an early Christian basilica interior, all topped by a Christopher Wren spire, much taller and more ornate than its cold, hard Protestant neighbour.

Cavan Cathedral is not unique, Mullingar, some 40 miles to the south, having one of the same period and similarly grandiose. After that, however, there seems to have been a failure of nerve – or the purses of the faithful were just not deep enough to sustain such episcopal megalomania. The intention is clear: 1,000-year destinies were in the air and Catholic Ireland was anxious to participate in such a celebrated second coming. Photographs on display in the narthex show Cavan's inaugural ceremonies: flurries of clergy, bishops by the score, a military guard of honour – a great day for Cavan. At the rear of the nave is an icon of high kitsch which commemorates John Paul II, the only Pope to visit Ireland. The tawdry medium is described as 'kinetic stained glass', the object as grotesque as the art form suggests.

The significant distinction which these adjoining religious buildings reveal in historical style overshadows other considerations, such as who is considered worthy of commemoration. In the cathedral, princes of the Church, bishops awaiting the Resurrection. In the Protestant church, military men receive the honours (a single aristo, the Earl of Farnham, has had his marble effigy wedged inside the communion rail), with the occasional cleric distinctly in second place. The Catholic dead in wars of the Empire are nowhere mentioned, excised from the public record. A quarter of a million Irish men and women served in the British forces and 50,000 died during World War I. The names of a dozen local men are mentioned in the Protestant church, their Catholic comrades in the trenches of the Somme and Ypres disowned and forgotten. In Enniskillen, a few miles north, on the other side of the border, the Regimental Museum displays the bugle used at the Battle of the Somme, the only memorial some of the local dead will ever receive; in the five-month-long bloodbath of the Somme, a million men, German, English and Irish, died – a 'victory' still popularly celebrated in the North.

In the streets of the town these preoccupations appear distant. History has been banished here by the lack of evidence of any earlier epoch; not a stone remains of the friary founded in the fourteenth century by the Lord of East Breifne, Giolla Iosa Rua O'Reilly. One is left with the living place, its cattle mart, its drama festival and the concerns of modern business: employment, tourism, emigration. On a Saturday afternoon, the streets are crowded with shoppers, the pubs overflowing with men watching a soccer match on television. There is a brisk trade in Easter eggs in many of the shops. A tall, grey man comes towards me, carrying an apple tart in its see-through cling-film wrapping, held before him formally, like an ecclesiastical object in a church ritual. Catching my eye, he nods gravely; one of the bishops in civilian clothes, taking a break from theological discussions back at the narthex, or maybe bringing back some grub for the guys in the dorm, for a midnight feast?

To travel north of the border requires negotiating the border posts of the official crossings. 'Unofficial roads' abound, less threatening, and sometimes more chancy. In my frequent journeys across the border in the early months of 1996 there is a tension in the air, yet it is very different from when I made these same journeys a year previously, before the announcement of the now-abandoned August 1994 IRA cease-fire. The border defences which greet the traveller from the South resemble those on the American embassies in Saigon and Beirut during respective sieges. Massed blank concrete walls, towers draped with anti-rocket screens and netting, observation slits with one-way vision glass, surveillance cameras, formidable arrays of detection equipment, huge bollards constricting traffic. It is enough to intimidate the most innocent traveller, to make one feel guilty of something, and all this without the presence of soldiers, off the streets at least temporarily. With soldiers on the street, there is real reason for fear. The soldiers are young, afraid; they cannot recognise the enemy. He has no distinctive colour, uniform, badge of office; he could be anybody, even me. Having seen these same British soldiers in the full flood of riot from army bases on the south coast of Cyprus at Episkopi and Akrotiri and been pinned to a wall by drink-mad British squaddies in Paphos, they thinking I was some species of Greek Cypriot terrorist merely because I stood out in the crowd, I know one is dealing with the irrational and potentially out of control. The fact that more innocent people have not been killed by the Army must be due to luck rather than discipline. They are young and prone to violence; men trained to kill make inadequate peacekeepers. To look sideways at a soldier on Royal Avenue in Belfast is to guarantee that he will stick his submachine gun up your nostril, stare into your eyes with icy ruthlessness. It is not a pleasant experience, yet people must live with it.

When I arrive in a town, why does everybody leave? Caledon, a few miles north of the border, could not be more deserted. An elderly lollipop man in a white plastic coat reaching to his ankles awaits custom at the bottom of the hill, waving his standard vainly in the empty street. The demon traffic from which this gentleman is protecting the schoolchildren passes in the singular down the broad main street; the promised inundation of children fails to materialise. Perhaps the pace of life here is more hectic on other occasions. Visiting country towns and villages which have been struck by the *Marie Celeste* syndrome can be an eerie experience. Obviously, life proceeds at its normal pace, the outsider's view a distortion. Here some of this atmosphere pervades the empty streets. I resolved to return at a different time of day and catch Caledon unawares, when something is happening and people are about. A little notice, pinned to a tree at the approach to the village, states: SEEK YE THE LORD.

When I do return, the streets are as deserted as before, giving Caledon the popular 1900 look. Two loungers on a street corner gape at a stranger. More seriously, on a stretch of wall between two houses, a discreet mural of the Red Hand of Ulster, the Union flag, the date 1690. In the Church of Ireland parish church, the dead of the two world wars are remembered, as is Reserve Constable Joshua Cyril Willis of the RUC, 'Killed in the execution of his duty, 1990.' A sign in the Spar supermarket announces the activities of the 'Field Marshal Alexander Pipe Band'. Alexander of Tunis, another local boy, was a son of the Big House.

Caledon is the estate village of the earls of Caledon, whose park and mansion lie behind the village, and it is superbly maintained. The various blights of the twentieth century appear to have bypassed it; such development as has taken place is in harmony with its attractive early nineteenth-century character. Alastair Rowan, author of the 'Irish Pevsner' (*The Buildings of Ireland*), remarked in 1979 that 'Caledon is one of the few places to merit exploration on foot', as though 'drive-by viewing' would suffice for the remainder of the province. The two things I had heard of Caledon before I visited it were that it is exceptionally pretty, and exceptionally bigoted. The first at least is manifestly true; on the second characterisation, I can only speculate. In 1968, 19-year-old Emily Beattie was provided with a council house, an allocation which was resented by other prospective tenants with large families. Miss Beattie's only crime was that she was Protestant and that the system favoured her application over those of higher priority tenants who were not. Protests led the local SDLP Westminster MP, Austin Currie, to squat in the offending council house until he was ejected by the police. The Northern Ireland Civil Rights Movement, galvanised by this abuse in the distribution of public housing, organised meetings and protest marches, which inexorably led to confrontation with loyalists and with the police. Out of this small spark, the troubles of the last quarter-century were born. It seems utterly improbable that such a pretty place could be the source of such agony.

In 1968 the political culture of Northern Ireland could find no room for non-sectarian civil protest, a fact which distinguishes the subsequent history of Northern Ireland as a society from present-day Europe and North America. From a loyalist perspective, *all* protest was by definition nationalist outrage, irrespective of the issue. Student revolt in Paris and the popular protests against the Soviet/Warsaw Pact invasion of Czechoslovakia following the 'Prague Spring' and Jan Palach's self-immolation also happened that year, as did student protests in the United States against the Vietnam War, and the continuing Black Civil Rights Movement. Internationally, the quest for civil rights was in the air. Only in Northern Ireland did this lead to civil war. The entrenched nature of the establishment, intellectually sand-bagged by 300 years of mind-numbing rhetoric and theological culs-de-sac, found itself unable to adapt; for those outside the sand-bags, it was unfortunately all too easy to slip into the complementary position, a revival of the armed struggle.

In 1973, by way of returning the compliment in Caledon, the IRA blew up a column which carried a statue of the Second Earl. This ritual slaughter of Ireland's sculptural heritage by nationalists is a product of utter narrowness of view, the tunnel vision of the ideologist. Not a single equestrian monument remains in Ireland because of the IRA's hatred of symbols of British rule; like woolly-mammoth-hunting cavemen, they hope with sympathetic magic to defeat their enemy by destroying his symbols, experiencing only the impotent joy of vanquishing a host of bronze-cast generals. Regrettably, the symbols are gone, all the art blown to smithereens, yet the IRA and the British remain, still glaring at one another in mutual incomprehension. In a secluded garden of Dublin Castle, safely removed from republican temptation, are the beautiful attendant figures from the obese statue of Queen Victoria by John Hughes which once graced the front of Leinster House, now seat of the Dáil. In the 1980s Victoria was sent packing to the city of Victoria in New South Wales: she would not have survived long if returned to public view in Dublin.

Inadvertently, I had parked my Dublin-registered car in front of the 1690 mural. Since most of the street was empty, I might have chosen a better spot. When I return, two long-haired youths of an appearance which I would avoid in Dublin were staring into it. The less attractive of the pair said, as I nodded cheerfully, 'Yer not welcome. Go the fuck out of here,' adding some appropriate insult about the Free State.

Caledon is one of a string of towns and villages running in a loop along the border, east to west across the landscape of Northern Ireland from

Armagh through Aughnacloy to Enniskillen, which mirror their counterparts south of the border. The 'look' is the same – or is it? For connoisseurs of security, the Aughnacloy border post is a superlative example, so intimidating that the Ministry of Defence might, in less fraught times, rent it out as a film set for features on the Cold War era, its defences a response to numerous IRA bomb attacks. The public road zig-zags through a labyrinth of high, featureless walls, observation towers and military paraphernalia of unspeakable grimness. You pass through, watched by soldiers behind tinted glass, seeing nothing. In the maw of this security apparatus, it is not difficult to believe that you might just disappear and end up in the Lubyanka – or dead in a ditch. On the other side of the chasm is a look-alike for Cootehill, a wide and windy main street with the parish church tucked into one side rather than punctuating its end; otherwise they are hardly distinguishable.

The dereliction and shabbiness which is a feature of many towns and villages immediately south of the border is also seen here, with gaping wounds on the main street where prominent buildings are just abandoned. There is a seedy air about the place, and it too gives an impression of the Ireland of 1900, the era of black-and-white photographs of grey, cement-rendered towns. This is the negative effect on business of having such an unwelcoming entrance to the town, and of its reputation as a potential trouble spot. Whatever the explanation, being on the border cannot be a bonus in promoting Aughnacloy as a place of trade. It has become a jetty rather than a bridge. Coming south through the crossing, I notice on a tree by the road another one of those little notices which appear all over the border region, casually placed in unlikely locations, like the business cards of cold-calling life insurance salesmen; this one aptly stated: PREPARE TO MEET THY GOD.

The population of Northern Ireland is permanently on the move, the traffic on the roads proportionally greater than in the Republic; as in Israel, everybody is on the move because there is nowhere to go (everywhere I have been in both Northern Ireland and the Republic, people remarked on the unprecedented post-cease-fire influx of cars from either side of the border). Prior to the cease-fire, cross-border traffic tended to be localised, Cootehill shopping in Aughnacloy, or vice versa, rather than Cork people in Belfast, Armagh people in Waterford. It is both a tribute to the civil administration of the province and its fatal flaw that so truncated a part of the island should manage at all to have become a coherent entity, not socially part of the island of Ireland, nor socially part of Great Britain either, merely linked politically to Britain and sustained economically by subvention from British tax revenues, its 5.642 square miles of territory nearly equal to that of Yorkshire.

On any map of the North, all roads lead to Enniskillen, the town poised, hour-glass fashion, on the junction between Upper and Lower Lough Erne, the northern lake being the Lower and the southern one the Upper, an appropriately disorienting metaphor for the meandering dementia of the border. In the museum I am intrigued by the relief map on display, a fine rendering of the island of Northern Ireland, sans Britain, sans Republic, sans Donegal. I must have travelled there by amphibious craft from Monaghan. The main street of Enniskillen is interchangeable with any part of Ireland: local names on shop fronts, as regional as in Kerry or Wexford, churches, the town hall, pubs, department stores, coffee shops, a chip shop, a Chinese takeaway. At a widening in the High Street is the Great War cenotaph, a monolith on which a head-bowed Tommy in tin helmet stands in repose, gripping his rifle. Around the base are piled those poppy-red British Legion wreaths, tokens of the recent Remembrance Day ceremonies. Below the feet of the melancholy bronze soldier is a frieze of birds in flight, spirits released in death. This feature of the cenotaph is a recent addition.

During the Remembrance Day ceremony on Sunday, 8 November 1987, a bomb which the IRA had placed in an adjoining house exploded, demolishing the building on top of the crowd, injuring over 50, killing 11. There are 11 birds in the frieze, poised in mid-flight, at the moment of departure, to fly over the waters of the lakelands. The Enniskillen bombing proved to be a small turning point, for individuals in the North, and on a political level in the South, one of many such cathartic incidents which chart the simultaneous progress of some quest for peace and reconciliation, and its converse – retrenchment. Although these signs of movement are no more than hair-cracks in the rigidity of Irish antagonisms, they are significant. Gordon Wilson, injured in the bombing and whose 20-year-old daughter was among the dead, publicly responded to the outrage with a spirit of forgiveness. In 1993, Albert Reynolds, Taoiseach and leader of Fianna Fáil, the southern political party most absorbed in nationalist rhetoric and ideology, appointed Wilson a member of the Seanad, the upper house of the Irish Parliament, his voice representing to the South the sentiments of Northern Protestants.

At the opposite end of the street, a plantation star fort which, in Victorian times, was transformed into a public park. The paths wind upwards like on the ziggurat of Ur, ascending to a narrow platform with another memorial column, a tall Doric pillar on which stands a victor of the Peninsular War, chilly in a toga, a poor choice of clothing for an Ulster winter. The inscriptions declaim military triumphs: MARTINIQUE, GUADELOUPE, EGYPT, MAIDA. A disenchanted demotic hand has added: 'Sex kills – die happy.'

There seems no escaping reminders of the grim reaper in Enniskillen. In the foyer of the town hall, a plaque commemorates a soldier of the Sixth Inniskilling Dragoons, Lawrence Oates, a member of Captain Scott's doomed expedition who died in March 1912 during the return journey from the South Pole. All families have their private language, phrases which take on a meaning through usage. In mine, Oates's words to his comrades as he left their tent, intent on sacrificing his own life in order to increase the chance of their survival, are a frequently referred-to code – 'I am just going outside, and may be some time.'

Armagh and Enniskillen are representative of the twin sources of settlement in Ulster, the former an early Christian site, the latter a plantation fortress, replacing that of a Gaelic chieftain. Religion and politics: political power deals in land ownership and authority and it is easy to manipulate; religion is less susceptible.

Armagh is awash with 'heritage'. If it isn't St Patrick, it's the Red Branch Knights, driving their opponents off opposing precipices. Below the cathedral, by tradition founded by St Patrick in AD 445, the 18th successor to the original building (none of them fell down naturally), posters cling to every electricity pole: PEACE NOW, FREE THE PRISONERS, TIME TO GO. All slogans of republican support groups rather than expressions of widespread popular sentiment, they reflect bogus aspects of the peace process. The peace sought here is one which conforms to a strictly nationalist formula, the prisoners referred to: the local Hizbullah activists; those being urged to leave: the British. Around the corner on the Orange Hall, need one ask? NEIN DANKE – to practically anything at all, Ireland's contribution to existentialism.

I park outside a newsagent's and go in, looking for directions. A fat woman is behind the counter, tearing the mastheads off the previous day's papers.

'I see you are up from Dublin.' (My car registration is always a giveaway.)

'Oh, yes, for a few days.'

'We see a powerful lot of cars from the Free State these times, since the cease-fire.'

(The 'Free State' became the Irish Republic in 1949; 50 years later, many citizens of the North (including nationalists) have chosen not to notice. It would raise a few eyebrows in Germany if someone said, 'I see you come from the Weimar Republic.')

'I imagine you don't read the newspapers much.'

'Ah, no. Sure I'd have no interest at all in them politicians, they have this country ruined, that John Hume and Trimble and the other ones, wasn't everything all right? They should 'ave listened to Paisley now. My wee lad plays a flute in the band and the RUC won't let them march in our own streets. Them Roman Caath-liks are ruining everything, no respect for democracy. My wee lad came home from practice and he put on his Man. United outfit, he has all the different jerseys, he said he was not going to practise no more because the RUC wouldn't let them march. Isn't that just terrible? The British government should stand up for their own.'

I commiserate on the treacheries of Perfidious Albion.

She changes tack and continues:

'They say that Princess Di is going to marry an Eye-gyptian, would you believe that? I heard it on the telly. I am sure he's only after her money. Isn't she a sweet wee girl?'

I buy a bar of chocolate and ease my way out of the shop, wondering if the 'wee lad' is a thug of 25. What if the entire British royal family were wiped out in a massive skiing disaster (or terrorist bomb), making way for the Egyptian connection to ascend the throne? Hussein I, King of Great Britain and Northern Ireland by the grace of God, Sovereign of Enniskillen and Armagh – would he care more for his troubled subjects than the present incumbents? Would they be as loyal?

Later in the day, stuck in traffic in Armagh, my absent gaze is concentrated by a large black-and-white photograph of a man's face with a disquieting furtive expression displayed on the advertising space at the rear of an Ulsterbus. The slogan ONE OF US, ONE OF THEM? succinctly expressed a pervasive Northern obsession: the gnawing urge to establish a person's ethnicity. Under this question, the small print read: 'If you catch yourself thinking like a bigot, catch yourself on.'

THE BIG HOUSE

'The light of evening, Lissadell, Great windows open to the south.' Yeats's image is of a world now lost, annihilated by extravagance and debt (slow horses and fast women), leaking roofs, land acts, family losses in World War I, political change and, finally, indifference. From the beginning of the nineteenth century, the great estates of the various periods of plantation were beginning to decline. Great houses were abandoned, sold to religious orders of nuns to be used as schools and orphanages; later followed a phase of burning – a few even by their owners for the insurance money – and, last of all, an unsympathetic political climate and increasing costs. This last has led to a rash of stately hotels and houses open to the public to earn their keep, with milord standing at the door, car-park attendant to publicans and grocers from Mulhuddart, rock musicians from Miami. Georgian and Victorian mansions, the 'big house' of Irish literature and landscape, has had to adapt or expire, the latter often the easier option.

On my way north I pass by two patrician eighteenth-century houses on a river estuary, separated by some miles of countryside, their rich, open, demesne land wooded at its edges. Neither has been converted to a convent or luxury hotel. They exist still as family homes, their land farmed, their roofs (the Achilles' heel of all aristocratic houses) unleaking. What might appear to be bastions of Anglo-Irish landed wealth and privilege become, on closer scrutiny, examples of change and evolution. The Jepsons of Dunderry House (inherited a generation ago from a distant relative) took over the estate and attempt to run it as a business. There is little sentiment for the glories of the past, no nostalgia for the lifestyle which the house once sustained. Their children, educated in Ireland instead of being, as in the past, sent to British public schools, lack the distinctive Anglo-Irish loudness, the 'English in Africa' syndrome. This bray, hallmark of a distinctive Irish cultural group, appears best suited for communicating across distant paddocks, particularly when encountered at a dinner table. Family portraits hang everywhere. 'But who are they?' 'I'll look them up for you, if you're interested,' the husband replies. They are certainly somebody's family, ancestors of the ancestors, orphaned by time and social change. A poster of the Irish World Cup team hangs in the family dining room, its members closing the circle of English involvement in Ireland. Far more people of Irish birth or extraction now live in England than English ever settled in Ireland.

For the Dalys of Ballylongford Hall, the path to ownership was even more disjointed. The last descendant of a great name expired, the demesne was sold. Their grandfather purchased the land – and the house came with it. Three generations later, the family has expanded to landed gentry status, riding to hounds, having an assured position in local country life. On the stairs and in the principal rooms the portraits hang (those of the previous family, that is). They know whom the paintings represent – well, vaguely. In both great houses the ancestral portraits remain, documentary relics of the tradition which created the houses, and of the world of exclusivity based on caste, creed, blood and land, now almost extinct. As long as the portraits remain, there is a continuity. After they are auctioned, all that is left is an empty trinket box, even if it is a gloriously decorated one.

In County Monaghan, a short distance from the border, Annaghmakerrig House has metamorphosed into The Tyrone Guthrie Centre, eschewing nuns, orphans, tourists or being torched in favour of a more engaging future. A thread of pitted avenue cuts through woods from the east; another, from the opposite direction, skirts a reedy lakeshore surrounding dark waters. Both tracks meet in a broad clearing of rising parkland, the southern slope of a drumlin, crowned by a ringfort. Poised between the fort above and the lake below is Annaghmakerrig, a pinnacled and Dutch-gabled Victorian gentleman's residence, with a long tail of meandering extensions, farmyards and outhouses. The name, like nearly all Irish place-names, is topographical: *Annagh Mhic Dheirg* – the Solid Place of the Son of the Red-haired Man. This landscape is the antithesis of a great demesne, with lands rolling to the horizon, nothing between the landowner and destiny but his rich acres. Here the house is contained by the natural contours of the land, wrapped around by its estate of hills and forests; only by climbing the wooded rise behind can its relationship to its hinterland be understood.

The window frames and doors are painted pillar-box red, an assault and shock to the eye among these bosky, greeny-brown hills. The colour announces a change of direction, the abandonment of a sedate tradition and espousal of something new – it might be a gourmet hotel or a transcendental meditation retreat centre. Annaghmakerrig, theatre director Sir Tyrone Guthrie's maternal family home, was willed by him, at his death in 1971, to the Irish State; it is now administered by the joint Arts Councils of Northern and Southern Ireland. The idea was that it should become a borderlands meeting place and residence for those engaged in the arts in either part of Ireland, a 'place of retreat for artists and suchlike creative people' (latterly from any part of the world), its *raison d'être* the drawing together of the diverging peoples of the island through artistic co-operation. This interaction of writers, composers and artists has, since 1981 when the house opened to the public, been an increasingly successful enterprise. Since then, The Tyrone Guthrie Centre, associated by greasepaint with the two theatres in North America which Guthrie founded (the Guthrie Theatre in Minneapolis and the Shakespeare Festival Theatre in Stratford, Ontario), has established itself as a significant oasis in the international network of communication in the arts. During my month-long stay at Annaghmakerrig, the residents, whose arrivals and departures flow through the house like an unstoppable torrent, included, other than those from every corner of the island of Ireland, representatives from Canada, Bulgaria, Denmark, England, Greece, and more. The house would provide the ideal circumstances for a country house murder mystery: a bronze bust of Tyrone Guthrie falls on a Swedish playwright – who could have done it?

I am installed in the Purple Room, overlooking a swathe of parkland and ragged wood over which a silvery mist is hanging. In the early morning the landscape around the house dissolves into a Chinese watercolour of subtleties, pearl grey upon ice blue, every shape half-defined, the lake and a single giant sequoia fixtures in a shifting haze. During the month there was a lunar eclipse; the whooper swans on the lake rose at midnight and in agitation swooped over the lakewaters, flying back and forth, circling in eerie protest against an alteration in the natural order – the Children of Lir in perpetual exile.

In the centre of my room, a metal staircase – actually more of a stepped girder, a Jacob's ladder of sorts – rises to a doll's bathroom under the eaves. It looks as though a leg of the Eiffel Tower had crashed through the ceiling, its presence disconcerting in an otherwise comfortable Victorian environment. A century of the family's books crowd the bookcases: obsequious biographies of British royalty, forgotten novels, sermons and tracts, intermingled with current literature and European classics. On the mantelpiece, daguerreotypes of distant Guthrie ancestors; among the contemporary art on the walls, the work of the many painters who have stayed here, cheek by jowl with steel engravings of military men, battles of the British Empire. All over the house it is the same, a blending of Guthrie family possessions with current work, as though the actually childless Guthrie's next generation were happily and productively still living here. In a sense, spiritually, they still are. One could hardly put to better use a no-longer-needed Big House. The house is now arranged to nurture whatever task the visitor needs to perform – to luxuriate rather than to starve in a garret. Quiet prevails: no radio or television breaks the silence of dark carpeted corridors or bright rooms overlooking the grounds; musicians work in isolated padded rooms.

Residents are summoned to dinner by the sounding of a brass gong in the front hallway. At dinner, a communal meal (the table seats 20), 13 people are present: the director of the centre, Bernard Loughlin, three composers, two playwrights, a brace or so of painters, some translators who are fashioning works of current Irish writing into Middle European languages, other practitioners of the various arts. It is often difficult to establish who is doing what. This is the only communal gathering of the day, a country house dinner party, Sir Tyrone present in spirit. The food represents the gourmet hotel persona of the architectural identity, cooked by Mary Loughlin, covertly running the gourmet establishment, educating the taste buds of the creative, under cover of the arts.

At breakfast and lunch, residents graze in the kitchen, feeding insatiable appetites or ascetic tastes. Personal conversations tend to take place off-stage, at the breakfast table, in studios, or during walks in the woods. Depending on the make-up in age, gender and disciplines of those in residence at any specific time, the dynamic in the house and at the dinner table can alter radically. With more males present, the talk is impersonal, theoretical, factual, career-based. As the pendulum swings towards more women, the conversation becomes more personal, actual lives being discussed rather than just careers, the attempt made to balance creativity with domesticity, family, friendships, sex and society. The men fall silent, having little to contribute.

Dinner is a more formal occasion and the conversation tends towards a series of monologues. Bernard Loughlin has a distinctive manner of speech, product perhaps of an Ulster childhood; he ululates on the subject of Big Ian Paisley, describing with sinister force the Reverend Doctor's habit of closing his eyes when orating, a mannerism he considers an indication of mental instability. Bernard closes his eyes to demonstrate. I glance around the table, eyelids flap down like drawn blinds in sympathetic unison, a sightless Last Supper. The composers swap notes.

First Composer: 'I keep everything I write, and use it all in my compositions.'

Second Composer: 'I write an enormous amount, but it is mostly worthless, so I throw it all away.'

Feminist Art Historian: 'My writing is concerned with the physicality of gestural painting of women by women. Male dominance of painting the female body has interposed gender tyranny, colonialism of the female soul, appropriation of the id.'

Listening more attentively to Bernard Loughlin's speech patterns, the singularity which I detect appears to be based on phrasing; this must be inherited, regional, not conscious. It consists of a momentarily longer than normal pause between words.

'Ben - Kiely, - Paddy - Gallagher - and - Andreas - O - Geall - a - hoir, - came - here - for - a - television programme. - When - the - television - people - came - to - collect - Ben, - he - had - one - of - the - maids - cornered - in - the - linen - cupboard, - telling - her - about - her - grandfather's - people.'

Many Northern talkers have the same conversational style, an inheritance from nineteenth-century fundamentalist pulpit rhetoric: they are, conversationally, all sons of the manse. Big Ian sports the same oleaginous delivery, crossed with that of a rottweiler; Mr Adams, with that of a pekinese. The dinner-table conversation proceeds undimmed. Dessert has been served and all the smokers strike up, led by a three-packs-a-day playwright. As a non-smoker with rabid views on the subject, I find myself continually enveloped in a noxious pool-room smog.

A Conceptual Artist: 'My installation will be composed of over 3,000 personally selected sea shells which I have gathered from the five continents and the four hemispheres. They will be arranged on the gallery floor in the pattern of the Great Nebula. Over this I will pour water from the Shannon, Ganges, Mississippi, Nile, Euphrates and Plate. The theme is unity in diversity, the curative and regenerating nature of water, the unity of the human and natural worlds.'

Self: 'But why shells?'

Artist: 'A symbol of pilgrimage, you know, Compostella, Botticelli's *Venus*, the pearl within the shell, life in the primal ooze.'

Self: 'Yes, but shells! Anything would have done as well.'

Artist: 'It's true, I might have used sea pebbles, grass, bits of bark, human hair. It's a real dilemma.'

Song Writer: 'I want my work to reflect a challenge to the music industry. It would be a bad day for me if I had a number one hit. I would be failing in my purpose of representing living music rather than static commerce.'

So it goes on, the private worlds of creation clashing with the need to communicate, welding the intractability of artistic media into something meaningful. It is not easy, even in such pampered surroundings.

In personal conversations much is revealed. Among Northern Catholics some have grim stories of intimidation by loyalists. They are not recent experiences but childhood memories, yet they bear no rancour. Significantly, none of them come from the ghettos. Those of unionist background tell another story: not mob violence but lone gunmen, neighbours picked off to equal the score; they too have a fatalistic response to their shared history. It is immutable, part of the experience of being from a divided people. Residents from the south of Ireland listen, as though Bosnia were being talked about. This is not their heritage or experience; they have nothing useful to say.

The 'Big House' of the Irish past has by both its residents and those living beyond its gates been so denounced, satirised and trivialised that the creativity which came from within Big House walls is a forgotten feature of landed life, submerged beneath a history of rack-renting landlords and conspicuous waste, and latterly great architecture or stately home nostalgia. Maria Edgeworth, George Moore, Somerville and Ross and Molly Keane have between them laughed the landed gentry to scorn, all from inside the fanlighted hallway, yet Coole Park, Edgeworthstown House, Drishane and Birr Castle were each in their way Annaghmakerrigs of creative energy, housefuls of art, writing and inventiveness.

The front drawing room of Annaghmakerrig has hardly altered since Guthrie's time, occasional later additions merging with the household objects: glass-fronted mahogany bookcases, a grand piano, couches, pictures and bric-à-brac. Unobtrusively, behind the door, is a set of tiny black-framed etchings by Daniel Maclise. One, entitled *A Patron Day, Sketch Taken at Ronogue's Well Near Cork*, shows a crowd gathered at a holy well. I looked closely into this tiny picture; in it, all the essential elements of the holy wells which I visited in West Cork can be seen. Maclise, a superb draughtsman, understood what he was looking at. Central to the view is a beehive-like building with an opening, evidently the well-house; from behind or out of it a hawthorn tree is growing. This is festooned with fragments of cloth, one quite clearly a human sock. To one side of the well, beggars stand like a grand-opera chorus, while in front a crowd kneels – a woman in a hooded cloak, a man in a buttoned tailcoat. The scene is filled with the crippled and disabled, people seeking cures. In the foreground the water flows on the ground and barefoot pilgrims either queue for the well or drink its waters. A man on crutches, with one leg held off the ground, carries two babies in a sling around his waist (a returned soldier and widower, owner of the sock on the tree?). 'Peasants' brandishing cudgels fill the background, while two women are vigorously thumping each other above the heads of the kneelers. On one side another pair of women are bound in a single shawl, one possibly carrying the other. The date is 1836.

This scene, along with others which are part of the set, concentrates on the life of the rural poor – those outside the gates of the Big House – before the Famine, and shows stock images which are also historically accurate. In another Maclise print, a cabin, the exact size of my original 'cabin' studio in Rossard, is inhabited by a couple, four children, a grandmother, three ducks, four hens, a sow and two piglets; the wife spins, the grandmother watches the iron cauldron on the open fire, a child rocks the cradle and the husband plays with one of the children – simultaneously a rustic idyll and an image of degrading and wretched poverty. Bad weather and crowds are the constants. Represented here are the illiterate rural population of the early nineteenth century; the veneration of holy wells appears consistent with everything else that is shown. Nearly 200 years later, the ducks and chickens have been banished and replaced by video and microwave, yet, remarkably, the religious practice of visiting and leaving tokens at holy wells and trees on their patron day has prevailed. More remarkably, the pre-Christian animist veneration of the nature spirits in trees is preserved by this ritual, a voice from 1,500 years ago still heard.

In a dim corridor of the house is a second representation of the same subject: a large cross-stitch rendering of Frederick William Burton's *Blind Girl at a Holy Well*, painted in 1869 and a popular subject of its day. The fabric must have been worked by one of the women of the household in the late nineteenth century. The subject would have been regarded as quaint and sentimental, an image of popular Catholic 'peasant' life, as well as adhering to conventional European artistic taste for sentimental genre subjects. Today in Armagh, bishopric of St Patrick, seat of both Protestant and Catholic bishops, in the grounds of the Protestant Archbishop's Palace is a holy well dedicated to St Brigid. This particular well survived the new broom of the Reformation within the very walls of the new dispensation, proof of the enduring nature of the tradition.

A few miles from Annaghmakerrig, at Cootehill, is Bellamont Forest, one of the most beautiful early eighteenth-century houses in the country, designed by the 25-year-old Edward Lovett Pearce, the Irish architectural genius of the period. Its name is not an anglicisation of an Irish topographical one but the grand tour equivalent, an Italianate name for a Palladian villa, 'Bella Monte'. Bellamont sits on top of a drumlin like the knob on a teapot lid, as contrived as a stage setting, convenience sacrificed for dramatic effect, the avenue circling through the parkland so that the house can be seen to maximum advantage. I go to draw it on a day which threatens rain and end up doing a sketch sheltering under an ancient beech tree in the grounds. As I draw, I notice far off on another venerable tree a small, square sign, presumably of the 'grounds private' variety. I decide to ignore its message.

The house is closed, its windows blind and shuttered, no sign of life. I wander in the demesne, an occasional jogger for company. The two lakes which flank the rise on which Bellamont stands appear between the trees of the park, over which can be seen the steeple of the parish church. To the rear of the house, not looking where I am going, I stumble in a rabbit hole. This, on inspection, proves to be an opening to some subterranean chamber, into which light is streaming from another source. The small boy in me has never been able to resist underground passageways. I search for the entrance, which is easily found – leading from the basement area of the house. From there a long cobbled and vaulted passageway slopes darkly down to the farmyard, a few hundred yards from the house. Among eighteenth-century foibles, one of the least attractive was the gentry's aversion to *seeing* servants in the immediate vicinity of their houses. Means had to be contrived to prevent the comings and goings of menials from intruding on the view. Hence this tunnel, skilfully devised to allow communication between the house and farm, out of sight of august eyes, the drama of the house's setting unspoiled by any current reality.

Ignoring common sense, I enter the tunnel, the far end only a speck of light in the distance, and am halfway down before I hear the sound of someone moving in one of the side chambers, a few feet from me. It is not light enough to see anything. I freeze and listen, remembering where I am, a few miles from the border, Injun territory, IRA homeground. Had there not been nasty incidents in this immediate area? What gruesome news had I read in the papers about Cootehill? More foot-shuffling follows, then the person, clad entirely in black, leaps at me from the shadows. With a terrified whinny, a tiny all-black pony races past, up the passageway to the light, leaving me petrified, heart thundering like a Lambeg drum. Later, recovering my equilibrium under a tree with a gentle drizzle falling, I come face to face with the sign I had seen earlier from far off. It states tersely, to any squirrel or thrush that might be passing, CHRIST DIED FOR THE UNGODLY

DUBLIN INTERLUDE

Coming east from Monaghan, and before turning south for Dublin, I stop in Drogheda. In St John's Catholic Church is displayed the severed head of the canonised Oliver Plunkett, Archbishop of Armagh, a suspect in the 'Popish Plot' who was hanged in 1661 at Tyburn. Plunkett occupies a large, brassy reliquary in a side-chapel, a tall, space-rocket-like container for his small, nut-brown head, shrivelled like a preserved apple, indistinguishable from that of Tutankhamun or the Tollund Man – an old, old person who remembers it all, yet does not care any more. He looks indifferent to his surroundings, his person as self-sufficient as any Amazonian shrunken head, simultaneously a person and a non-person.

On a kneeler a spare and solitary man prays fervently, his anguished face pinched with grief and concentration. He is as oblivious to my presence as is Plunkett's head, yet they might have been cousins, the same aquiline line of the nose, leaf-shaped eyelids cupping the eye-sockets, a mouth tight and drawn. Not far from Drogheda live some of Plunkett's blood-relations; it is not too preposterous to think that they may call occasionally on their ancestor, and kneel awhile among the devout. There is something macabre and preposterous about the idea of witnessing one's contemporaries entreating a family member many centuries dead for favours in the future – a wife cured of cancer, an ill child made well, a win in the Lottery. In the North Cathedral in Cork, in a more modest box, is Plunkett's arm-bone; doubtless his other members are scattered across the Catholic world: his heart in Rome, his silver shoe-buckles in Santiago-de-Chile, his Bermuda shorts in Miami.

A little nut-brown elf man, a tribal shrunken head or juju doll – who is this person, trapped and obscenely displayed in a gorgeous brass display case? The small carapace of the creosote-painted head looks tiny in its vast container, lonely and forlorn; it is just a head, no body, nothing else. The Egyptian mummies in the British Museum, far from home and laid out in the glaring light of a public mortuary, at least have bodies attached to their heads. This Drogheda specimen has suffered the added indignity of the separate body parts being trundled about Europe like a reluctant tourist; some are lost, others end up here, there and anywhere at all, Rome, England, Germany, Ireland.

I regret my visit to Plunkett's head. This is voyeurism of the most vulgar kind, little better than being a member of the crowd screaming for blood at Tyburn, awaiting the disembowelling with relish. The abuse of human dignity in displaying the parts of a real human person as an object of public 'religious' curiosity and veneration is hardly less offensive than the eighteenth-century viewing of the insane as an entertainment. A time must come when this barbarous form of Christian ritual is no longer acceptable, when Plunkett's gory remains will be given proper burial. I feel a strong urge to kidnap the head and take it home, inter it in the garden and plant a mountain ash on the spot, telling nobody. When eventually, a month or so later, I am back in Rossard, I mention my revulsion at its display to Pat Connor, a sculptor with a profound interest in hieratic images of the human head. 'Oh yes,' he said. 'When I was a child, we went on a school tour to visit Drogheda, and were brought to see Plunkett's head.' The zoo, Nolly Plunk and an ice-cream cone, very educational.

The display of Plunkett's head may be seen as a last and unlikely survival of the European Celtic cult of the human head. To the Celts the most important symbol of divinity and supernatural power was the head, as container and embodiment of the human spirit. The Janus-like male idol on Boa Island in Lough Erne is the finest surviving Irish example of this pre-Christian cult, which continued as an important motif into Irish Romanesque and medieval figure sculpture.

Either it is acceptable to preserve the heads of one's ancestors, and every family mantelpiece and piano should be decorated with a row of ancestral faces between the photographs of the living, or it is unacceptable, barbaric and offensive to human dignity, and what is happening in St Peter's Church is just pagan ancestor worship. If this is to be considered an acceptable practice, perhaps it should depend on the eminence of the person to be preserved – might the grizzled head of W.B. Yeats be displayed in the Irish Writers' Museum (his heart in Sligo, his kneecaps on the Shankill Road)?

I return to Dublin for a rest, to see my family and prepare for the next leg of my journey, a more extended tour of Northern Ireland. My studio-cum-office is on the sixth floor of a mid-nineteenth-century granite sugar mill, now known as the Tower. It is a few minutes from the centre of the city, and overlooks a stretch of the Grand Canal Harbour, an expanse of water inhabited by swans and cormorants. Sometimes I just sit at the window and watch the cormorants dive for fish, counting the seconds until they surface, attempting to calculate where they will reappear. Invariably I am wrong, yet it is a pleasant and peaceful way of managing not to do anything more pressing. Last year the pair of swans which nest at the far end of the harbour produced six chicks; only one survived to become a cygnet.

Around the water are an assortment of stone warehouses and high-rise granaries; the atmosphere on a foggy day resembles the world of Fritz Lang's *Metropolis*. I live nearby, further along the canal, in an alternative 'Kavanagh Country', where the poet spent the latter half of his life, and about which he wrote as evocatively and with as much feeling as he had done about Monaghan in his early years. I make the journey between home and studio a couple of times a day, under trees along by the water, across a lock-gate, under a low, skew-arched railway bridge. If you must live in a city, this is not a bad compromise. Sometimes I come and go in the middle of the night, the locality at its most *Metropolis*-like.

On Saturday morning I drive to see some friends in Dun Laoghaire and return towards the Tower at midday. Grand Canal Quay runs between the warehouses, under the skew-bridge to the Tower. Halfway down, trucks are parked on either side, leaving only a narrow alley for passage. Visibility under the bridge and between the trucks is severely limited. A small, blue pick-up truck is approaching at speed from the opposite direction. It pulls in halfway down, between the trucks, and I negotiate the passageway, stopping at the narrowest point to see if there is room to proceed.

Suddenly the driver's door of my car opens and a man, screaming obscenities, hurls himself into the car, knocking me across the passenger seat where I lie with him on top of me as he punches me and pours a torrent of incoherent abuse into my face. Terrified and pinned under him, I try to feel with my free hand on the floor for the car crook-lock in an attempt to defend myself, but with his weight on top of me I can't move. This is the ultimate urban nightmare, a chance meeting with some deranged individual – being in the wrong place at the wrong time. With a savage scream he puts his hands on my throat and shakes me. I think, 'This is it; just back from the border and I am murdered by a maniac on my doorstep – the final indignity.' With a further torrent of obscenities, he jumps back out of the car and vanishes. I sit upright, shocked, and fortunately look around. He has run to his pick-up and taken a sledge-hammer out of the back. With this raised in the air, he is now running straight back at me. All the while the car engine has been running, so I just push the accelerator and shoot between the trucks. In the rear-view mirror, like on a small television screen, I see him running in the street, the sledge still above his head, his mouth wide open, screaming. Had I not turned and seen him coming, in a few minutes I would have been dead, or severely brain-damaged. I drive unthinkingly past the sanctuary of the Tower, mindlessly crossing the city, my eyes constantly searching the mirror for a blue pick-up. I see about twenty in the next quarter of an hour.

Tragically, such incidents have no meaning. Cities are full of deranged individuals, people so stressed that the next human being to cross their path ends up dead. Fortunately this man did not have a gun, much more immediate than a sledge-hammer if you have murder in mind. However, has a man who reaches for his sledge to attack a stranger perhaps done so before? I attempt to reconstruct the persona of my assailant. All I can produce is the smell of his breath (he was not drunk) and the sound of his hysterical voice. I don't think I really saw his face at all, he was so close to me and I was so terrified, but I understand now what Francis Bacon was painting all those years, the scream of anguished despair, in this case become aggressive. In retrospect, I realise that I cannot even adequately describe my assailant – male, a Dubliner, maybe 35 and below average height, the driver of a blue pick-up truck, make and registration unknown; he was, one might say, nasty, brutish and short.

He could have been a jobbing builder, a small-time drug dealer, or, quite plausibly, an IRA fellow traveller who has been engaged in punishment beatings (the sledge-hammer is second only to the nail-studded baseball bat as the most-favoured weapon among paramilitary vigilante groups). It is hard to accept that this individual never behaved thus before meeting me, an anonymous motorist blocking his road on a pleasant Saturday morning in Dublin. I found the experience deeply depressing; it destroyed my equanimity for weeks afterwards, still does if I think about it. As an unbeliever, I find such intimations of mortality profoundly unnerving; even for a believer, it would be difficult to fit a demented sledge-man into the divine plan, but no doubt they can manage it somehow. I lack this luxury.

As I meander across the city without purpose, a motorcycle policeman suddenly appears on my side, indicating that I should pull into the kerb. I do so and he regards me coldly. Am I aware that a digit is missing from my rear number plate, that I am driving too fast, erratically and dangerously in a built-up area, that my car looks as if it should not be on the road at all? Do I have my insurance papers and driving licence on me? I attempt to explain my recent encounter with a representative of the 'Sledge-hammers for Peace' brigade. The garda gives me a poke with his leather-gloved hand and responds, 'Your insurance papers and driving licence, please?' Of course I am without the necessary documents. The motorcycle cop drives off in a roar, leaving me with a sheet of limp, white paper desiring my appearance at some district court, some time in the future.

Inevitably, needing sympathy, the first person I meet after my encounter has to hear of my adventure; as I talk, I have the uncomfortable sensation that she is just waiting for me to finish in order to share with me her own encounter with danger. I am right, but it turns out to be much worse than I have anticipated. She too has had a near-death experience, but hers was an 'out-of-body' one! It is alarming how quickly one can descend into anarchy. I reach for my out-of-body sledge-hammer.

Punishment beatings are the lower end of the level of violence which the population of the North have had to live with, and one which passes for justice in the ghettos. On the daily news in the South, the references to 'punishment beatings' are so commonplace that one might legitimately wonder if the term is just another Irish euphemism for some form of social behaviour. A few days later, as I walk along Nassau Street, past Fred Hanna's Bookshop which has Tim Pat Coogan's book *The IRA* in its window, I bump into an aquaintance who is looking for a copy of some book of mine, now out of print. My mind still moving upon the subject of violence, I recollect that the same publishing house also publishes Gerry Adams, president of Sinn Féin, and Alice Taylor, a West Cork rustic raconteur. I envisage Adams, Taylor and self meeting for high tea in the deep plush of the Shelbourne Hotel on St Stephen's Green.

Perhaps it would not be such a good idea, however. Instead, I phone the

Sinn Féin office in Dublin and speak to a cheerful young man with a strong Derry accent. Does he know when the annual Sinn Féin commemoration of Wolfe Tone takes place at Bodenstown? Assuming automatically that only a fellow republican would bother to ask such a question, he replies, 'Do you have your latest copy of *An Poblacht*? There was an article in the last issue which mentioned it, I think.' Not being a subscriber to this republican newspaper, as convincingly as I can manage I plead incompetence. 'Can't put my hand on it right now.' He is not bothered, and goes off to look for the information.

Back on the phone with the details, he offers to find a seat for me and my family on buses provided by Sinn Féin for the pilgrimage to County Kildare; evidently the party faithful regard this as an occasion for a family outing. I say that I will let him know. Visions of sitting next to party activists and managing not to reveal that I am a spy for the Enlightenment could be difficult. What if I had to sit next to Adams? I am comforted by the consideration that even in revolutionary organisations there is a pecking order, and the leaders are unlikely to travel with the proletariat. Could I actually carry on a conversation in republican dinosaur-speak? 'Tell me lads, how goes the armed struggle?' Should I refrain from mentioning my brief acquaintance with Mrs Windsor, monarch on an adjacent island? I plan to go, but do not contemplate the occasion with much pleasure.

Later, by way of comic relief, I phone the office of Fianna Fáil and ask the same question. (Many Irish political parties make the annual pilgrimage to Wolfe Tone's grave – on widely separate dates.) An altogether more suave young man deals with the matter. 'I will check it on my screen. Be back to you in a moment.' I imagine that he must be the type who wears red braces and works in financial services, but this image is instantly destroyed by telephone music of massed bands playing appalling *Soldiers of Destiny* theme music. After only two phone calls, I feel disinclined to accompany any of these groups on their annual symbolic blood-letting at the grave of a martyr.

Having left Northern Ireland and its collective religious obsessions behind, I am glad to be out of a society that feels obliged to place signs in every thicket reminding one of eternal damnation. A society so wedded to the language of symbols has little interest in abstract thought. However, in Dublin you merely exchange one style of bigotry for another. The underlying prevalence of sectarianism is hard to avoid in any part of Ireland; in the South it is just less overt.

A friend invites me to lunch. Her fine house stands on a quiet street in Rathgar, a leafy suburb of Victorian Dublin. This is not the world of wayside pulpits and shopkeepers fulminating against their Caath-lick neighbours; if people have religious beliefs, it is their own private business, or so I thought. My host is a Dublin socialite, a charming woman who has spent a lifetime involved in the arts, whose friends are ranged widely in positions of cultural influence. The guests are myself, the director of an important private art gallery and his wife, other people involved in the worlds of literature and music.

The conversation has trawled through scandals of the moment, books published, exhibitions seen; it could be anywhere in the developed world: educated people discussing culture over a convivial lunch. On my right the gallery director's wife has drifted from the artistic to the personal, and the power of prayer. This is not a subject with which I am comfortable or experienced, so I listen to an account of wonders seen. My neighbour has been well rewarded for her faith and an impressive list of unexpected cures, poodles lost and found and diamond rings recovered is delivered to the table. The others listen but do not contribute miracles of their own, umming and ooohing as the occasion demands. I neither contribute nor ooh enthusiastically, preferring silence and to let this rigmarole of populist faith pass me by. Perhaps misinterpreting my lack of keenness, the miracle-worker turns to me with a leading question. 'What about you, then? Have you experienced the power of prayer?'

I like to keep my powder dry when the winds of prayer are blowing, say nothing, not reveal my actual views. However, a direct question demands an answer, so I respond, 'Well, as an atheist, of course, I do not have such experiences.' She screams shrilly and, placing her podgy, ring-covered hands beneath her chair seat, quickly moves herself as far away from me as table and guests will allow. With a gasp she says, 'Then you must be a very evil person.' Her remark cuts through the table conversation like an axe, followed by a gabble of talk as everyone rushes to smooth the tension. The miracle-worker and I do not exchange any further conversation, but during the remainder of the meal I can see her observing me distrustfully, her eyes probing beneath the tablecloth to see if my cloven hoof has burned a hole in the Turkish carpet. So much for appearances. I might never have left the borderlands. I feel like sneaking around to the miracle-worker's house in the middle of the night and placing a placard in her garden hedge, emphatically stating GOD IS DEAD. It could be news in Dublin 6.

In the 1950s, my great-aunt's maid, Lizzy, showed the initiative of a truly modern woman in a perilous situation. She was cycling home at night from a country dance and met the Devil on the road.

'And what did you do, Lizzy? Did you pray for divine protection?' asked my great-aunt.

'Well, ma'am, I just rang my bell. He didn't like that.'

DERRY AS A SUBURB OF BEIRUT

'When the burning starts, your place will not be torched.' Andy mentions that his mates have been talking again, their words intended to be reassuring. These 'friends' are West Cork small farmers, tradesmen, builders, a postman and some others, his drinking companions, not representatives of the Combined Loyalist Military Command, the Red Hand Commandos, or the IRA's Army Council. Andy is an immigrant, English, a stranger in so far as you can remain a stranger in the place which has been your home for over half a lifetime. To those who are native to the place, you will always be a stranger. Nonetheless, he has built a house in the Skibbereen area and brought up his children here, and this is the place which he regards as home.

The threat I have heard often enough, yet I had never seen it carried out. Timmy Sullivan, small farmer, builder, game poacher and aggressive drunk, had to be restrained in Duggan's Bar when he screamed out, 'I'm going to burn out that fucking Dutchman.' He did not do so and, even without restraint, would probably have balked at the actual deed. He might have broken a few windows, cut down a tree, lurched drunkenly into the

Dutchman's kitchen in a flood of accusations – and later parted in an effusion of sentimental alcoholic affection. The offence need be no more than the inadvertent blocking of a gap between whin bushes, some minor failure in the protocols of rural life. Alternatively, the problem may be more fundamental: a non-national's understanding of the rights of private property and the freedom of the foreshore in Ireland and elsewhere may have different meanings.

This burning is a recurring theme, an atavistic urge towards violence, an irrational desire to destroy. Rather than have recourse to the law, there is an ancestral urge to see what one cannot have reduced to embers. The 'Dutchman', archetypal foreigner, will have paid the market price for his house and land, employed local people to build or alter it, be a relevant component of the local economy, yet however much he may contribute to maintaining life in some isolated area of the western seaboard, a miasmic fog will occasionally descend on his neighbours, who tend to become men of spirit when drink has been taken. Then the talk is of when the burning will start. It does not happen, or only very rarely; the occasional burning of a neighbour's haybarn has more to do with blood feuds and neighbourhood spite than any reference to nationalist fervour aimed at newcomers or those of different denominations.

Change location, from the largely untroubled south of Ireland, where conflicts are concerned with the arcane rituals of envelope-farming, party politics and the persecution of the travelling community, to the North, and the emphasis changes also. In Ulster, the same braggadocio of drunken louts takes on the reality of dangerous words – and without too much pressure, the word becomes the deed. The sanction of political unrest validates the urges of every freelance pyromaniac in the land to torch his neighbour's chip shop with a petrol bomb, or to destroy the entire commercial and cultural centre of a town or city, because the burner is unemployed, one of the have-nots. The received version of Irish history, whether it be from a loyalist or nationalist perspective, does not encourage subtlety of thought; the gut reaction precedes by many generations the reflective response.

In his nineteenth-century rendering of a poem from the Irish, 'O'Hussey's Ode to the Maguire', James Clarence Mangan ends a lengthy lamentation for Gaelic nobility brought low by conquest with the words:

But the memory of the lime-white mansions his right hand hath laid
In ashes warms the hero's heart!

Just so. If the generations who have grown up in the South, far removed from any sense of immediate threat of ethnic or religious conflict, can still empathise with the sentiments of Mangan's hero, those on this island living in a volatile, divided society have little hope of distancing themselves from the adrenaline of burning lime-white department stores and corner shoe shops, let alone a challenging supply of church, chapel and meeting hall; Orange, Masonic and parochial halls are an added bonus.

A month later I go North again, this time making a journey as far away from the contamination of the border as is possible, skirting the coastline on the north-east of Ireland. In one respect Northern Ireland is the most interesting part of the island because Irish 'history' is still being lived there. The North represents a fascinating opportunity for time travel into the labyrinth of Irish political mythology, historical preoccupations, sectarian antagonisms and colonial inheritance. In the South, Irish history and its concepts are becoming muted, beginning to be relegated to doctoral theses and popular films; people are attempting to live in the now. In the North there is no dividing line between the past and the now. *This* is the true 'seamless garment' of Irish consciousness; the participants have not noticed that they live in a different age, one which is indifferent to the question of whether the Eucharist is blood or a metaphor, unaware that there ever was such a burning question.

In a series of hops I move up the coastline of Down and Antrim, foolishly believing that manifestations of aggressive politics were confined to the borderlands, and that a more benign spirit of Ulster might be encountered elsewhere; I hope to find a society at peace with itself rather than at war. The north-east coast of Ireland possesses two of the most outstanding areas of natural beauty in the whole island: the Mournes and the Glens of Antrim. The former are an unlikely series of mountains hugging the coast. They are not real mountains, but a child's idea of them, very steep, much too close together and rounded on top; I find them rather too improbable to take seriously.

I stay for the night outside Newcastle in the first of a ghastly sequence of shrines to the Laura Ashley cult, designed to offend the eye and sedate the senses: the classic Irish bed and breakfast where the hospitality is as overpowering as the visual taste is bad. In the morning I suffer an abrupt introduction to those who are to be my constant travelling companions, off-season tourists of advanced age, massive corpulence and extreme views.

The nonagenarian Canadian couple at breakfast carry on the North American tradition of public conversation; even this early in the morning they are wearing the warpaint and tribal costume of Miami Beach, plaids which had been sadistically designed to nauseate the hung-over traveller, enough make-up to disguise the Elephant Man.

'That Ben Franklin was here in Ulster. Wasn't he an inventor or something?'

'My ear is still bothering me, Harry.'

'Listen to this, what I read in the brochure: the National Trust is the largest single purchaser of toilet tissue in the UK. Just fancy, pity we are not in sanitary supplies.'

'Harry, my ear is all swelled up.'

The German couple opposite are anxious to contribute their Deutschmark's worth to public debate; the man has evidently OD'd on Irish trivia and desperately needs to off-load. He starts to explain about drainage in the Mournes, annual rainfall, agricultural potential of the area and the benevolence of the Earls of Roden, an extinct landowning family who made some major contribution to upland drainage. The Canadian, not impressed, turns to me.

'Young man, if you are from Dublin, how come you do not have an Irish brogue?'

'You must have a very poor ear for language.'

'He is not trying to be rude, Harry; they are just like that.'

The Canadian male moves to another topic to counter the Germanic drainage, now overflowing and in danger of inundating the breakfast room.

'Canada is being ruined by the Indians. They want everything now, and when the Métis get in on the act [people of combined French and native Canadian origin] white people will have nothing left but their clothes. The Indians should stay on their reservations and take what they are given.'

'That's right, Harry. Canada is just like Northern Ireland; the minority have no respect for democracy.'

I leave them to their soda farls and shiny brown sausages as large as Zeppelins; neither couple looked as though a cholesterol breakfast, the proverbial 'Ulster fry', was exactly what their girth required. This talk of 'the minority', a commonly used term among unionists and nationalists to imply the latter, interested me because it reminded me of the same phrase as used in Israel, but with considerable liberty. To my ear – or sense of proportion perhaps – the phrase is aptly used to describe small segments of the population who are minorities in Ireland or anywhere else: Asians, Muslims, Bosnian refugees. In Israel, Ashkenazi (or European) Jews refer to the Oriental (or Arab) Jews as 'the 60 per cent minority' in defiance of mathematics or logic, the implication being that they might represent large numbers, yet are politically or economically disenfranchised. In Northern

Ireland, to refer similarly to the 45 plus per cent Catholic proportion of the population as 'the minority' may be factually correct, but it implies far more than it states, being closer to the wishful thinking of Israel's European cultural elite than to any democratic respect for major sections of the population. Recent population statistics from Northern Ireland record 855,000 Protestants and 645,000 Catholics. What will happen when the 'minority' become the '60 per cent minority'?

I imagine that I am inured to rain, yet my heart sinks because the mountains have disappeared when I set off towards Downpatrick and Strangford Lough. In Downpatrick I visit St Patrick's grave, the most eloquent bogus antiquity in Ireland. Under a mammoth boulder inscribed in Irish characters with Patrick's name reputedly lie in ménage-à-trois bliss Patrick, Brigid and Columba, three of Ireland's most important saints. This grand cyclopean boulder was placed there in 1912; it is a pity that it is a fake because it is more satisfactory than anything else in the town, where, as in many other parts of the North, warfare has ensured that precious little from earlier than the eighteenth century has survived. Some municipal clod has erected a sign right next to the stone, informing the public (incorrectly) of what it is.

I cross the Narrows by ferry to the Ards Peninsula and continue up the coastline in a fine, grey drizzle. This lifts at Portavogie and I begin to enjoy the sight of the sea and the seaside villages, each with its World War I cenotaph, some with a figure of a uniformed Tommy, others just a record of names. Wherever there is a cenotaph, the kerbstones are painted red, white and blue, the colours of the Union Jack. Occasionally the tarmac of the road has a mural of the Red Hand and 1690, each little place asserting its British traditions, should anybody be in doubt. I am ruminating on these fairly muted statements of identity as I round a corner outside Grey Abbey and read in large lettering on a wall facing the junction:

WE WILL NOT FORSAKE
THE BLUE SKIES OF ULSTER
FOR THE GREY AND MISTY CLOUDS
OF THE REPUBLIC

I have to pull in dangerously to the verge and go back and read it again. This is rather more interesting than requests that we remember 1690. It is the first inscription I have seen that expresses a present-day thought and fails totally to mention the past. This is something one could discuss as an objective comment on how loyalists regard the society of the Irish Republic

— these are metaphorical skies, the blue of private conscience versus the grey mists of dogma. In its limited way it makes a fair comment on the states of mind involved in the conflict. In truth, the dark soul of Ulster mirrors that of the Republic; the more either concept is identified with, the deeper into a bloody cul-de-sac it drags the believers.

The weather becomes so bad that I abandon my plan to continue along the coast to Belfast Lough and cut across the country to the city, staying the night in a small hotel next to Queen's University. In the university I go to an exhibition celebrating Seamus Heaney as the new Nobel Laureate. This verges on gathering up the poet's nail parings with all sorts of objects, short of beer mats, decorated with Heaney's words. I find the adulation depressing: no use to poetry and surely an embarrassment to the author.

Across the road in the students' union building, a debate has been organised to discuss the 'marching season'. Two hundred students crowd the Mandela Hall. They look like students anywhere, embossed with Walkmans, Coke cans, spilling armfuls of books. Deirdre McAlliskey from the students' union is chairperson. Other speakers are Peter O'Reilly of the SDLP, Gerard Rice of the Lower Ormeau Residents Association, Chris Ryder of the Police Authority. Letters declining the invitation to be represented are read from the Orange Order and the Royal Ulster Constabulary. The absence of these organisations deprives the meeting of the prospect of achieving anything, as is pointed out by speakers from the floor before the meeting has even begun. During the 1960s, Bernadette McAlliskey was one of the most dynamic and vocal leaders of the civil rights movement; the chairperson of the meeting is her daughter. In 1981 the UVF attempted to assassinate McAlliskey senior, shooting her nine times. The IRA's response was to successfully obliterate two generations of a single political family, Sir Norman Stronge and his son James, then burning their house to the ground.

I shift with impatience as speaker after speaker gives an account of his or her position. All this might be read in the daily papers; am I just wasting my time? The man from the Ormeau Road reiterates the hurt of his community through which Orange marches annually pass, with the accompanying content of deliberate threat and insult. An articulate girl from the floor reminds the audience that the Orange Order is a Christian body, the violence a product of fellow travellers and yob elements among their supporters. Here is another rehearsal of the long-standing absence of debate on the rights of one community to 'invade' the territory of another, with or without malice aforethought, 'because our fathers and their fathers before them did so'.

Chris Ryder, of the Police Authority, casts the discussion into some perspective, emphasising more than all the other speakers some essential malaise in Northern Irish society. His point is that the position of the RUC is an impossible one; that whatever they do, they are on the wrong side; that the problem lies with the society, not its police. Annually in Northern Ireland there are over 2,800 marches and every one of them has to be policed; all take place during the marching season (12 July to 30 August). Of these parades, a quarter are nationalist, three-quarters loyalist; many march through areas which, due to demographic change and population growth, have changed in ethnic/denominational character since the marches began a century ago.

In Annaghmakerrig, the night-time discussion had occasionally moved to this topic. Three of the women had grown up in religiously mixed suburbs of Northern towns, and in all three cases their families had moved as tension rose during the 1970s. One was from the only Catholic house in a friendly and peaceful Protestant street where the family had amicable relationships with their neighbours. The bands habitually paused to play outside their house, then moved on. This happened every year: an implicit threat, clearly stating, 'We know who you are.' The other two recounted similar incidents, bearing no animosity towards Protestants, but much towards the Orange Order as a catalyst for bigotry. By chance, on that occasion the speakers were Catholic; although for Protestant the type of incidents differ, their experiences are essentially the same.

The meeting proceeds. The Ormeau resident becomes impassioned, attempting unsuccessfully to seem reasonable – the grievances of his community are too deep to be concealed. A betting shop where some nationalists had been gunned down is repeatedly mentioned; here also the Orange marchers pause to sound the triumphalist drum of victory. The speakers from the floor who are Protestant carry no writ for violence, yet seem imbued by naiveté, asserting that the 'yob element' is unrelated to the Orange Order. Perhaps so, yet they are a significant product of it. Many whose political background could not be identified ask why the prime protagonists had chosen not to be represented. The most disquieting speaker is a close-cropped young man who says, 'The RUC will have nowhere to hide, nowhere to run to,' as though the RUC is the source of the trouble.

To an outside observer, the encounter appeared both impotent and tragic, the loyalist tradition choosing not to articulate its position in this most appropriate of stages, that of university student debates, leaving itself to be represented on the streets by its most rabid elements. By choosing not to speak in such a forum, the only platform left is the confrontation of the Lower Ormeau Road, where sectarian antagonisms are the language of communication. The meeting ends – a damp squib, nothing achieved except a reiteration of the intractability of dissent. The chairing of the meeting by Deirdre McAlliskey was symbolic of paralysis: another generation of the same family saying the same things, the civil liberties voice talking in a democratic forum, the forces of reaction choosing not to debate, the IRA and UVF waiting in the wings, ready to deal their own aces, precisely as it was in 1968 – failed civil liberties agitation drifting into anarchy.

My journey takes me further up the Antrim coast, witnessing some of the finest seaboard landscape in Ireland, then through the Glens to the northern coast. It rains steadily, downpours savagely lashing the hillsides, yet through it I enjoy the high seas and deep valleys. Across the straits the outline of the Mull of Kintyre and the coast of Scotland appears and disappears, seeming at times unnaturally close. In Ballycastle I spend the night in a run-down modern hotel, new ten years ago, already decaying. Conversations there are unpromising; this is international commercial traveller territory, employing dull people, patronised by the same. I go walking along the seafront, towards the remains of a medieval abbey on the coast. Inside its walls there is no need to walk bent double from the wind. I potter around looking for I do not know what, and find it. In a corner is a plot devoted to sailors lost at sea during World War I, commonplace in any part of Britain or Ireland; what is unusual is the memorial: a Celtic cross decorated with a harp, shamrocks and an interlace design. Clearly in 1918 it was not considered inappropriate for Irish men serving in the British forces to be commemorated with Irish symbolism. Today this would be anathema. Northern Ireland's unionists have so wished to distance themselves from what they perceive to be 'nationalist' culture that they have alienated themselves from what used to be a strong part of their own identity.

I wander on from town to town – Coleraine, Limavady, Strabane, Omagh – and stay in a succession of chapels of the Laura Ashley cult, a belief system which transcends politics and ethnicity. In Limavady, something about the place-name, a familiar resonance, attracts my attention; I consult my travelling library for the origin of the name and am not disappointed. Limavady and Leamawadra are variant anglicisations of my old friend from Rossard, the *Léim a Mhadra* river. Because the Irish-language origin of Northern Ireland's topographical place-names is not acknowledged on road signs as it is in the South, this information acquires a subversive quality. Whether the unionist population accepts it or not, this is its own cultural loss, a conscious self-deprivation of the richness of language.

Everybody I meet is anxious to talk: all wish for the abandoned cease-fire to be restored; no one seems overly optimistic. In an Omagh pub I share a pint with a stranger, a small, quiet man with receding ginger hair and grey freckles. He is a retired RUC man, as innocent of political realities as any other occupant of the dream landscape in the Republic. He is friendly, a committed Christian, anxious that I should realise the importance of peace to Northern Ireland. 'After the cease-fire we went to Dublin. I had not been there for 25 years; it was so nice, so friendly. We walked about, the wife shopped in Henry Street. We stayed in the Gresham. We met many Southern Protestants when we attended service in St Anne's. They told us that Ulster people, Catholic or Protestant, were different from people in the South; we did not mind, it was good to be there.' He continues to express enthusiasm for the people of the South, rather in the manner in which German tourists admire Greek peasants for their hospitality, and then he moves to his central theme. 'You know, *I* too am in favour of a United Ireland. I would love to be able to travel freely to any part of Ireland, as we did when I was a child. Yes, I am in favour of a United Ireland, but under British rule, of course. That would be best.'

He looks at me sideways, to see how I might receive this proposition, and when I do not blink he expands his theme, explaining how really the British system is more egalitarian, that the British Isles are a natural unit, that this could bring Irish people together rather than the opposite. He might have been a Southern nationalist talking: the innocent assurance is the same; the zeal also. His views are characteristic of many people I talked to in Northern Ireland: seeing the eventual triumph of a single solution, nobody, absolutely nobody, mentioned compromise, the forging of some lateral alternative which must be the only possible solution, the thawing and flowing together or in parallel of the twin icebergs of the Northern Irish mind. I change the conversation to policing; on this his views are sanguine. Too many of the 'wrong elements' had been drawn into the force, the accusations of bias were frequently justified. He is optimistic about the future, if Roman Catholics of the 'right sort' would join. He is in this respect a realist, acknowledging the failures of the RUC, in which he had worked all his life. Politically he belonged with all the other Irish dreamers, light years from any understanding of the possible. Without the sublimation of received positions and attitudes on all sides, no progress can be made.

When on the road between stops, I turn to the car radio for news. Today's contribution is presented as a new perspective on the minority. A Northern academic has published a report asserting that 'the minority was more likely to be unemployed because they have more children than Protestants and, lacking ambition, are employed in the construction trade'. This is a classic profile in any society of the most vulnerable socio-economic group, be they Puerto Ricans in New York or Turkish Gastarbeiters in Berlin. In Ulster it is news that what is generally understood to be a by-product of sectarianism might have a more acceptable explanation – a preoccupation with large families and a lack of economic ambition!

Derry over the last 20 years has become like Beijing during the Cultural Revolution, the wall inscriptions a platform for declarations, what passes for dialogue: PEACE OR WAR? – RELEASE THE POWS – NOT AN INCH – DEMILITARISE NOW – ALL PARTY TALKS NOW. I stay in a Georgian house on the edge of the walled city, one of the few not occupied by offices. Protestants have deserted the holiest shrine of loyalism, abandoning the Georgian streets for Bungalopolis on the east bank of the Foyle. The minority have occupied the citadel.

I have been touring Derry for some hours in the company of a leading citizen, a plain-speaking, self-made man, proud of his homeplace, aggressive in its defence. All conversations in Northern Ireland begin with one's tribal identity: are you 'one of us' or 'one of them'? When this factor has been negotiated, communication can continue. This interrogation can take the form of a direct question or, more normally, that of discreet yet pointed enquiries as to your address, school or other giveaway details. The need to know is not necessarily based on bigotry or prejudice, although they are there in abundance, so much as being an accepted social convention, the better to understand the speaker. My guide has tried all manner of stratagems to discover if I am 'us or them'. I remain uncooperative. Eventually, in the middle of a crowded pavement, in tones as loud and hectoring as the Reverend Ian Paisley in full parliamentary flood, he roars at me, 'Well, then, are ye a Prod or a Taig?'

Such determination to establish one's religion and ethnicity is worthy of the Middle East, where the prevailing understanding of the nation-state is synonymous with that of the dominance of a particular ethnic group: minorities are not willingly accommodated. Northern Ireland's population still exists in this time warp, lost to the post-Holocaust need to put seventeenth-century religious wars behind them. Both sides to the conflict enjoy their intolerance, even thrive on it; the savagery of terrorism is merely the stewpot occasionally coming to the boil. Most of the time it simmers, emitting jets of acrid steam when the temperature rises. Satan, a character distinctly unfashionable in current Christian theology, is, like the binman, an acknowledged neighbourhood presence, his influence mentioned with familiarity as though he lived a few streets away, in the church, chapel or meeting house where 'they' worship.

My host of the thundering voice has not abandoned hope of categorising me like a war orphan with a label tied to my overcoat reading 'Prod' or 'Taig'. He has another strategy up his sleeve. 'Let us', he says, 'visit the new genealogical centre; you might like to meet some of the people working there.' This seems like a fine idea, although I do not realise that I am walking straight into a bigot's web. Irish family names are still regionally based, despite all the turmoils of the past: an O'Dogherty is likely to be from Donegal, a Ryan from Tipperary; the Lalors originate in Counties Kilkenny and Laois. The religious affiliation of the individual, however, cannot be taken for granted from the possession of an Irish, Norman, Scots or English name. Intermarriage has been far too common for centuries for any actual ethnic divisions to exist. The barriers are substantially those of received cultural identity and religious orientation; ethnic identity is largely myth and wishful thinking.

Leading Citizen (to genealogist): 'This is Mr La Fontaine from Dublin. Put his name into your computer there, see what comes up.'

Self: '*Lalor*, not La Fontaine.'

Genealogist: 'Well, let me see now, how do you spell your name? Ell ay ell oh arr? There are also Lawlor, Lawler, Llalor, O'Lalor, McLalor, one of the 'Seven Septs of Leix', derivative of *O'Leathlobhair*, *leath* – half, *lobhair* – a sick person or possibly a leper, the name of two early Kings of Ulidia, that is pre-Christian Ulster, whose lines are extinct; an alternative reading, of course, could be 'son of the half-book', meaning a story-teller, a sage or scribe, and then the name might be a corruption of the English 'Ligger' – a drunk or thieving person, principally found in Yorkshire.'

He waffles on, to the Leading Citizen's evident irritation.

Leading Citizen: 'Get on with it, man; we do not have all day. See if he has any namesakes in your records.'

The computer wheezes and groans through millions of baptismal and other records derived from church and civil documents, covering all Ulster throughout the previous century; eventually it churns out three distant kinsmen (or possibly Gaelicised Liggers?), each with a variant spelling. They are Catholic, Church of Ireland, Presbyterian. My Citizen is not amused. Ethnic cleansing becomes more difficult when people are not ethnically clean.

In search of some common ground with this xenophobe, I mention Mary Robinson, assuming that he would respond positively. I forget that in the ultra-conservative political world of Northern Ireland, there are no women MPs of any denomination, the only EU 'nation' so stigmatised. He replies with vehemence: 'It was a sad day for republicanism when a woman like *that* was elected President. The nationalist cause was put back a generation.' I wander off and stand on a street corner, despairingly repeating to myself 'Prod/Taig; Prod/Taig; Prod/Taig' as people pass on the pavement; they just looked like people to me. In Jerusalem you can play this game too, and in Beirut with even greater variety: Armenian, Copt, Druse, Bahai, Sunni, Shiite, Ismali, Orthodox, Russian, Latin, Sephardic, Ashkenazi, Kraaites, Samaritan.

From Derry I wander south towards Strabane. Today's news from the province is even more farcical than yesterday's: Belfast City Council is in uproar; the State and British culture are under threat. Conradh naGaelige, an Irish-language organisation, has attached tasteful signs saying *Bruscar* to the litter-bins of the city. This subversive word means 'litter' in Irish. Belfast City Council's Councillor Dodds considers English to be the only language of the Northern Irish State. The signs must be removed; Conradh naGaelige must pay for the vandalism of council property. On the television news, Councillor Dodds looks like an extremely British bulldog, short of temper and not overly bright. In *Gulliver's Travels*, Swift maintained 'that whoever could make two ears of corn or two blades of grass to grow upon a spot of ground where only one grew before, would deserve better of mankind, and do more essential service to his country than the whole race of politicians put together'. The same principle might apply with regard to language. Councillor Dodds is clearly a single-blade-of-grass man, his gift to the province a minus: 'Never know two words when one will do.' The irony of such tribal narrowness is that by articulating his bias, the Councillor contributed to adding a new word to the vocabulary of the citizens of Belfast; *Bruscar*, so good they named it twice!

I pass through Pettigo in order to look at Station Island. As far as I am concerned, looking is as near as I wish to go to this San Quentin of the spirit. Floating out in the middle of Lough Derg, the pilgrimage island resembles the prison of Chillon, a mass of conventual buildings surrounding a green-roofed basilica. It looks intimidating and I am pleased not to have to investigate this survival of medieval pieties, the pilgrims now praying for planning permission for their bungalow rather than eternal salvation. I stop on my way back through Pettigo. Here the border runs through the middle of the village, with different currencies circulating at opposite ends of the street. In the southern sector, a naif monument commemorates a local War of Independence fighter. He wears his cap peak backwards as did countrymen of the day, a style now embraced by rollerblading teenagers; a few hundred yards away in an adjacent street, yet across the border, is a tree planted to celebrate the taking of Sebastopol.

In Strabane, at Grey's Printing Shop, a National Trust property still functioning as an eighteenth-century jobbing printer's workshop, an audio-visual programme relates the career of John Dunlap, an apprentice of the firm who became the printer of the American Constitution. The American War of Independence is the field of conflict in the audio-visual show, and the behaviour of the British Army in 1789 is held up to scrutiny. 'The Redcoats left five civilians dead on the streets of Boston – there was to be no turning back.' They might have been talking about Derry in 1968. Can it be that no one in Northern Ireland applies these lessons of history to their own situation? In every museum, heritage centre or historical tableau I visited, the parallels of the North's present with its own and others' past seemed to me to be inescapable. What is so wrong with these people that they appear incapable of coming to appropriate conclusions?

Outside Strabane I pick up a young man with a lugubrious expression who is hitching towards Omagh; his features are so long they might have been on the rack. He talks, as did many others from the nationalist community whom I encountered, about politics, the cease-fire and the IRA's intentions, assuming without question that anybody from the South is a closet republican. By the time we have gone a few miles, he warms to his theme: that the British could be defeated; that it was a matter of time, five or ten years; that they would leave and the unionists would see sense and accommodate themselves to a United Ireland. I suggest to him that the IRA actually have little support, that even after the breakdown of the cease-fire, people are more interested in peace than slogans. With this he agrees, but he says that it does not matter: the IRA could carry on even with almost no support, the hardcore were not liable to be swayed by compromise. When I suggest that the population of the South *is* prepared to compromise, he is not impressed. 'It is only a matter of time. The British will go, Ireland will be united, we will come into our own.' He could have been talking about Sheffield Wednesday or the 4.15 at Doncaster; he had the same assurance that this favourite would win. The odds are not promising.

In Omagh I had expected to find the town devoted to the memory of its most famous son, Jimmy Kennedy, born there in 1903. But I find no sign of the 'Red Sails in the Sunset' pub or 'The Teddy Bears' Picnic' cake shop, no bronze monument in front of the barricaded courthouse of a couple dancing the 'Hokey-Cokey'; the happily frivolous and ahistorical nature of Kennedy's compositions do not recommend them for public or private commemoration in the province. In Omagh, 'South of the border' acquires an entirely new resonance, *mañana, mañana!* The cenotaph is decorated with a bas-relief of a Flapper with bobbed hair, hovering Wendy-like over two dead soldiers in the trenches; she carries a garland saying 'From Tyrone'. My hotel room has a four-poster bed, deep and restful, a comforting womb of mahogany and faded purple curtains; on the wall I contemplate an attractive poster relating the familiar Ulster-American legend: Presidents, inventors, civic leaders, millionaires.

Onward to Enniskillen again. The local newspaper, *The Impartial Reporter*, carrys a headline about the Remembrance Day bombing of 1987: REVEALED: WHY THE IRA LIED OVER ENNISKILLIN BOMBING. The IRA had then claimed that an army radio had accidentally triggered the bomb. Now it is revealed that this had been a damage-limitation exercise, designed to save face in the light of international obloquy. Among the green-eyed faithful it matters little what the world thinks. The newspaper was merely reiterating what everybody knows: that this is a dirty war and you, the readers, are expendable when compared with the vision of Pearse and Plunkett, the virgin soldiers of the General Post Office.

I go in to Blake's for a drink and to read my newspaper. On Saturday afternoon it is thronged with couples and their young children. Groups of men at the bar watch soccer on television. A young couple sit down beside me with a package like a large sausage roll – an infant enveloped in rugs. I enquire how old it is, what gender. The girl responds, 'It's a little man, a week old. His name is Clive.' The father, a slim youth with limp, trailing hair, smiles sheepishly, insists on buying me another pint, asks me what is my team, is disappointed when I plead ignorance of soccer. We talk about the cease-fire, children, pubs. I say that I like 'brown pubs', dark and unaltered Victorian pubs with the grime of ages on them. My companions agree that Blake's is a quality brown pub; they think that it would be interesting to see the South; they have heard that it has all the best scenery – and that Dublin is cosmopolitan. Clive's mother gives me the package to hold; it requires some probing to see that the little man is actually inside it. After they have gone home, I speculate on the prospect of a bomb in the pub. What would be achieved for Pearse's dream to incinerate week-old Clive, his 18-year-old parents, the fellows at the bar, the barmen, myself and all the other couples with their children? Precisely this in many permutations has happened in Northern Ireland, time out of number.

Further down the street, two eight-year-old girls in first communion outfits are coming out of a pub with their parents — an archetypal Irish nationalist image and an appropriate target for blowing to smithereens. At the town hall two RUC men in bulletproof vests are harassing a young busker, in keeping with the universal antipathy between policemen and anything harmless.

It is a relief to proceed to my bed for the night and to encounter the bed and breakfast from Hell, Westville Friendly Home, a mile outside the city. As though attracted by a magnetic force, all the house accessories in Christendom have accumulated in one building: no conservatory, loggia, gnome or pond has escaped this grotesque environment. Dimmed lights, chandeliers, home-improvement accessories and Brighton Pier fairground prizes lie like snowdrifts along the mantelpieces; the knee-deep carpets probably accommodate the province's entire allotment of carpet mites. All the toilet rolls have lace hats, the loo seats are enclosed in fleecy anoraks, signs around the outside of the building point to the 'Ornamental Pool', 'Rose Garden', 'Mini Golf', 'Fairy's Grotto' and more. Small dogs are scattered about the house like abandoned floor mops; I step on one and it displays the snarl of a piranha. In my bedroom, a 'hostess pack' is placed in a prominent position, claiming to include 'all a visitor should know about staying in Westville'. I diligently read until I come to the part which advises what action should be taken if you have an accident while in bed. I assume that this refers to the possibility of the three ceramic ducks falling on me in my sleep, or the fairies emerging from their grotto to steal my belongings. At breakfast the following morning, I am directed to a table with a panoramic view of the 'Olde Wishing Well', a feature which I had missed the previous day. The other guests are lavish in their praise of Westville; they must have passed an accident-free night.

The 'Ulster Way', Northern Ireland's long-distance waymarked walking route, bisects the Enniskillen to Armagh road, just beyond Clogher. I follow it for a few miles south in among plunging fields and little hills like inverted pudding basins, the visibility reduced by infinitely winding roads and heavy vegetation. I am looking for Altadaven and 'St Patrick's Chair', an early Christian site associated with a holy well for which I have seen a map reference.

The site is adequately signposted and I find it without difficulty. At the roadside are slopes closely planted with trees, with a path winding down into the forest; this I follow, past rocks and stones with arrows painted on them, then a crude timber sign pointing up into a thicket on a mound. Inside the wood visibility is limited, the sunlight barely breaking through. I follow the path upwards and am immediately struck by the hardly believable colours of the mosses and lichens which surround the narrow path: luminous green and ochre-coloured, as intense as in a rain forest. The path has a thick carpet of ginger pine needles, and everywhere the trees have seeded and saplings are filling in the intervening space. It had rained not long before and the leaves are shiny with a light sprinkling of wetness, the ground springy with moss and dead leaves. Almost at the top of the ridge, the path diverges among the trees and reveals a rock formation which might be half-quarried stones, a Victorian folly or a natural rock formation. A large boulder in the middle resembles a stone seat. This is 'St Patrick's Chair', a mysterious and unlikely antiquity, associated with the saint's perambulations in the area. Looking down through the trees I see the holy tree, in this case just branches growing from the lower trunks, festooned with the usual pilgrim tokens of torn scraps of cloth. Below the branches in a large rock are cup marks, bowl-shaped depressions carved during the early Christian period, brimful of water and acting like small fonts.

This little wood of the whisperings has a fair claim to being among the most mysteriously beautiful places I have seen during my recent travels around Ireland; to have stood there on a sun-filled morning, alone and untroubled by the daft megaphone religiosity of wayside signs and church banners, is to have experienced something of the freshness of belief when churches were centres of learning and humanity. I stand among the moving branches and draw the scene. It is difficult to establish its atmosphere, which is more an experience than something tangible; even in my drawing, the place looks rather improbable. To do justice to the colours of the vegetation is exceptionally difficult. I wonder who visits these pre-Christian holy places. Are they all Catholic, or do members of the Protestant churches also regard holy wells as places of spiritual experience? Are the attractions purely superstitious or is there more? The fact that a nature-lover's highway passes through this wood, and that St Patrick's Chair has become one of a series of last outposts of unspoiled nature, unites pagan religious belief, early Christianity and present-day environmental priorities in circumstances of complete harmony.

Instead of returning to the main road, I continue on in what I assume is the direction of Armagh. The quality of the roads deteriorates and their directions change abruptly every few miles. I am clearly in 'unapproved road' territory, unloved and unrepaired also. I drive on, wondering on which side of the border I am, in which country; how would I know? At road junctions, there is nothing so convenient as a road sign, sparse in all parts of Ireland, non-existent in this region. For an hour I drive, turning hopefully whenever a road looks as if it might be heading in the correct direction, but I do not pass a single occupied house or person. As I come round a corner I see a car, half-parked in the roadway, the windows misted, a figure inside. Close up I can see it is a uniformed garda of the Mad Cow Patrol in an unmarked car. It is a curious fact that the government of the Republic should show rather more determination to restrain Northern cattle from entering the Republic than preventing paramilitary forces based in the South from crossing the border at will to carry out ethnic cleansing of Protestant farmers in border areas. Economics speak louder than lives. The Cow Patrol establishes which side of the border I am on, but I quickly lose it again until I come to a stretch of good tarmac which indicates the North. Half a mile along this bovine strada, around a corner I come to another unmarked car with a sleeping garda recumbent behind the misted windows. Between these two sentries I have evidently slipped into and out of the Republic. With relief I finally find a road sign which indicates the direction of Armagh, the reverse of that in which I am travelling.

I might as well have camped in a field as attempted to find something to do in Armagh on a Sunday night. There are no pubs open, of course; no restaurants either. I want to sit down and read an archaeological report on Eamhain Macha, a site which I have visited in the afternoon, not stand in the wet and windy ravine below the cathedrals with a paper of chips in my hand. Around the corner from where I am sheltering come a group of soldiers crouching in single file, guns forward, bushes in their helmets; they pass me as though they are tracking a lynx in the empty street. I watch while they continue their pantomime manoeuvre into the distance. Having trudged around in the rain, refusing to believe that there is not a single place to eat except hotels on the outskirts of the city, I see a sign for an upstairs restaurant in a darkened building. At the top of steep stairs, a closed door suggests a pool hall or an illicit drinking den – it turns out to be a gloomy restaurant serving alcohol. The decor resembles a restaurant which I used to frequent in the Gaza Strip: deep flock wallpaper, on the walls hideous landscapes of improbable tropical islands, a smell of something which is not food. The staff hover in the darkness of a distant niche, occasionally emerging for a foray among the tables. The only feature missing is the Palestinian flag and old men in a corner smoking hashish from a water-pipe. During the two hours which I spent there, the groups at the tables talked in a conspiratorial manner, heads bowed over their tables. After I have left, I meet the poster campaign again: TIME TO GO.

Each day I have visited a museum, heritage centre or historic site, looking for evidence of a unionist self-image – 'this is who we are'. Artefacts and symbols of Gaelic culture are displayed in abundance, stretching from the Bronze Age to 1798, then declining abruptly to but not progressing beyond the 1920s. I find symbols of unionist culture very hard to identify, difficult to pin down. It is debatable if they are represented at all in these public collections. In nearly all cases 'tradition' has been substituted for 'culture' – traditions of military service, loyalty to the British Crown, traditions of emigration and striving in new worlds. The ever-present cenotaphs are as close as one can get to a unionist icon: they express perfectly a loyalty to British traditions and sacrifice, as though 1690 elided perfectly into 1914, the Boyne and the Somme twin moments of triumph over the enemies of Protestant conscience. (Both battles began coincidentally on the same day, 1 July – a matter of deep meaning to the seekers of tradition.) While this image may be apt for 1690, which confirmed the plantation of Ulster and does represent a climactic military and sectarian victory, how do the carnage and disasters of the Somme and Ypres, fought against a 'Protestant' enemy, belong to this same understanding? I suppose they do if you want them to.

Among all the heritage centres I expect to find some answer. What I do find is bizarre in its implications – that the culture of Northern Ireland, as presented in its major historical displays at, for instance, the Ulster Museum, Eamhain Macha and Derry Tower Museum, has little to say about unionist culture; the concentration is invariably on the Bronze Age, Celtic and Christian past, the visual language of which is now embraced only by nationalists. The Regimental Museum in Enniskillen or the Battle of the Somme Heritage Centre on the Ards Peninsula are nodal points for unionist history, indoor equivalents of the cenotaphs; all those tattered ribbons and dented tin helmets, faded photographs of grinning, foolhardy young men or ancient survivors wearing medals like chain-mail emphasise the tragic folly of what is commemorated. It is hard not to come to the conclusion that the unionist society of Northern Ireland in fact regards World War I, its greatest social disaster, as its finest hour. In this it is truly in harmony with nationalist opinion – that there is nothing so glorious as a defeat. The torn regimental flags which hang in so many churches are each one of them a Turin Shroud to the faithful, beloved emblems of lives needlessly lost.

The Battle of the Somme Heritage Centre in Newtownard is one of the few centres which attempts to present the complexity of Irish history. Here the significant fact that regiments from the South as well as the North, Catholics as well as Protestants and nationalists as well as unionists had shed their blood is confronted, and the difficulties of the Home Rule crisis which led to the partition of Ireland are addressed. One comes away with the impression that somehow it was all worthwhile, that such a loss of life was meaningful because it was for King, Country and Ulster. The Ulster American History Park in Omagh is designed around the tradition of Ulster Presbyterian emigration to the United States – 15 Presidents of the United States have Ulster roots, a truly remarkable level of achievement. The park, and other similar displays in the North, all celebrate the same factor: our sons and daughters who have died fruitlessly or prospered – elsewhere.

I come south again towards Dublin, passing through Crossmaglen in south Armagh, as solidly nationalist as the towns of north Antrim are loyalist, another small village with its cenotaph, another pleasant, quiet place with few people on its pavements. In this instance the glorious dead whom the cenotaph commemorates are the hunger strikers of 1981. On this Soviet-style socialist-realist monument, a ghastly emaciated human figure rises above a phoenix; he looks like a concentration-camp victim, skeletal and gaunt. Self-immolation is being commemorated in Crossmaglen, rather than trench warfare. The sentiments of its inscription might have been from Patrick Pearse, the wording less literate:

GLORY
TO YOU ALL PRAISED AND HUMBLE HEROES
WHO HAVE WILLINGLY SUFFERED
FOR YOUR UNSELFISH AND PASSIONATE LOVE
OF
IRISH FREEDOM

Crossmaglen is hunger striker territory, local man Raymond McCreesh one of its sacrificial victims.

On each approach road to the village are IRA scent-markings: bogus traffic signs, circles and triangles, each carrying a grim message with appropriate graphic: SNIPER AT WORK, accompanied by the silhouette of a man with raised arm holding an automatic weapon (a smaller sign has been tacked to one of these saying ON HOLD; a more recent update states WE ARE BACK); another sign has RUC with a line across the letters like a no-parking sign. The Irish taste for gallows humour seems to thrive in adversity. These political images are the most accomplished form of political art to be seen in Northern Ireland, belonging to an entirely different category from the not-very-well-drawn murals of King Billy on

(TOP) *Macnas drummers celebrate the legend of St Patrick;*
(ABOVE) *Paddywhackery at the St Patrick's Day parade in*
Dublin; (RIGHT) *One of the wise virgins, well prepared for the*
Irish weather

Evening sunlight on Roaring Water Bay, West Cork

Like a pair of Russian dolls, the farmhouse at Rossard contains within it a famine-period cabin

In Dublin Castle, a dead imperial soldier lies at the feet of Hibernia with her harp and laurel wreath – one of the few British monuments which have not been blown to smithereens by the IRA

The head of Oliver Plunkett faces believers from its shrine in St Peter's Church, Drogheda

The brassy reliquary, like a Gothic space rocket

O'Connell Street, Dublin. A man and child applaud during the peace rally which followed the breakdown of the cease-fire

IRA sympathisers with their explicit signs infiltrate the Dublin peace rally. The peace they seek is strictly on their terms

World War I cenotaph, with Remembrance Day poppy wreaths, on the County Down coast

The Red Hand of Ulster, unionist symbol of defiance and blood-sacrifice, in Portavogie

A British Army bastion squats between private houses in the square at Crossmaglen

The figure of a dead hunger striker rises above a phoenix to confront the tower of the RUC barracks in Crossmaglen

*The language of signs: an IRA road sign sits comfortably among local authority equivalents.
No attempt is made to remove the non-official signs*

IRA armed struggle road sign in Crossmaglen, with post-cease-fire update information

his charger, or portraits of 1916 leaders. Some activist, aware of the international pop art of the 1960s and the work of artists like the Spaniard Juan Genovés who specialised in similar outline political graphics, has introduced a new concept of militant art to Northern Ireland's visual language.

The most sinister of the signs shows a small figure of a man with an Armalite raised above his head. It commemorates 'Volunteer Edward O'Brien', blown up on a London bus by a bomb that he was carrying to its target. The inscription, referring to the fact that O'Brien's family and community in Gorey, County Wexford, had condemned his actions, states: 'Gorey disowned you, we will always remember you.'

On a brief trip to Dublin during February, I attended a peace rally in the city centre: this was a public response to the abandonment of the IRA cease-fire. An enormous throng of adults and their children, organised by 'Mothers for Peace' and following banners which announced GIVE US BACK OUR CEASE-FIRE, had crowded into the city centre, packing O'Connell Street and spilling into the adjacent streets. In the midst of the earnest mass of hopeful citizens was a small knot of IRA supporters, cordoned by a squad of gardaí – whether it was for their own or the crowd's protection was not clear. A grim-faced woman carried a sign commemorating the same bomber with the statement that he 'died working for a lasting peace'. This was followed by *Tiocfaidh ár Lá* – Our day will come.

In Crossmaglen's Sinn Féin office, the 'Armed Struggle' T-shirts do not exactly suggest a separation between Sinn Féin and the IRA. I expected the dry-cleaners to advertise 'ethnic cleansing a speciality'.

If the IRA signs in Crossmaglen are intimidating and sinister, the British military presence is equally dreadful, as though the gun towers of Auschwitz had invaded the landscape of *The Crock of Gold*. Cheek by jowl between neat little two-storey houses on the square is a military excrescence of spirit-crushing violence. It is such a visual intrusion into the normality of the street that its presence is barely credible – a khaki-coloured, steel, bulletproof medieval bastion and monument to the Westminster Politburo. Behind and above this outpost rise the observation towers of the fortified RUC station, from which the army can look into the kitchens of the town, observe the families of Crossmaglen eating their Ulster fries. Across the square by the post office and the Northern Bank, a large placard on a telephone pole states with grim authority:

DEAR BRIT
IF YOU MESS
WITH THE BEST
YOU WILL DIE
LIKE THE REST

'The best' referred to here is the South Armagh brigade of the IRA, noted for its vigorous pursuit of the armed struggle.

To the people of Crossmaglen, a village caught on the northern side in the swooping curves of the border, there is no conceivable reason why they should by ruled by Britain. For sheer ineptitude, arrogance, unrepentant colonialist attitudes and cultural ignorance, British institutions in nationalist areas of Northern Ireland emphasise the universal truth that no people can rule another whose autonomy and culture they fail to hold in respect. To the lives of Crossmaglen's population, the British presence is utterly repugnant. This is a different perspective from that in the loyalist camp; loyalists dislike and distrust the British government, yet identify with a Britain of the mind, a combination of loyalties and religious belief. For loyalists, the British are both a bulwark against Irish nationalism and suspected of being nationalist fellow travellers. To nationalists, the picture is less complicated: TIME TO GO, that is all.

The search for identity has brought the three communities on the island of Ireland to seek what are totally divergent goals. The citizens of the Republic strongly identify with Europe, a relationship which is to some degree reciprocated, amply so in a flood of ECUs. Unionists in Northern Ireland wish for integration with a strongly monarchist and monocultural Britain of 1900, a Britain that does not exist. Similarly, the nationalists of the North wish to be united with the rabidly Catholic and patriotic Southern Ireland of 1922 – another unavailable option. Of the various seekers of nirvana, the unionists are in the least promising position. Not only has that with which they identify forever vanished, what has succeeded it, the Britain of today, does not need or care for them. The white-supremacist societies which occupied both parts of Ireland until the 1970s have left behind a legacy of nostalgia for a past golden age, one in which all the bowler-hatted and green-flagged verities remained unchallenged. To the wraith of Lincoln Steffens might be attributed the observation, 'I have seen the past and it cannot be improved upon.'

During the students' union meeting at Queen's, a shabbily dressed man stood up and announced that there was insufficient humour in discussions of Northern difficulties, a statement with which there could be little disagreement. From under his coat he withdrew something resembling a felt tea-cosy which he placed on his head. It was a large, white shamrock. The stalks fell about his ears and made him look like a Tibetan monk. He announced that the hat represented the white shamrock of peace; on the side facing me he had attached a red shamrock – the red shamrock of Ireland – and on the other was the green hand of Ulster. Everybody had been accommodated by this comic manipulation of familiar symbols. The audience laughed and clapped and the man sat down, to be followed by further reiterations of all that had gone before; a girl with short bleached-blonde hair stood up and said of the Orange Order: 'These people do not represent my culture.' I should have liked the opportunity to ask her what did.

That the divided peoples of Northern Ireland might find a common symbol is not a bad idea – a pair of Staffordshire dogs for the collective mantelpiece, one a British bulldog, the other an Irish wolfhound, might be a start. Predictably the unionists would buy the bulldog, the nationalists the wolfhound – not such a good idea after all. Anyway, dogs of different species fight. Something more anodyne perhaps – a postage stamp which everyone would use: Seamus Heaney folding sheets with the Queen, a co-operative image for a divided people?

On my last night in Armagh I stay in a decayed eighteenth-century mansion on the outskirts of the city. No gnomes here, or lace hats on loo rolls. The bookshelves in my room are crammed with Biggles books, school stories and nature books for the young; an antique bell pull is ready to summon the non-existent Molly from the servants' hall. Outside the breakfast-room window, grey squirrels probe in the grass; no sound of the city penetrates through the dense trees. The guests are the standard complement of retired people on a golfing holiday, their conversation appropriately witless. Surrounded by family portraits, Hogarth prints, militaria, the accumulation of generations, the voices of young children playing in a distant room, one of the women made her definitive comment.

'Jim, sweetie, it's so peaceful here. Quiet, you know. We could live like this too.'

'Sure, heart-throb, sure we could, if we did not have all those goddamn television sets on 24 hours.'

I did not come to Northern Ireland in order to listen to television dialogue from real-life soap-opera characters – these breakfast encounters are beginning to spoil my appetite and hamper my ability to do justice to a daily Ulster fry. As I chat in the hall to the young couple who are the latest generation of the family to own the house, my eye wanders to a hand-tufted rug on the floor which looks like an arts and crafts product of the 1920s. Its colour scheme of red and white emphasises the central motif: the Red Hand of Ulster, fingers erect and palm forward like an old-fashioned stop sign, marking the moment in Ulster when paralysis became institutionalised. When my computer feels aggrieved by something inappropriate which I have done, a similar hand appears on the screen; on the Ulster screen the message might read: 'This province has not been formatted for the twenty-first century.'

CUMBERLAND STREET BLUES

In anticipation of Bloomsday, 16 June, due to fall on a Sunday this year, I go on the Saturday morning to the James Joyce Centre in Dublin's North Great George's Street, to consult their programme for the following day. The Centre is housed in a Georgian townhouse in one of the few streets of eighteenth-century buildings still, at least in part, residential, other than those which remain as tenements. Looking down from Great Denmark Street is Belvedere College, where Joyce attended school. The street overflows with historic associations: the Earl of Kenmare lived in this house, Isaac Butt in that; here somebody famous, there a notorious one. At the Joyce Centre, young tourists – Japanese, American, European – are perusing the arrangements for Bloomsday, anxious to miss nothing. I get my information and depart. The interiors of some of the houses of North Great George's Street are furnished in sumptuous period style, not the homes of Dublin's wealthy, but lovingly restored by those most dedicated to preservation of the city's eighteenth-century past.

Behind the fractured brick façades of reds and browns are fine interiors, eighteenth-century buildings with eighteenth-century rooms, stairways, plasterwork, marble fireplaces. This integrity is increasingly under threat, with Georgian Dublin rapidly degenerating into the style of a Wild West town. Its eighteenth-century terraces have become like the shop fronts of Dodge City and have nothing behind them; eighteenth-century façades preserved at the expense of the interiors, or worse: entire buildings being demolished and replaced by office buildings with pastiche façades of beetroot-red brick, Georgian only in their resemblance to George III's apoplectic complexion. The conspiracy of folly which has contributed to the annihilation of the essence of what was Dublin's glory is led by Dublin Corporation planners, private developers and both modernist and conservative architects, all apparently incapable of comprehending that the core of the city's beauty does not consist of a dozen grand-manner architectural set pieces, but the fabric of its streets and squares which came into being in the Georgian period and have been the background to the life of the city for 200 years. This quadriga of barbarians has collectively done as much damage to eighteenth-century Dublin as British or German bombers did to Dresden or Coventry.

John Pentland Mahaffy, scholar and conversationalist, tutor to Oscar Wilde and later Provost of Trinity College, lived in the street from 1865, more or less a century after the great houses were built. An early lover of Dublin's eighteenth-century architecture, Mahaffy in 1908 founded the Georgian Society to gather details of the city he saw declining around him and to preserve some visual record of its decaying mansions. After Wilde's disgrace he coldly remarked, 'We no longer speak of Mr Wilde at Trinity.' At the bottom of this still-elegant street which slopes steeply down towards the city centre, the grandeur abruptly disappears. In Parnell Street the shabbiness of an unfashionable quarter is all too evident. It seems that the poorer the area, the greater the proportion of premises used as betting shops, pubs or fast-food outlets. Yet the tawdry atmosphere of the street is no preparation for what is around the corner, in Cumberland Street. The Saturday market extends across street and pavements, a mass of people, clothes, household bric-à-brac, rubbish. Here the have-nots gather each Saturday morning to prove that the grinding poverty of medieval Dublin, Swift's Dublin, Joyce's Dublin and O'Casey's Dublin is as much a part of the modern city as are the intellectual pursuits of Joyce scholarship a street away.

The day is a glorious one, so warm that even this, the most neglected quarter of Dublin, has a Mediterranean look to it, some semblance of a day in Genoa or Piraeus. Dublin had many street markets in the past; a few remain – Moore Street, Camden Street, Thomas Street. In these markets, fruit and vegetable stalls daily line the pavements where vocal, quick-witted women command the sale of their wares, engaging in repartee with the shoppers. There is an ordained order to buying in such markets, a balance between getting good value and being given what the stall-owner considers you deserve. I do not come well out of such shopping encounters, being either ridiculed by some woman who is annoyed that I should have the temerity to consider that I might choose my own fruit, or come away with a bag of semi-putrefying bananas. 'Jus look at him, willya? He wants to choose his o-awn, doesn't trust me. Mister, them mush-er-ooms is perfec, picked today in the County of Meath. Ladies [to the other shoppers], isn't he a trial to be picking and pulling at me dis-pla-ay? I swear to God, men shouldn't be allowed out on the street!' The crowd laugh. I pay for a bag of mushrooms, half of which will be weeks old and taste like sawdust. Mahaffy remarked, 'In Ireland the inevitable never happens and the unexpected constantly occurs.'

In Cumberland Street, the pavements are the traders' stalls, or the street is if there is not enough room on the pavements. Dublin's poorest shop here, from Corporation tenements, Georgian tenements, traveller encampments, cardboard boxes in doorways, park benches where they sleep under newspapers. The entire street resembles an ant hill, the shoppers (surely too grandiose a term?) crawling over piles of clothes strewn on the ground, children sitting among the debris, babies placed for convenience in boxes or anything which might safely contain them. For sale here are household objects so wrecked that it is hard to imagine that even the destitute would want them — clocks dropped once too often, odd shoes, smashed china, broken plates, broken everything, bits of things, damaged objects which seem totally beyond any kind of utility.

I ask the price of an occasional item, a pair of African elephants in fake hardwood, once painted to look like ebony, now tuskless, peeling and with only five legs between them. 'Two pounds.' As I move away, the seller responds, 'Fifty pence would do.' I decline; even the reduced price sounded exorbitant for such damaged goods. Among the detritus of clothes, carpets, broken furniture and rusty objects no longer identifiable are abandoned toddlers, children everywhere, of every age, colour, complexion. Among evidence of such humiliating poverty there is an abundance of good feeling from those who have brought something to sell. Perhaps it is because the day is so gorgeously sunny: the entire market appears full of promise to the buyers and sellers in this world of dross.

It might have been the crowd at the hanging of a highwayman, a Hogarthian jumble of the poor, the curious, the halt, the lame, the disturbed and the disabled, all shoving up and down the length of the street, seeking that one object neither too destroyed nor too expensive to be still capable of performing some domestic function. A demented man, over six feet tall and clothed in tatters, his feet so swathed in rags that they resemble pods, patrols the open spaces of the street, his mad eyes receiving some terrifying vision. In the darkness of an open side door in a transit van, an elderly couple sit passively, waiting for something to happen; they have the immobility of a Rembrandt portrait of old people, flesh the colour of ivory, some coloured garment visible in the gloom, their faces a map of experience and tranquil resignation. On the ground in front of a rubbish skip piled to the top with ruined books, broken furniture, wrecked typewriters and kitchen equipment, the street is piled with clothes for sale – T-shirts, jeans, sweaters, everything and anything – and in the middle of the clothes a young girl sits grinning, queen of her heap of merchandise, full of joy, laughing because it is good just to be alive.

Most of the clothes come from South-east Asia; those who worked the machines to produce them were probably not paid any more than the garments are now being sold for. The scene might in fact more plausibly be in the street market of some desperately poor Asian state than in one of Europe's affluent capital cities, priding itself on its urbanity. The shoe department of this pavement supermarket stocks only worn shoes for the down-at-heel. Here the market appears to reach its nadir – elderly women sifting through cast-offs which are beneath contempt as footwear, Mother Hubbards seeking shoes for their too many children.

A few Saturdays later I return to do some drawing in Cumberland Street Market. I need some material on which to base a woodcut for this book. I find a box on which to sit and open my pad. As soon as I have begun to work, an audience of small children gathers around me to watch. Without intruding, they look over my shoulder, and an older one delivers a commentary to the others on the progress of my drawing, which they can perfectly well see for themselves. Boys and girls, tough looking and outspoken, snigger as the commentator disparages my work. They question me about everything: who I am, why I am there, where I have come from, whether I have children – and more. A more thoughtful little boy looks straight into my eyes and asks with great seriousness, 'Hey, mister, are you a faggot?' Evidently, in his domestic world men are expected to engage in more masculine occupations than drawing. He was seeking an appropriate explanation.

BLOOMSDAY

Under a pale blue, cloudless sky and against a backdrop of the ruffled grey waters of Dublin Bay, smartly dressed church-going couples hurry along the seafront at Sandycove, anxious not to be late for the service. Men in striped blazers, white ducks and straw boaters, women with pleated ankle-length skirts, lace blouses, flat, flowered hats and pale gloves, accompanied by children in sailor-suits all stride purposefully southwards, the shipping in the bay behind, trudging remorselessly in and out of the port, seeming to belong to a more mundane world. Each earnest soul carries underarm a thick and well-thumbed tome, a book of common prayer, missal or church hymnal. The chapel of ease which the crowd is approaching looks like no ordinary church, the featureless granite exterior wall sloping gently upwards to a high and bevelled parapet, already busy with heads bobbing in the early-morning light. This is the Joyce Tower at Sandycove, the volumes carried by the crowd are tattered copies of *Ulysses*, the occasion Bloomsday.

On this day in Dublin, the city reels with an acute sense of *déjà vu*. Is that a faded sepia photograph of past life in Sandycove, or is this the now, the best part of a century later? It is the latter, an eccentric and nostalgic indulgence for a day in a sepia-tinted world, during which the events of 1904, when three young men – James Joyce, Oliver Gogarty and Samuel Chenevix Trench – lodged uneasily in this small Napoleonic observation tower overlooking the southern shores of Dublin Bay which Joyce used as the location for the opening sequence in *Ulysses*, are recreated and transmuted through literature back into daily life. Bloomsday is annually celebrated in Dublin as one of the major cultural events of the year, during which literary homage, a fancy-dress-party atmosphere and alcoholic indulgence collide in bizarre circumstances, each year contributing further to the consolidation of Joyce as the ultimate Dubliner and modern secular saint.

My feelings about Bloomsday are ambiguous. Being a reader of Joyce rather than a worshipper, I usually dip my toe into the Bloomsday festivities, but balk at the obligatory Edwardian music-hall garb and prescribed pork kidneys for breakfast. This year I decided to succumb to total immersion; 16 June is both a Sunday and a day of glorious and uninterrupted sunshine, ideal for perambulations. At 8.30 the Martello Tower is already busy. My photographer Allegra and I edge our way through the crowd, predominantly 'Edwardian', with interlopers from the late twentieth century such as ourselves. I manage a straw boater; Allegra, hopelessly compromised in shorts and an appalling T-shirt, looks like a spy from a surfing movie.

The interior spaces of the Tower are small and tortuous (like being on the inside of a gorgonzola cheese), designed for the accommodation of a small garrison, armament supplies, a powder magazine. The rooms – sparse, functional and austere – have been overcome by Joycean memorabilia: the writer's embroidered waistcoat, his cane, correspondence and books. A tableau on the first floor, like a stage set, recreates the room as originally occupied by Gogarty, Trench and Joyce. On Bloomsday it is hardly possible to move between the bodies and exhibits, or communicate up and down the duodenum-like spiral staircase. Grasping their prayer books, the members of the First Church of Joyce Polymath gradually assemble on the rooftop gun-emplacement for a reading. We lounge against the granite parapet, another row of people at our feet, sitting on the step, others on the gunrest, packed closely together: Edwardians, babes in arms, small children, smart and fashionable couples, the old, decrepit, eccentric, and, even at this early hour, the statutory happy drunk, greeting strangers as though to his home. With a tipsy grin and slurred diction, he bows extravagantly, 'Elcome to Bloosssday, elcome.' In the centre of the gun-emplacement at the flagstaff/chimney, Barry McGovern, celebrated interpreter of Beckett, prepares for his reading.

Other than the occasional interruption when the drunk welcomes a late arrival – 'Blues-day, a fine day, elcome, Joice, elcome' – the 60-odd babes and adults, straw-boatered or bonneted, listen captivated for an hour as McGovern reads, many of his audience following him in their own copies. Elegant-suited and waistcoated young men who look as if they might be more normally studying the Dow Index are absorbed in their texts. All around to the horizon, the sea now sparkles and the sky begins to brighten; the idea of holding a reading up in the air and enclosed only by sea and sky on a day of summer sunshine transforms the claustrophobic and often subversive-seeming atmosphere of many literary readings into something life-affirming and joyful; for such a life-affirmer as Joyce, this could hardly be more appropriate. Gradually, as he reads, McGovern circles around the flagstaff in a balletic manner; when he has finished, the drunk rises and makes an incoherent speech, strangers prompting him when he forgets what he had intended to say: 'A fine breeding od *U-ly-ssses*. May I offer con-drabilations, I –'

In slow motion, the audience funnel down the spiralling stairs to wander in search of the next venue, or just stare aimlessly at the Forty Foot Gentlemen's Bathing Place below on the shore, where a few nude elderly men, as pink as babies, lazily go about their rituals of daily bathing. A sleek black barouche with matching black horse is parked by the entrance to the Tower. The top-hatted driver in green and gold livery flicks his whip in the air, awaiting the Lord Lieutenant, or, perhaps, two dentists from Drumcondra.

Allegra and I feel the need for food, and follow the straw boaters back along the Sandycove seafront to the South Bank Restaurant, where a Joycean breakfast has been available since 6.30 in the morning. I ask a passing waitress, 'Did anybody come at 6.30?' She looks at me wearily and replies, 'Oh, yes. Germans.' As we arrive, nineteenth-century parlour songs with piano accompaniment are being delivered. By the time we have been served with lavish plates of animal organs and puddings, a two-handed reading of the pub encounter between Bloom, the odious Citizen and his wretched dog, Garryowen, is in full progress. Somewhat later, a woman in period outfit who had been among the congregation at the Tower becomes Molly Bloom, and improbably exposes her most intimate thoughts to a roomful of hungry breakfasting strangers. *Ulysses* may be all things to all men, but I doubt that its contents are appropriate to every occasion, ' . . . and yes I said yes I will Yes.' I thought rather, 'not while I am eating my pork kidneys, please.'

Time passes between meeting new arrivals, further supplies from the kitchen, and an inevitable lethargy induced by overindulgence in the organs of fowls and beasts. While all this is taking place in Sandycove, alternative itineraries at other locations throughout Dublin are exploring variant versions of the same themes. At the James Joyce Cultural Centre, the Irish Writers' Museum, Bewley's Oriental Café, the Mansion House and the Ormond Hotel, there are Bloomsday breakfasts, readings, outings, excesses of all kinds: literary, gastronomic, the vulgar and the pointless. Each venue is authenticated by being a major or minor location for some event in the text; the audience, like at *The Rocky Horror Show*, know the words as well as the actors do. Fortunately Joyce never mentioned throwing water. As we leave the South Bank, the Tower drunk arrives and welcomes the diners; outside, in the sunshine, a crocodile of gingham-bloused, sensibly skirted Edwardian cyclists pass, mounted on antique bicycles and a tandem, silhouetted against the sea, another sepia-tinted image of past times, Cissy Caffrey and Co. heading for Kingstown Pier; horse-drawn open carriages, barouches and landaus pass in stately defiance of enraged car-owners in a state of imminent cardiac arrest, the carriage-folk determined to extract any possible grain of verisimilitude from the occasion.

Back in the city centre, Allegra leaves to take photographs elsewhere. I sit at a street café in South Anne Street and contemplate my next move. As soon as my coffee has been served, I notice that at the next table is sitting an odious character who has been running a handy business trading in forged versions of my woodcuts. I abandon my coffee, stifling a temptation to pour it over him, and wander around the corner into Grafton Street where an altercation is taking place at the entrance to Bewley's Oriental Café: two gardaí are removing a man carrying a substantial leafy branch from the premises. I recognise him as an eccentric artist of considerable reputation. His unharmonious clothing, flowing hair, Messianic gaze and accoutrements declare his various allegiances: a Keffiah for the Palestinians and Islam, a woven shoulder bag for tribal peoples everywhere, a necklace of cowrie shells for spiritual communication, the ashplant for the rain forest. The gardaí unceremoniously propel him into the street from where he stands at a safe distance and abuses them, a Biblical prophet denouncing those corrupted by power and vice; Dr Paisley might have picked up a few tips in invective. With a smile, I pass into Bewley's and go upstairs to the Café-museum (an archive of catering-trade memorabilia), where a reading of the Nighttown episode of *Ulysses* is about to take place.

The audience is composed of devotees: a German scholarly type with a fistful of papers, furiously taking notes even before the performance has begun; an undoubtedly American academic, deadly earnest, rapt in attention; a motley crowd of students, tourists, the curious, myself. The actors are lined up before the counter, facing the audience. Behind the counter a waitress stands, bored by the proceedings, her expression vacant.

The performers, a group of actors in period costume, each take a number of parts: prostitutes, the Madame, Bloom, Stephen, the soldiers, the crowd, Edy Boardman, a holly bush. The dialogue is fast and funny, well delivered with appropriate accents. German and American scholars are captivated, pencils poised, suppliants at the shrine. Behind the counter the waitress has woken up and is laughing heartily. The funnier the performance, the more she tries to stifle her giggles, yet more solemn become the listeners. Eventually, heaving with amusement and suppressed laughter, the waitress stuffs her apron in her mouth and disappears beneath the counter. The reading over, audience and academics applaud enthusiastically. The waitress resumes her post, her face suffused with pleasure. She has discovered Joyce.

Afterwards, I notice an old friend, Sadhbh, and join her group. I am introduced to a woman who informs me that she was 'the real Molly Bloom'. Could this be? Had not the buxom Nora Barnacle died in Zurich some years before? She means, however, that before some rival actress had made a career of reclining on stage in a negligee, declaiming Molly Bloom's soliloquy as though she were Electra, she herself had originated this performance at a Bloomsday of yesteryear.

Fantasy and reality carefully evade each other's gaze: Ken Monaghan, a nephew of Joyce and director of the James Joyce Cultural Centre, lived under a shadow as a child. The incubus was 'Uncle Jim', commonly believed in the Ireland of the 1940s and '50s to have brought disgrace upon the family and the nation. His parents warned Ken never to reveal the relationship. Joyce's great work, *Ulysses*, the basis for his infamy, was then read by neither his relatives nor his detractors; like the Devil in Derry, its presence was felt but not seen.

Times have changed, if not utterly; Joyce is now widely commemorated in Dublin, and his works have become a quarry for all manner of allusions, generally commercial. From the Riverrun Gallery (*Finnegans Wake*), to the 'heroine' of *Ulysses* in Molly Bloom's Flowershop, there is no escaping the man or his work and the disgraced citizens are determined to forgive.

Despite the mammoth breakfast of inner organs at Sandycove, lunch (or a drink) beckons, and I move across the street to Davy Byrne's pub where Leopold Bloom paused in his 1904 rambles for a glass of Burgundy and a gorgonzola sandwich; the same fare is available for Bloomsday, in tandem with the conventional supply of pints and bulging triangular ham sandwiches served with enough English mustard to give the eater heart failure. In the dark interior, pub life is as usual: drinkers undisturbed by any particular date on the calendar hover expectantly over their pints in earnest conversation. I dutifully order my Burgundy and gorgonzola and place myself at the rear of the pub, where I have an appointment to meet some other journeyers. The Duke Street doors are wide open, the pub bouncers solidly silhouetted against the brightness outside; passers-by appear and vanish abruptly in the golden opening.

In the rear room of Davy Byrne's, a woman in a large feathered hat, whom I had not previously noticed, stands up from one of the tables. She seems ill at ease as she tentatively addresses the customers: quite clearly some of these people are not aware that it is Bloomsday; possibly they have never heard of Joyce. After some hesitation the woman – 'Molly' again, I presume – produces some letters from her crocodile-skin handbag. I am mistaken: this is not Molly Bloom but her alter ego, Nora Barnacle, who then proceeds to read out loud in a public bar the real letters written to her in intimacy by her actual lover, James Joyce.

The lunch-time crowd in Davy Byrne's are not impressed by this tabloid exposé; they have been talking about the prospects of Noble Lady winning the 4.15 at Down Royal, with Tim Tracy up; Ireland's chances in the World Cup; the latest Walrus and Carpenter quadrille of Northern Ireland's politicians. Jim's outpourings to Nora are not welcome. A thin man wearing a grimy woollen cap, with a grubby cigarette-butt permanently attached to his lower lip like an offensive mole, takes umbrage at the delivery. His voice intrudes on the reading like the hiss of a disturbed python.

'Would you feck off to the stage of the Abbey The-atre with your fecking oratorio, missus. I'm on me lunchbreak – this is a fecking bar, not a lit-ter-rary meeting.'

Undaunted, Nora reads on. Two young men in blazers and boaters appear, possibly a supporting cast of Jim and Gogarty. The objector decides, correctly, that a song would end the reading, and growls out a few bars of a tuneless 'The Oul Triangle'. Instantly the barman intervenes. 'That will do, Tony, the young lady is entitled to give her recimitation.'

At the Duke Street entrance another altercation has broken out and the bouncers are grappling with someone. I forget about Jim and Nora's love life, and concentrate on this fresh diversion. A man whose voice sounds familiar is attempting to enter; the bouncers are determined to keep him out. In the mêlée, above their heads waves a healthy leafed ashplant – it is the rain forest prophet again. With a heave he is toppled into the gutter, the ashplant flung after him. Back at my end of the bar Jim and Gogarty are commiserating with Nora, aka Molly, while the Citizen orders another pint. From behind the gesticulating prophet in the street, now gathering a crowd of passers-by, Allegra reappears, accoutred in a becomingly Edwardian ankle-length dress and less historically accurate but demure cloche hat. We abandon Davy Byrne's for the next stop on our itinerary – the northside, to which the impoverished Joyce family retreated as their father Simon Joyce's fortunes declined and they were overcome by squalor and humiliation.

The street life of northside Dublin is stylistically unlike its counterpart south of the Liffey; on a Sunday afternoon this is emphatically so. As though the quarter had never quite emerged from the previous century, a pervasive torpor grips everything. The broad Georgian streets are hot and empty, inhabited only by straying cats and solitary individuals dozing on the front steps of their terrace houses, the dark ironwork of the railings like radiators, throwing heat back into the streets. From a deserted side street comes a whir of wheels as the Edwardian cycling group of the morning passes into and out of our gaze, like a dream recollection, a cardboard cut-out, determinedly pedalling. The street returns to its somnolence until a walking tour appears, 20 individuals guided by a young man who places himself before an abandoned-looking house and explains its position in the Joycean firmament; the sleeping woman on the adjoining step awakes and regards them with distaste. A self-appointed parking attendant in dark clothes and shapeless peaked cap enters the street; he is small, withered and smelling of drink. With rolled newspaper he begins to marshal the non-existent traffic. Inevitably, this pantomime conflicts with the speaker's words and gestures; the tour guide capitulates and hastens his group to the next sad Joyce residence or *Ulysses* location.

Number 7 Eccles Street was the fictional home of Leopold and Molly Bloom. Its timber door is now in the Dublin Writers' Museum; the stone Georgian doorcase was still standing in 1979 when I drew it for a book on Dublin, inscribed then with a pilgrim's message, like the graffito of lost French soldiers of the Grand Armée, wandering in the Sinai Desert: SUR LES TRACES DE BLOOM, 24 AOÛT '79. Today, the Mater Hospital's most recent extension has blandly obliterated all trace of the building. By way of reparation, the hospital has for ten years been hosting a Bloomsday street party: this is the alternative Bloomsday, during which other concerns have taken over, and despite its being on Bloom's spectral doorstep, little reference is made to the man or his creator. In the hospital foyer is a tenth birthday cake, as large as a tractor tyre.

A '60s-style rock band performs under an awning. Buddy Holly and Elvis seem as close as the band is prepared to go towards 'Love's Old Sweet Song'.

Nurses from the hospital jive on the tarmac. A not-too-proficient face-painter works somewhere among the crowds, turning small, hopeful faces into deranged midgets; stilt-walkers strut, one dancing gracefully with a person dressed as a polar bear; children are everywhere. On one side of the street there is an extensive barbecue provided by the hospital for the occasion – no organs here, but distinctly un-Joycean spare ribs, hamburgers and Coke.

North Great George's Street is only a few streets away from Bloom's house. The James Joyce Cultural Centre, rival omphalos to the Sandycove Tower, has been busy all day with similarly appropriate events. By the time we arrive there in the afternoon, it is closing to prepare for the night's Bloomsday Ball, a £60-a-head, costume affair. At this juncture, foiled by a closed door, I feel that a rest is required. I do not think that I can listen to another 'Stately plump Buck Mulligan' without violently attacking the speaker. We temporarily abandon Bloom to the company of Elvis (both are in the hills with Simon Bolivar, Finn MacCool and Che Guevara, awaiting the call), and repair to a friend's sunny garden to sleep under the trees and gather our resources for the evening's events; as I snooze, briefly, I dream:

Stately, plump Elvis Presley came from the stairhead, bearing an electric guitar. A high-collared yellow satin sequinned cape, ungirdled, was sustained gently behind him on the mild morning air. He held the guitar aloft and intoned: Introibo ad altare Dei, wah, wah.

Later, refreshed and prepared for further revelations, we emerge, accompanied by Peggi Jordan, a 78-year-old bon viveur, ready for whatever the evening might have to offer.

The Mansion House, residence of Dublin's Lord Mayor, has also been busy throughout the day with Bloomsday events. The evening's offerings are musical interpretations of Joyce's period, Edwardian songs, both the appropriate and the banal. One group of songs, part of a song-cycle by Maureen Charlton, takes Jim and Nora to a further plane of encounter, and comments wittily on the period. Alas, there was much of the banal from other contributors. This is the point at which Bloomsday might be decently abandoned, as the event nosedives into the anything-will-do bracket of bad poetry, inaudible delivery and uncomfortable chairs.

The Mansion House is deserted in favour of a sprint around the corner to Buswells Hotel, where more serious business is in progress. Gathered in a darkened room (with two doors to the bar) are assembled the hard men of Bloomsday, serious Joyceans, reading *Ulysses* with passion and cunning. Instead of, as in our previous port of call, people talking about Joyce, here are those who know his work intimately: David Rose, director of the Oscar Wilde Autumn School, poised to be painted by Whistler; Robert Nicholson, curator of the James Joyce Museum, in impeccable if slightly raffish whites. We might have been in the *Els Quatre Gats*, circa 1900, young Picasso intense in a corner, Erik Satie drunk under a table. People from the floor go to the front of the room and read their selected pages; the main performance is a simultaneous English/French reading with thunderous (French) piano accompaniment. All this is delivered with extraordinary gusto and involvement, the proximity of the bar enormously assisting delivery. The Edwardian clothing, previously dapper, is now decidedly frayed. Straw boaters lie in piles like empty biscuit tins, bonnets are askew, bow ties have swivelled under the ear. One of the readers goes round with a bowler hat, soliciting contributions to pay for the room. We stagger out through the bar into the night, vastly relieved – Ms Bloom had not been mentioned.

Allegra and I are beginning to wilt, while Peggi is merely getting into her stride and suggests the United Arts Club, a den of artistic iniquity founded by W.B. Yeats and Lady Gregory a century earlier, just when Jim had safely left the country (he would not have been welcome as a member). A short journey of another few Georgian right angles brings us to Fitzwilliam Street and 'the Club', its door opened by speaking into an intercom, like a prohibition speakeasy, 'Knock twice and ask for Molly.' In the bar a cloud of depression hangs over the drinkers: independent, confident women, listless men – where had we been? They have missed Bloomsday, wasted the day, now feel bereft, abandoned. After midnight Allegra decides to desert the cause and departs. I lie down on a couch and rest, then more revellers arrive.

From the Joyce Tower of the morning reading, the South Bank Restaurant, Davy Byrne's, Eccles Street, Buswells and other venues throughout the day, familiar faces reappear, dressed extravagantly; one of the 'carriage-trade' groups, carried away by their enthusiasm for Joyce, now ecstatically voluble, approaching lift-off. As though enough were not enough, the ragged volumes are produced again, and the manners of an Irish music *seisiún* invade the staid behaviour of literary readings. Individuals vie for the opportunity to read, arguments develop, nobody can agree. Abruptly, Peggi begins to sing and instantly everyone falls silent, listening intently to her lovely rendering of 'On the Banks of the Lee'.

> When true lovers meet,
> Down beside the green bower,
> When true lovers meet,
> Down beside the green tree.
> Where Mary, fond Mary,
> Declared unto her lover,

You have stolen my young heart,
From the banks of the Lee.

Oh I loved her so dearly,
True and sincerely,
There's not one in this wide world,
I love more than she.
Every bush, every bower,
Every wild Irish flower,
Reminds me of my young love,
From the banks of the Lee.

Her pure lilting voice cuts through the raucous clamour of the drunken celebrants; order has been restored. A handsome Scotsman reads softly in a Glaswegian burr; one of the other readers, in mutton-chop whiskers and formal dark jacket, appears to have lost his shirt, another his command of the English language. Reading after reading follows; by this time the level of literary karaoke has been reached, and delivery is approaching laryngitic spasm. Mental weariness is certainly setting in. A lengthy, possibly exhaustive, delivery of J. Milton Hayes's ' The Green Eye of the Yellow God' seems to mark a point of no return; after this, anything is possible.

At 2.30 a.m. we leave.

Further down Fitzwilliam Street, where it opens to the square, another small group of wandering Joyceans has gathered on the front steps of a Georgian house, from which one of them is declaiming enthusiastically, like Lenin on the hustings in Moscow, one of the parodies, the broad cod-Anglo-Saxon in revolt against the flaat-ness of his Cork accent. A scuffle develops and the book is pulled and grabbed by other hands – someone is thumping another with his ample copy of the master's work. I drive slowly past, gaping out of the window in disbelief, as the loose pages of *Ulysses* begin to rise and fly about like slates in a gale. On the corner of the square under a street lamp, best thigh forward, two mini-skirted teenage prostitutes contemptuously observe the fracas; such rowdy behaviour is bad for business.

From the ridiculous to the sublime, certainly. In recent years critics have begun to lament that the phenomenon of Bloomsday is in danger of trivialising Joyce's work, that honouring his achievements is becoming submerged in fancy-dress parades and farce. Never! Without doubt the trivia abounds, yet what is more important is that Bloomsday has wrested *Ulysses* and *Finnegans Wake* from the exclusive possession of scholarship, and brought them a wide and appreciative readership. All the end-of-Bloomsday crowd, irrespective of the amount of drink taken, know both their *Ulysses* and their Dublin. Joyce's work is being celebrated for his love of language and affirmation of life's multiplicity, his image of Dublin confirmed by reciprocity. There are few themes in current Irish life which Joyce failed to touch on; the language, culture, humour and foibles of his fellow citizens have changed totally, yet changed not at all, in a century; the gloss may be different, but the fundamentals have hardly altered.

On the midsummer solstice, I attend a garden party in a substantial Regency house in Blackrock on the southern shore of Dublin Bay, across the street from one of the Joyce family residences before the disastrous hegira to the northside began. Also nearby is the site of 'Frescati', childhood home of Lord Edward Fitzgerald, whose mother Emily Lennox, Duchess of Leinster, invited Jean Jacques Rousseau, then in flight from France, to come and tutor a batch of her 22 children. The savant (who had waxed lengthily on the subject of children's education) sensibly declined the offer of a close encounter with the Fitzgerald household, yet his educational principles were put into effect by a tutor who ended up as the Duchess's lover, then husband. This proxy Rousseau, tutoring the young Edward Fitzgerald, caused as much domestic havoc in Blackrock as at the same time the red-hot Mary Wollstonecraft, tutoring another vast aristocratic nursery, did in Mitchelstown in County Cork.

The demure and elegant surroundings of a 'salon' echo the comfortable world of the Edwardian Dublin from which Joyce had found himself cast out. This might have been the setting for any Joycean occasion, too elegant perhaps, not quite petit bourgeois, yet the cultural tastes of the evening are 1904 in aspic. A young girl sits at the piano and plays parlour songs and operatic arias popular in Joyce's time; 'Love's Old Sweet Song' comes again and echoes through the room and out on to the lawns as the sun is setting. 'I dreamt that I dwelt in marble halls, with vassals and serfs at my side.'

Jim, with his light, tenor voice, would surely have been a welcome addition to the evening.

HALLUCINATION AND KRISTALLNACHT

At the beginning of July, I flee from Dublin and return to Rossard in West Cork. From here I intend to travel up the west coast towards Donegal. The weather is as an Irish summer should be: warm and sunny, with day-long regressions into bleakest winter.

After some months' absence, the house has more or less disappeared under an overenthusiastic spring and summer growth – the signature of West Cork is mild weather, rain at every atmospherically possible moment and manic growth of all wild and uncultivated species, the rude good health of weeds generally challenging the growth potential of all planted crops. The hedges of the approach road through the townland of Ardura are not to be avoided: they reach into and across the narrow roadway. Ox-eye daisies as large and white-petalled as paper flowers, foxgloves and fuchsias in shades of pink and purple, and New Zealand flax about to erupt into its once-in-a-generation flowering all tumble from the hedgerows. Honeysuckle, dandelions, nettles and docks fill the spaces in between. Hawthorn and intense hollybushes enclose darkness in their crusty leaves.

Days pass as I strim, hack and mow, just to let some light in the windows and to discover what might be growing in the garden. Among nettles as tall as sunflowers, raspberries lurk. A fig tree gasps for air among its more quick-witted neighbours. Fuchsia *triumphans*, growing in a fervour of waving branches, dominates everything. Ferns, like some species brought back by Darwin from the Galápagos, threaten to make access impossible. Vegetation vibrates with the burden of recent showers, the slightest movement bringing cascades of moisture into the air. In the midst of all this fructifying nature, the house stands, stoical and uncomplaining, hoping for some attention for its own slatey needs. Around the gardens, large, drugged bumble-bees hover in the air, buzzing in sonorous contentment.

During a visit, Allegra wanders around in the fields. Soon she comes in from the upper garden and announces the unlikely presence of three dead mice under a pear tree – the characters from a nursery rhyme in combination with a Christmas roundelay. I grab my gardening gloves and go to inspect. One mouse has unaccountably revived and departed; the other two I bring into the house, place on my worktable and draw. Their death is without explanation. The whim of some passing cat? I arrange their silky bodies and long tails, like sleeping babies. Afterwards we take them to Allegra's temporary darkroom and they are photographed on a bed of ferns, *nature morte*, stark and unsentimental.

During the 1970s, as I walked, cycled or drove the eight miles to and from Skibbereen, particular configurations of landscape would attract my attention. The features of the return journey west were always more alluring than those on the eastward direction. The main road from Skibbereen skirts the wide reaches of the navigable Ilen river just outside Skibbereen, then turns away from the coast to travel through rising fields and jumping hedgerows, towards a long straight stretch, where every element of the landscape, at a particular point, is arranged with accidental perfection.

This superb combination of the natural and the man-made never failed to impress upon me the delight of harmonious forms. Kilcoe, a nineteenth-century Church of Ireland parish church, was enclosed in an aureole of mature trees. These were probably planted simultaneously with the building of the church. A steep and severe gable end faced the traveller, the line of the roof disappearing into the trees. Far behind them, and enclosing in its contours the wind-sculpted treetops, was the overshadowing outline of Mount Gabriel, the Mont Sainte-Victoire of the region, which rose dark on the horizon. The mass of the mountain contained the trees which, in their turn, enclosed the church, itself guardian of the quiet graveyard of local

Protestant farming families: Connell, Sweetnam, Jermyn, Berry, Townshend, Kingston, names closely associated with the immediate hinterland of Kilcoe.

No matter how many times I passed this chance grouping, I could not do so without admiring the perfect balance of building, trees and mountain, a model for the relationship of architecture and open landscape. In July, after an absence, I again pass this way and unconsciously acknowledge the timeless beauty of the same composition. Later, I make a drawing of the scene from memory. In the process of drawing, some sense of unease makes me conscious that I am not doing justice to what I have seen and thought I knew intimately. I feel the need to look again.

The following day, I again come west from Skibbereen. As the Kilcoe trees rise into view, I look more critically at the scene and realise that all is not well. The church (which I had seen and drawn the previous day) has, apparently, been taken by aliens. It has gone! I slow down, turn into the side road, park in the graveyard gateway and stare in bafflement at the absence. I clamber around among the gravestones, where a flat space like a helicopter pad represents the church's former presence. Stone and roof, windows and bell, pews, lectern, monuments and memorials, all have vanished, vaporised like the buildings of Hiroshima, leaving only a shadow.

Derelict or ruinous buildings can be brought back to life. The abandonment of tradition implicit in the destruction of this building removes with it the history of the local Protestant community which has lived in the area for almost 300 years. I resolve to ask my neighbours for an explanation, but suspect that this was a church decision, a sort of ritual self-annihilation, prompted by the commercial value of the building materials: a numerically threatened congregation selling the roof over its spiritual heads.

So powerful was my attachment to Kilcoe that I had drawn it, a few years after its disappearance, in full confidence that I had just seen it. I wonder what else I have drawn that was not actually there – a disturbing thought. There is, of course, always another explanation – the lateral view of things. At the top of the Kilcoe hill is the Old Rectory, a fairly undistinguished farm building close to the road, its pleasant, white-painted gable visible through the trees. The English writer Mary Norton, author of *The Borrowers* series of children's books, lived in the Rectory for some years. These 'Borrowers' are a race of small people who live below the floorboards of houses and 'borrow' things others may not need, pickers-up of unconsidered trifles. Is it perhaps too much of a coincidence – a missing church, known kleptomaniacs (well, borrowers) in the parish?

Intelligence of things sought always comes from the least-expected source.

Eve, my youngest daughter, announces that of course *she* knew all the time that Kilcoe had been demolished. Had not some other child on the school bus told her that the bell was being sent to Dodoma in Tanzania to grace the cathedral there?

I return to my strimming. It is useful, therapeutic, uncomplicated. July is such a pretty month in the claustrophobic superabundance of the Irish countryside. July is also the marching season.

In the North, as the tension increases daily, I am glad to be elsewhere. Old antagonisms erupt at Drumcree in County Antrim, where Orangemen assert their right to march through a nationalist area. The RUC forbids the march, then capitulates: a recipe for further anarchy. The conflict festers in Derry, where the acrid whiff of burning is in the air. The lime-white mansions are topical again, burning merrily on the Northern skyline among the flying petrol bombs, the looted hi-fi shops and the riot police. The nine-o'clock news on television has the discomfort of an old movie which you did not care for at first viewing. They might as well show footage of 30 years ago – nobody would know. Perhaps they are doing just that?

Politicians in the republic of dreams express themselves 'surprised' at the recurrence of violence in Northern Ireland. Nobody in the North, of whatever persuasion, appears to share this feeling that the unexpected has occurred – rather the opposite. When I attended the students' union meeting at Queen's University in March, the writing was on the wall: 'the burning season' was on its way. Now, in July, Southern commentators express themselves 'surprised'. Ostrich farming is a fairly recent development in Irish agriculture, a touching metaphor for the times we live in.

People watch the Drumcree developments in dismay, each side to the conflict interpreting the same facts in a diametrically opposed manner. Unionists affirm their civil right to 'walk the Queen's highway'; nationalists assert their right to oppose them. The violence of extreme nationalism rallies in the face of a festival of loyalist bone-headedness. 'The blockish presbyters of Clandeboye' was John Milton's phrase, and that was not said yesterday.

The phenomenon of the dustbin of history being emptied in the faces of the living is widespread in its implications. The North's carefully nurtured tourist industry burns along with the primary schools and churches. Tourists head for the airports and the border, just as in any sub-Saharan African nation which is experiencing another military coup. At least in the North they don't shoot tourists.

Generally, in the South, if I say that I have been in Northern Ireland and find the behaviour and attitudes of the people there archaic and reactionary, all automatically assume that I am referring exclusively to those of unionist politics. It does not seem to occur to people in the Republic that northern nationalists might be living in a corresponding time warp to their unionist fellow citizens. Having made a broad survey of friends, acquaintances and strangers on this issue, it appears that Catholic, Protestant, Jew and unbeliever in the South are united in seeing unionists as the sole culprits in maintaining the flame of sectarian bitterness, their perspective of little consequence. Few Southerners of whatever politics or persuasion seem interested in crediting the unionist version of reality with any validity.

In Bantry something untoward has happened. The great market square, among the largest of its kind in the country, has, since I was here in January, been metamorphosed into a municipal sanitary engineer's idea of urban improvement.

I like to refrain from pronouncing on 'the Irish'. Nineteenth-century travel books are generally good at this sort of broad generalisation: the 'Irish' (or Kurds, Polynesians, British, Belorussians) are an arrogant/loveable/friendly/duplicitous people (choose as many options as you like, then apply them to the nation of your choice). The issue is generally more complex, national character more elusive. However, Irish people do seem to experience collective myopia when there is a question of the conscious architectural improvement of their built environment. Those entrusted with this role in public life appear to have been educated at the Hibernian Institute for the Visually Deprived. Yet, if the matter is left to traditional local building methods, nothing too alarming is likely to happen.

Bantry is a case in point; almost every other Irish town might fare as badly. A wave of Eurodollars has flowed over the market square of cattle market memory, washing the past into the bay and replacing it with what appears to be the elevated lid of a scud missile silo, or, more mundanely, a sewage works. The very modest yet pleasing architecture of the town, the customary assemblage of shops and houses, previously defined the character of the square. Until, that is, HMS *Eurodollar* sailed into the bay, with a shipment of orange bricks, bogus Edwardian streetlights and park benches. It is a pity it failed to join the *Surveillant* and other French ships of the 1796 invasion at the bottom of the bay.

What might have become welcoming, with grass for children to play on, trees for lovers to sit under, planting to curb the icy winds from the sea, has instead become arid and pretentious in a metropolitan way. A hard and windy expanse has been created, which is consistent in only one factor: contextual inappropriateness, attempting to impose on a country town what would be soulless in a city.

From Saddam Hussein Square, I move away into the town. Bantry's streets are comforting in an old-fashioned yet interesting manner: good pubs and enough hairdressers to coiffure the French fleet of 1796. I have a meal in Vickery's Hotel on the main street. The oddly shaped atrium, created long ago before such features became fashionable, has the atmosphere of a Bianconi Coaching Inn, complete with aged retainers.

Across the street the rotating lighthouse beam in the window of the Anchor Tavern beckons. I enter, and emerge as rapidly. Inside, there is hardly room to breathe. In the evening there will be a firework display to inaugurate the square: the pubs are doing good business.

Further down the street, I try another pub. It is marginally less crowded. Here the bar counter is also busy, but the noise level is more tolerable. I strike up a conversation with Ilse, a petite German woman with a bob of bleached-blonde hair, somewhat in disarray. Long settled in the area, she runs a small export business. Intelligent and articulate when sober, she becomes vocal and demagogic after too many gin and tonics have been downed. When she is drunk, her sentiments do not endear her to a bar of townspeople. Truth (particularly with a German accent, and loudly delivered) is nobody's favourite dish.

'Ze Irish ar stupid, jus stupid. It is only vee Germans who care for the enwironment in Ireland. Zay ar dirty people, dirty. Zay vill throw ze zigaret package out z'car vindow. In Germany you vill never zee zuch a zing.'

Having observed this sort of joyous Irish abandon 20 times a day, I nod uncommunicatively. Ilse assumes assent – she would, whatever I had said or done. Her diatribe continues.

'Ireland is ze last free country in Urope – zuch air, vater, aupen spaces – but my neighbours vould destroy it all iv they could. Id maks me zad.'

She stares at me with a melancholy expression and, above the rising crescendo of sound, for fear I might not have understood, roars:

'ZAD!'

As this unpalatable news is being voiced, the patrons at the bar divide like the Red Sea before Moses, moving away to right and left. I now remain sitting at the bar with this depressed and tactless woman, as though I were her fellow national, denouncing the natives. She warms to her theme. Fortunately the noise in the bar is sufficiently loud that not too many customers can actually hear what she is saying.

'Ve Germans are bringing good daste to Ireland, showing zis persons how zay should live, and zay do not like us for id. Ve ar doo honest. Of course, zay are zuch lovely people, but ignorant. Zay vould destroy everything if zay could. Id mak me angry. Vee Germans are ze only people who can save Ireland from the Irish.'

Conversations with Ireland's friends and admirers tend to be profoundly depressing. Not only are the friends frequently both insensitive and arrogant, but there is usually a strong element of truth in their observations. In this case, the central point – that Irish people have a poor record with regard to 'enwironmental' issues – is beyond dispute.

Ilse's monologue is being listened to with distaste by the nearer drinkers: young couples, girls with polished faces and frizzed hair, men in leather jackets with short haircuts. I hope that no one is going to hit my companion – or, as would be more likely, me. A young fellow in fisherman's gear catches Ilse's eye.

'Right you are, girl, 'bout Germany, like. A right smart crowd of fuckers ye are, cute out, and hard workers too.'

Ilse murmurs in satisfaction. Even the Irish know the truth.

'Smart enough ye are altogether, yet stupid enough to vote for Hitler. Now isn't that strange, don't you think? Ye didn't look so shagging smart in 1945, did you ever think of that? All Germans are good for is working their shagging bollicks off. We all laugh at them – fucking eejits.'

There is a long pause, after which he adds:

'I *am* for Europe, natural like; *Germans* give me a pain in me gut. They talk such shite.'

He smiles sweetly, contemplates his pint, changes the subject, and begins to discuss his trawler. One of the shiny girlfriends jabs her man with her elbow and hisses:

'Buy her a drink, for fuck's sake.'

The boyfriend responds with a hostile scowl. She aims a swipe at him with her purse, then pushes through to the bar counter. I fade into the crowd as Ilse, now embracing the girlfriend, is crying bitterly on her shoulder. An hour later the hard Teutonic and softer Irish tones of their voices rise from their corner of the bar, singing in harmony.

By that time I am having my ear bent by Jams O'Donnell, a tall and gangling fisherman who describes himself as belonging to the republican tradition. He could 'sort out' the six counties in no time at all.

'It's a case of pursuing our destiny. The Brits are on their last legs, their power is gone. The day of glory is not far off, when the tricolour will fly over every Northern town.'

Jams's girlfriend gives a bored yawn. She has heard it all before. She joins some friends who are singing 'The Bantry Girl's Lament'.

> For Johnny, lovely Johnny,
> Is a-sailing o'er the main.
> He's gone with other patriots
> To fight the King of Spain.

Predictably, 'Johnny, lovely Johnny' fails to return, dying 'in the foreign land of Spain'. Despite the drunken rendering, the beauty of the melody and poignancy of the words are not lost. Jams interjects significant lines from the ballad into our conversation while continuing his polemic, an impressive feat of co-ordination in the circumstances of drink taken.

> And who will plough the fields now,
> And who will cut the corn,
> And who will wash the sheep now,
> And keep them nately shorn?
> And the stack that's in the haggard,
> Unthrashed it will remain,
> Since Johnny went a-thrashing
> All in the land of Spain.

Jams does not like my non-violent, non-partisan point of view. He laughs menacingly when I suggest that Northern Protestant culture is as valid as any other form of Irishness.

'Ahh, West Brits like yourself have no courage, yeer just all talk. Blood must be spilled. The Prods need a proper pasting before they come round, you can't alter the march of history. "Ireland unfree shall never be at peace," did you ever hear that now?'

I acknowledge that I am intimately familiar with nationalist rhetoric:

'It is from Patrick Pearse's oration at the graveside of the Fenian O'Donovan Rossa, 1915.'

Jams's eyes narrow to little dark spaces in his flushed face. He sticks out his tongue at me and, abruptly, joins the singers.

> The girls from the bawnoge
> In sorrow may retire,
> And the piper and his bellows
> Go home and blow the fire.

For Johnny, lovely Johnny
Is a-sailing o'er the main,
He's gone with other patriots,
To fight the King of Spain.

I am tempted to push my luck and mention *Kristallnacht*, but decide that although Jams has humoured me thus far, there are topics more sensitive than Irish nationalism and sectarian bigotry — such as, for instance, Irish racism. At this suggestion the gorge would rise and fists would fly. With his republican sentiments, he *knows* that he is right and doesn't really care what I think (a 'West Brit' in his eyes, merely because I disagree with him). Accusations of racism are different. Here he will be on shaky ground, and react with the passion of a broken glass in my face.

For Johnny died for freedom's sake
In the foreign land of Spain.

In Pulaski, Tennessee, outside a barber's shop, once the Law Office, a handsome plaque commemorates the founding of the Ku Klux Klan on 24 December 1865. As I sketched this nostalgic and historic site, a man of the town stopped to talk with me, ask me my business, where I came from, my reasons for being in Southern Tennessee. This was very much as might happen in Limerick, or Portadown. He approved of the fact that I was drawing the hallowed spot, sighed nostalgically and said:

'That was a real time to be around — a man's time. Show those niggers who's boss.'

He went his way, I concentrated on my work. The plaque mentions the names of those gents who attended the fateful meeting: Jones, McCork, Reed, Crowe, Lester, Kennedy. Now *that* is interesting, Kennedy being the name most frequently pulled out of the hat when Irish-American liberalism is being flaunted. There were, it seems, Kennedys and *Kennedys* — some we would prefer to forget.

It is easy to be unfair to Bantry, but then Bantry is an archetypal Irish country town. When talking about Bantry, one could be talking about Bray or Galway, Tuam or Wexford, or 200 others, all places in which there have been 3 a.m. pogroms against members of the travelling community.

Early in the morning of 19 September 1994, a group of ten men, Dublin thugs and local vigilantes, armed with iron bars and one driving a forklift truck, attacked the traveller encampment at the town pier in Bantry. To the sound of the smashing of glass and the screams of small children, the caravans and mobile homes were lifted into the air by the forklift and toppled over. This descent into the persuasive methods of the 1930s in Germany has become, in recent years, a commonplace in the Irish Republic. The ritual of intimidation against the travellers was designed to encourage them to leave Bantry, where their presence was not required. In a subsequent court case which took two years to arrive before a judge, a Dublin man was convicted of being involved in the harassment. He had, he claimed, been employed by a Bantry businessman to terrorise the travellers into leaving. Since he had no previous connection with the town, and had to travel from Dublin in order to carry out his brutal business, the responsibility seemed to rest squarely among some of the local population. It is probable that this action against the travellers, had it not come to the attention of the media, where it made Bantry appear primitive and bigoted, would have received considerable local support. Bantry Town Commissioners debated the issue, but chose not to condemn it.

During this summer of long, hot days of sunshine, the West Cork Music Festival took place at Bantry House: classical music performed in patrician surroundings. The 1796 bicentennial brought a flotilla of French sailing boats into the bay, and a summer school explored the politics of that year. It is hard in such circumstances to imagine that racism, the most searing and destructive of human preoccupations, lives also in this place. The Devil is not always so compliant as to depart at the ringing of a bicycle bell.

I leave the bar, and as I stand outside in the street contemplating my next move, I become aware of the inhabitants of a muddy car and trailer double-parked in front of me, occupied by a farming family. The driver is an ample woman in a rather crumpled sweater and jeans. In the passenger seat sits her husband, leaning his elbow through the open window, laughing at whatever was being said in the car, the back seat crowded with children, a grandmother and a dog. With a casual flick, the farmer throws his cigarette packet out of the window at my feet. Having suffered a serious personality change while in the bar, I instantly respond in my best Hiberno-Germanic manner.

'In Deutschland ve vould not do that!'

From under his curly hair the farmer looks at me quizzically, one eye closed. Then his face breaks into a great grin. He starts to laugh heartily. Grabbing his wife's arm, he bellows, 'Did you hear that: "In Deutschland"?' – imitating in best West Corkese my attempt at German-accented English. In the back of the car, all the children, the grandmother and the dog are laughing, the sheep in the trailer baa in hilarity; even the shopping in plastic bags seems to shake with amusement. The farmer leans his handsome face out of the window, his crest of curly brown hair tossed by the wind. Earnestly he contemplates this nosy-parker foreigner and then laughs again.

'God bless your innocence, man, have you nothing else to be thinking about? Go home and leave us to be who we are.'

Like Superman in a telephone kiosk, I slip out of my lederhosen, abandon my feathered hat and, suitably chastened, attempt to assume my former personality.

It is time to leave the south-west and head up the coast. As I round the turn of an idyllic little gorse-fringed bay to the north of Bantry, two teenage girls in identical bright summer frocks are hitching a lift. I stop and open the passenger door; they are going a few miles. Both proceed to get into the front seat. I suggest that one or both might get in the back, that there is not room for three in the front. They reply that they will sit together in the front.

I decline this proposal and the prospect of unasked-for intimacy, and drive on without them, ruminating at the peculiarly uncompromising attitude of people seeking a lift, insisting on smoking when you – the driver – have asked them not to, deciding that you should go to Omagh when you said that you were going to Strabane. A mile further on, an old man waves vaguely from the grass verge; he might equally have been scratching his ear. I stop and he gets in. I relate my experience of the two girls, then the conversation turns to other matters: he talks about 'the dreight', rainless weather. Soon we arrive at his destination. As he is leaving the car, he says in all seriousness:

'I was wondering about them two girleens you told me about; do you think that they might have been Siamese twins?'

I acknowledge this quite ludicrous possibility, and we part.

In country places everybody knows everybody, and their business. The prospect that a few miles from this old man's native place there could have been a publicly visible, yet to him unknown, pair of conjoined children is highly improbable. Yet he had clearly debated the possible explanations to my tale, and opted for the most fantastical option.

Such an appetite for the bizarre or the mystical is deeply rooted in Irish rural society, and their urban diaspora (most Irish city-folk are no more than a few generations off the land). Tales of bleeding images, moving statues, virginal apparitions – the gullible in pursuit of the invisible – are still, at the latter end of the twentieth century, common phenomena. Belief in fairies, the little people, may have been banished by electric light and television, yet the ingrained attitudes of centuries – if not millennia – do not disappear with the flicking of a light switch.

SINGING 'GALWAY BAY'

County rivalries are based on firm if chance allegiances: to this expanse of bog rather than to that lush hillside; to the debatable ascendancy of Mizen Head over Bolus Head. As you pass from one county to another, sometimes the landscape changes, but usually the boundary is neither marked nor noticed. I abandon Cork to embrace Kerry, conscious of leaving one loyalty while entering another.

My plan is to get back to Enniskillen in County Fermanagh, where I am due to join a cycling group for a tour of the north-west coastline. Unfortunately, I have chosen a very roundabout manner of getting there. Instead of going north from Dublin, I have come south to County Cork, and intend to traverse a large portion of the west coast.

At the August peak of the Irish summer, the roads are crowded with tourist traffic, and nowhere more so than on the Ring of Kerry. This is the most well-known and commercially developed tourist route in Ireland. The road from Bantry joins the circuit of the Ring, on the section between

Kenmare and Killarney. Suddenly, the relative quietness of the roads, even in high summer, is exchanged for tourist mayhem. Enormous coaches, like mobile catafalques with their peering occupants, monopolise the roads. They park in serried ranks at every viewpoint, and make travelling for others a not very pleasant experience. Walkers, cyclists and backpackers scurry for the verges of the roads as the coaches roar past on the tarmac, carrying their quiescent cargoes from one beauty spot to another. This can never have been an ideal way to view Ireland. Now, when the coaches, which are groomed for travel on interstate highways and autobahns, have expanded to be monstrously out of scale with local roads, either the scenery or the coaches must go. The tourist authority, in its relentless pursuit of ever-greater numbers of visitors, will naturally regard the scenery as expendable. I would forbid the coaches.

At Kenmare, an attractive and lively country town, I make a minor diversion in order to visit Sneem, one of the most charming villages of the region. The layout of the paired village greens is a geometric witticism: two opposing grassy triangles, meeting at their apex. The delightful scheme is pleasing to the eye, as well as both soft and gentle in its atmosphere.

Since the eighteenth century, the mountain and lakeland landscape around Killarney has been the most scenically celebrated area of Ireland. Its splendour remains, although now it has become necessary to wander further and further from the principal routes in order to appreciate the landscape. In fact, the only way in which the natural magnificence of the Killarney National Park can be viewed unmolested by traffic is either in the dead of winter, or by abandoning the roads and taking to the walking routes in the hills above the town. Here, the last remaining indigenous oak forests are to be found and, in their respective seasons, the variously berried and blossomed rowan, holly, hawthorn and rhododendron sprout between the rocks and the torrents.

The town of Killarney is so devoted to tourism that it is best left to the enemy. The troops of the occupying power seem relentless and insatiable in their appetite for pillage and rapine. They stagger from the looted shops, laden with green Aran sweaters and Irish crystal glass made in the Czechoslovak Republic. In late July, the town resembles Mecca during the Haj, only less organised.

I pass through the teeming mountains, escape the pressures of the strained and hectic town, and come out on the other side, unscathed. I will return to Kerry later in the year, after the human avalanche has subsided.

In the gathering dusk, I drive away to the north and then east, towards

North Great George's Street, Dublin. Late-eighteenth-century houses, until recently tenements, are being restored by lovers of the city's Georgian architecture

Bloomsday: the costumed participants listen to Barry McGovern reading Ulysses *at the Joyce Tower in Sandycove*

'Stately, plump Buck Mulligan'

Dublin street market. A child squats on the road among her wares

An elderly couple sit passively among the jumble of Cumberland Street Market

The pavement studio of Dublin's traveller child artists on Nassau Street

Michael Collins and the glass from the occult assassination

Cill Rialaig, looking east from Bolus Head. The author lived in the second cottage from the left, with fishing-net draped over the thatch

Cill Rialaig from above, overlooking Ballinskelligs Bay. Pats Ó Conaill's cottage is the roofless ruin on the extreme right

Fairyhouse race meeting: anticipation mounts as Danoli approaches the first fence

Limerick. I was once thrown out of a pub in Limerick – not because I was out of order, rather the opposite. I came in the door, a stranger to the place, and was instantly asked to leave. The length of my hair was sufficient to attract the barman's attention. Such encounters leave a bad impression.

Limerick City is a conservative place, with a dubious reputation for Catholic piety, urban violence and family feuding. In 1904, the only anti-Jewish pogrom in Irish history took place here. In the 1970s, a Maoist bookshop was burned. Although made notorious under the name of 'Stab City', inspired by an untoward enthusiasm among its citizens for knifing one another, there are, naturally, other aspects to the place – its better self.

The following day I visit the Hunt Museum, which is located on the campus of the university. This is a superb and eccentric privately-formed art collection, the sort of accumulation of treasures which required passion, and perhaps a little madness, to bring to fruition. Although created in the mid-twentieth century from the private means of John and Gertrude Hunt, who were astute antiquities dealers of moderate means, it is in the tradition of those great collections assembled by nineteenth-century megalomaniac millionaires: a Getty, Gulbenkian or Wallace.

The tiny rearing bronze horse which cavorts in a display case is believed by scholars to be a cast of a lost original clay maquette by Leonardo da Vinci. It is surrounded by an enormous battery of medieval ecclesiastical art. There are works by Picasso and Giacometti, Cycladic dolls, a leopard-head mask from the kingdom of Benin in West Africa. The core of the collection is its wealth in bells and crosiers, processional crosses, reliquaries and Gothic statuary. It must have been immensely satisfying to put together such a collection, knowing that one might be scholarly and daft at the same time, without inviting censure. The collection has now passed into the public domain through the generosity of the Hunt family, and is soon to move into the eighteenth-century Custom House in central Limerick.

Neither Irish nor British state policy regarding art or antiquities favours decentralisation. Little of great merit in the island's holding of historic art and antiquities has escaped from the possessive grasp of Dublin's institutions. Cork, Monaghan, Waterford and a few other places have small collections, but these are not significant. The Ulster Museum in Belfast is the only other major claimant. Limerick is a unique exception: a world-class fine-art and antiquities museum, located far from the banks of the Liffey.

After the art, the buildings. King John's Castle sits on the east bank of the Shanon with its Anglo-Norman feet in the water. From the far bank it is imposing, with great stone drum towers bolstering its sense of strength and impregnability. From behind, this grandeur falls to dust. The keep was previously occupied by local authority housing, recently demolished, to be replaced by an exceptionally arid steel and glass wing, inhabited by the Interpretative Centre. I perform my duty as an enquiring traveller by sitting through the audio-visual programme. As usual, I am accompanied by 200 schoolchildren, each separately and without co-ordination rustling a crisp packet.

Limerick is a Viking foundation, its name of Old Norse derivation. The Viking contribution to urban settlement in Ireland – to trade and medieval art and craft – is immense, as significant as that of any other invading force from the Fir Bolgs to the Tudors. The audience is treated to a presentation of the Vikings as 'Neanderthal' savages (apparently one-eyed), in horned helmets (which they never wore), attacking the Christian monks. This is Irish history from the monastic perspective, as taught 50 or 100 years ago, still being served up to impressionable audiences. I leave in despair.

I transfer my patronage to the visual, although not audio-free, safety of the café, established in the core of one of the drum towers. The only customer, I drink tea while the radio broadcasts a frenetic Gaelic football match. The impassioned voice of the commentator echoes around the rough, whitewashed, stone walls. The woman behind the counter speaks enthusiastically of the prowess of the teams, of which I have to confess ignorance. In Limerick, they do not mince their words, and she is a woman of definite opinions. Over the sections of rhubarb tart, she eyes me with distaste. She clatters the cutlery behind the counter, and declares with vehemence: 'Then you must be very lacking in national spirit.'

From Limerick, I cross the Shannon into County Clare, and late in the evening, with the setting sun casting the harsh landscape into moon-like relief, continue north, past W.B. Yeats's tower of Thoor Ballylee, silhouetted against an iron-grey sky. The continuity of past into present, and the poet's sense of indebtedness to all those who had gone before, are symbolised by his act of refurbishing this small Norman tower-house as a home for his family. It is part of the very tangible presence of Yeats, here and further north, in the countryside around Sligo.

The pace of Killarney has been left behind, and although the roads are busy with summer visitors, it does not feel as though the essential beauty of the area has been surrendered to the noise and pollution of motor coaches.

When I arrive in Galway, the annual Arts Festival and the Race Week which follows it, the social highpoints of the season, have just been celebrated. The narrow streets groan with the press of bodies – people who are suffused with the arts, or who have been liberated from their savings at the racecourse. A few lucky ones have winnings to spend. The sheer number of people in every bar, café, hotel and square inch of open space suggests a city suddenly filled to bursting point with refugees – Kabul with the Taleban at its gates – except that these refugees from the world of work are all in high spirits. They are loving the place, the weather and the traditional music which blares and eddies from every doorway. At the music *seisiúns*, forever taking place in back rooms, the prevailing state of mind is giddy abandon, verging on levitation. An inspiring cocktail of ozone, friendship and music envelops the crowds.

I place myself in a backpackers' hostel, right on the Corrib, in the thick of things. I had phoned a week before to book. When I arrive, late in the evening, there is no record of my call, nor any room for me at the inn. I protest. Mysteriously, a bed is discovered.

This is in a very small, hot, airless and claustrophobic room in which there are already five large young men who have an inordinate amount of luggage, backpacks, bedrolls, water bottles and assorted camping equipment. This confusion now occupies all the floorspace. They are Australian, taking a year to do a world tour: so many countries, so many days. If it is the first week of August, then it must be Galway. The previous week was London, that before, Amsterdam. They have a special kind of innocence, an awkward combination of street-wisdom and naiveté. To anything which I say, one of them responds in monosyllables:

'I am on my way to the north-west.'

'Rally.'

'There's no air in this room.'

'Naaah.'

'I think I might be getting brain fever.'

'Aaah.'

They are so tired of travelling that at the mere suggestion of a trip to Connemara, they become even less loquacious. They will find a bar and spend the evening there, drinking. I just climb into my bunk and abandon myself to sleep; the backpackers leave for their night's entertainment. The following morning when I awake, they are already gone, allowing me to see the floor for the first time.

'Naaah.'

After passing through a multitude of towns, Galway immediately strikes a different chord. Most Irish towns and villages appear as though designed for stagecoach viewing. You have already passed through the smallest hamlets before you realise that 'that was a place'. In those of larger size, including quite substantial towns, a grand tour is often possible without one ever needing to stop. The main street containeth all: churches, shops, pubs, courthouse, banks, and whoops, you are out among fields again – the town has been left behind. There is, generally, no complexity of structure which may not be absorbed in a passing manner. Irish country places evolved from being attendant on the road from the proverbial Oola to the unfindable Gowna: a case of less not being more.

Galway is the home of Macnas, the street-theatre company which had, in March, redeemed the tawdry image of Dublin's St Patrick's Day parade. Their performance in the recent Arts Festival was being mentioned by everyone with enthusiasm: local talent made good elsewhere; their success internationally is a cause of pride in the town. As the fastest-growing urban centre in Ireland, Galway is popularly regarded as one of the most vibrant cultural centres on the island. It is a place where enough is usually happening to justify any expectations. Beautifully sited, it is invaded from the north by the river Corrib, leading to the inland sea of the lakes, and from the south by the sea. As the threshold of Connemara – the essence of the west – it represented for previous generations the doors of perception. Beyond Galway the doors swing open.

Despite its enveloping urban sprawl, the heart of Galway is as vital as its reputation suggests, having more theatre, music and visual art to offer than any comparable Irish town. I say 'town' with caution. Although Galway is a city by right of its fifteenth-century charter, the atmosphere is of an engaging university town, teeming with students and visitors, gourmets of all ages.

Galway's medieval plan imposes on it a shape, form and character which instantly distinguish it as a more complex place. Kinsale and Kilkenny, also medieval in plan, have some of the same magic. These are places in which one might lose oneself, where the entire town may not be absorbed merely by standing between the bank and the chip shop and staring. In switchback manner, the principal street is a succession of separate bits, running from Eyre Square to the river, tracing the path of the sixteenth-century thoroughfare – William Street, Shop Street, High Street, Quay Street.

In the university library is a sixteenth-century map showing things as they were when Galway was an independent mercantile city-state. Then it was as proud and prosperous as any Tuscan hill town, equally devoted to trade and clannishness. This map penetrates the darkness of the Irish past, illuminating it in an extraordinary way. It shows what was there to be destroyed during the Cromwellian and later wars. The Irish past can be difficult to visualise, so little remains of early visual records.

Appropriately, the Galway map is the most detailed cartographic record produced in late medieval Ireland. It presents a bird's-eye view of the country's finest merchant city, a measure of what was irrevocably lost in Kilkenny, Carrickfergus, Ferns, Ennis, Kilmallock and Waterford. The Irish world of walled towns with stone-built houses, decorated in fine late-Gothic ornamentation, survived into modern history, yet fell into such decay after the depredations of the seventeenth century that, when they began to revive economically during the late eighteenth and nineteenth centuries, the continuity had been lost. Now what survives are mere shadows on the glass, memories preserved by street plans and by, as in Galway, many orphaned architectural fragments which once decorated the merchants' houses.

After St Patrick, Daniel O'Connell and Oliver Plunkett must, between them, have the greatest number of streets, squares, parks, bridges and local authority terraces named in their honour, more than all the other saints and local and national heroes put together. John Fitzgerald Kennedy has since his visit to Ireland in 1963, some five months before his assassination, run them fairly close. The centre of Eyre Square, Galway's only significant open space and traffic junction, is now the John Fitzgerald Kennedy Park, a place for backpackers to sit in the sun. Young people who have travelled to Galway from all corners of the globe arrange to meet in the square and wait for something to happen, other friends to turn up.

The square is actually a mess. The monuments are placed as though in a lumber room; nothing relates to anything else. Chance, and the moribund aesthetics of the 1970s, are everywhere visible. Above the lumber, the rusty metal sails of Eamon O'Doherty's abstract sculpture of Galway hookers – a type of local fishing boat – rise in determined defiance of their tawdry surroundings.

From Eyre Square, the principal streets meander towards the bridges of the Corrib. Here, the life-sustaining mystery of the salmon returning from the ocean to their spawning grounds in the waters of Lough Corrib remains a compelling image of the natural order. In the period of the spring salmon run, the river is a solid mass of moving life, the fish patiently awaiting their opportunity to pass over the weir, from which they are released into the fresh waters above the town. Then they will, by instinct, return to their ancestral pools. This area of Galway, the banks of the river and canal with its multitude of bridges, is in direct contrast to the narrowness of the town's streets. Around the circle of the waterways, people loll on the grass or gaze down into the moving stream.

On the quays at Wolfe Tone Bridge a monument, presented to Galway by the city of Genoa, commemorates a local legend that in 1477 Christopher

Columbus visited the town. This was his last European landfall before he sailed to the New World. The inscription has been vandalised by some Latin American indignant at the honouring of a Spanish-colonial fortune-hunter.

Local folklore is adept at colonising the colonists' world for its own purposes. In Spanish Parade is the Spanish Arch, popularly believed to be a relic of the strong trade links between mercantile Galway and Spain, and to be the place where the Spaniards traded. Actually it is the opposite: it was built as a British fort to maintain control over the hostile and volatile local merchant families. Folklore proves more appealing than fact. Barnaby Gooche, Elizabeth I's Provost Marshal of Connaught, wrote to London in 1583 (five years before the Armada), proposing to create:

> a voyd place bye the haven where the Govonor has desyned to have a cyttadell whych if here majestye thought good he could buyld wythowt any charges to her majestye, which, in my fansey, consydrying the pryde and great welth of the townsmen and how greatly they are addycted to the Spanyard were as necessary a maatter as myght be.

In the museum, I am taken to task by the attendant for asking questions; he is rather more concerned with spinning fantasies to tourists. I dislike museums such as this one, which has not moved from equating bygones with antiquities. The display includes antique babies' feeding-bottles, clay pipes, farm implements, more bottles, local photographs from the Galway of the past, and bits and bobs of handicraft: baskets, lace, old advertisements. It is a truly democratic collection in which everything is as legitimate as everything else. Some bars of soap from the 1950s are displayed next to a Bronze-Age axe. I object to the fact that the version of the great pictorial map of the city is a mere photocopy, while the guide continues to refer to it as though it were an object of great value. He does not care, and nor do the visitors.

Nearby on Nun's Island is the Catholic cathedral, the last and most monstrous example of church megalomania. It is not a product of the Fascist '30s but of the swinging '60s, when everything had evaporated from the Imperium of the Church but the money to create monuments to crassness and folly. An Italian Renaissance dome sits on the solid bulk of the building, suggesting grandeur within. No grandeur is to be found, except that of an empty cinema. Twin Peruvian Baroque minarets (surely the mezzo-American's revenge?) flank the entrance. Tudor Rose side windows strike a subversive blow for the Provost Marshal. Can the clergy or designers of this house of stone have been so hung over as not to feel that *Peruvian* and *Tudor* were perhaps stretching things beyond the point of credulity for a cathedral in the mid-twentieth century? Perhaps they were striking a blow for ecumenism?

Tourists flock to visit the cathedral. From a distance it looks like a place one would wish to see, something important on an itinerary. Inside they wander, looking for something beautiful or edifying to contemplate; they will find neither. Yet between the confusion of Eyre Square and the vapidity of the cathedral lies one of the most diverting, vital and historically important cities in Ireland.

In Bowling Green, a street behind the medieval St Nicholas of Myra's church, is Nora Barnacle's house which I visit a number of times, or, rather, attempt to do so. Nora, the wife of James Joyce, was born in Galway. The house, in a mean little two-up, two-down terrace, has a single window and door at street level. I peer in the window, but I might have been looking down a well; there is nothing to be seen in the interior darkness but a reflection of my face. A small piece of paper in the window, on which the ink has faded, provides some now-illegible information concerning opening hours. Perhaps the house opens after midnight. Certainly it failed to do so during daylight hours.

In the centre of the town, the pubs and restaurants are still bulging with custom, the streets in festive spirit. I go into Tigh Neachtáin on the corner of Cross and Quay Streets, a spit-and-sawdust interior, pub and restaurant combined, with the kind of dark, unpretentious atmosphere which is a modern attempt to evoke the dim simplicity of other days. Here the food is excellent. I succeed in steering clear of the Mount Vesuvius of mashed potato, overlooking a Pompeii and Herculaneum of chocolate-brown chops, with a fleeing population of tinned peas dyed in green ink. These scatter across the tabletop at any attempt to approach them with a fork. Instead, I eat grilled loin of venison in a date and honey sauce, drink an excellent red wine and have brown-bread ice cream for dessert. Later, during a traditional music *seisiún* in the bar below, I sip a slow pint of Guinness. The audience is composed of men and women in their twenties, Irish and Continental, American, British, Japanese. They exude a kind of joyous good-fellowship; the music can hardly compete with the laughter and conversation. They all have bags which spill on the floor, revealing books, travel guides, tin whistles. Like an anthropologist from Papua New Guinea, observing the customs of the tribes of Galway, I conclude that being a student on summer holidays in Galway may be an important social ritual related to the mating practices of the people.

Tigh Neachtáin is a late-medieval house, its fabric blandly concealed behind modern plasterwork. It is a survivor from the Galway of the medieval map. During the early nineteenth century, it was the town house of landlord Richard Martin, whose estates in the west covered 200,000 acres. Known locally as 'The King of Connemara', he was, for his love of animals, dubbed 'Humanity Dick' by George IV. At Westminster in 1822, he promoted the first animal-protection legislation, and in 1824 founded the Royal Society for the Prevention of Cruelty to Animals.

It wasn't in Tigh Neachtáin but in the cavernous interior of another medieval dungeon, The Snug, that I met Dave and Gráinne, a local couple in their early thirties. Dave is a builder, doing well in the housing boom: things have never been busier; Gráinne has inherited a pub from a bachelor uncle. They are passionate followers of horse racing, Gaelic football, soccer – strictly in that order – and spend many evenings in the pubs, not getting drunk but drinking convivially with friends. They appeared intelligent, hardworking and ambitious for success in their business, and I found in them an admirable mirror of attitudes and responses to all sorts of present-day issues.

A staple of Irish conversation is the revealing anecdote which is used like a New Testament parable. A direct or sometimes oblique tale is presented to substantiate a point. We had been talking about the farming community's use of illegal drugs in animals. The children of small farms, they know all about it. Dave's ire rises at the thought of one of his neighbours.

'Mick Fitz is a right case, a bloody savage. He treats his missus and his kids as badly as his stock, and that's fairly desperate.'

Dave begins and Gráinne continues. Their topic is evidently a well-voiced one. The farmer in question has a serious drink problem, spends all the time he can in the pubs, has long ago lost his driving licence, yet is still driving. The gardaí are always after him, but he does not care. He has been in court so many times that it means nothing to him; he had already spent eight months in jail for a long succession of driving offences. They shake their heads and laugh at his behaviour; what truly offends their sense of decorum is quite different.

The farmer has a large herd of dry cattle which he winters-out on rented land, irrespective of the weather. On a recent occasion he left a cow and some heifers locked for days in a shed, unfed and unwatered, while he was on a drinking bout. In the course of his building work at the adjoining farm, Dave had released the stock from their captivity. Gráinne contributes:

'I reported him to the RSPCA, the effing hoor. It was not the first time they had heard of him.'

Her expression darkens. Their mutual indignation at his mistreatment of cattle and their amusement at the farmer's alcoholic, uninsured driving and general fecklessness are in curious contradiction. Endangering animal life seems to have taken priority over that of humans.

Attitudes to drunken driving tend to focus not on the dangerous irresponsibility of the driver, but on the fact that he might kill somebody else while drunk. That was certainly reprehensible. The act of drunken driving in itself seemed to be within the canon of acceptable behaviour, perhaps because in Irish society everybody who is not a total abstainer does so at some point.

'Abaile' is a large, modern mansion overlooking the upper reaches of Lough Corrib, far enough from the suburbs of Galway to be surrounded by fine farmland, devoid of bungalows. The approach to the house is by a tree-lined avenue. In style, the house lies somewhere between stockbroker posh and *gaeilgeoir* plain (extensive half-timbered central block, flanked by thatched wings); in scale it has all the accommodation of a Georgian gentleman's residence. Reception rooms, a magnificent front hall, a rear courtyard with loose boxes for half a dozen horses: all are contrived to impress. The principal façade is decorated by a limestone, eighteenth-century Ionic portico, cannibalised from some demolished country house. The proportions of the portico are slightly out of kilter with the form of the house (and in violent conflict with both timbering and thatch), as though the porch had been purchased from a mail-order catalogue and turned out to be too large when it arrived.

The driveway of 'Abaile' is lined with new cars, a steward motioning in the darkness with a torch. The ground-floor reception rooms glow with the warmth of candlelight, and the moving press of partying people are clearly visible from outside the tall windows. I move through the public rooms. I know nobody here but my host, and him only superficially. Among the crowd I recognise a former cabinet minister, numerous TDs, some undertakers from the banks (active in the Cromwellian rather than the funereal sense), a decorative sprinkling of people from the arts and universities.

A chance invitation has brought me here. My host and his wife greet guests in the hall, the picture of well-groomed affluence. He and I have met only twice previously – at fine-art auctions in Dublin, where he had been successfully bidding on major works of an Irish painter on whose printmaking I had done some research. I am greeted as though the principal guest, and carried on the arm of my host to his study and then some of the main rooms to view his collection. Periodically, he introduces me to groups of guests: 'Brian Lalor, an authority on K's early work, come to give me a few tips.'

Neither of these claims is even remotely true, yet I do not protest. It is often simpler to be fraudulent than to explain who you actually are. Each painting that we view – restored, conserved, in appropriate period framing – sits under its individual brass-cowled downlight. All illumination in the rooms is designed to enhance the paintings. The works are exclusively of those Irish artists of the early twentieth century whose reputation and market value are beyond reproach: Jack B. Yeats, Roderic O'Conor, William Orpen, Walter Osborne.

A large and splendid late Jack Yeats, *Singing 'Galway Bay'*, awash with emotional energy and extraordinarily vivid colour, dominates one room. A lapis lazuli Connemara sky forms the backdrop for a heroic striding figure, singing as he goes. A set of Irish literary and political portraits by John B. Yeats (father of both W.B. Yeats and the painter Jack Yeats), the knighted Lavery and Orpen are in another room. In a third are further works: John Lavery's of the elusive Hazel, in raw beauty and in ethereal decline. The corridors between the rooms are hung with landscapes of the west of Ireland by Grace and Paul Henry, Maurice MacGonigal and Harry Kernoff. Evidently, the collector's skill is more assured than the architectural schizophrenia of the house might suggest.

The grand tour completed, I am deposited with guests – Bill, Tony, Deirdre – while someone else is fêted. Deirdre talks of her string of racers, Bill of his contracts to supply halal meat to the Gulf, Tony of his plans to extend his cosmetic surgery practice and to establish a major clinic in the region.

'Boob jobs are mostly local, nose jobs from the Med – Athens, Istanbul, Tel Aviv, Cairo. Those women are just *too* well endowed.'

Deirdre swings her dainty bust around, smirks at Tony and purrs: 'Amn't I a good advertisement for you, pet?'

Hospitality is lavish: the hundred-odd guests talk avidly and familiarly; jokes and anecdotes carry over the heads of the party. The buzz of fellowship grows as the evening progresses. Everybody here appears to be successful: professional and business friends, developers, architects, solicitors, estate agents, women of business acumen and men of ruthless determination.

Late in the evening, when the number of guests has thinned and enough alcohol has been consumed to tarnish slightly the glamour and wrinkle the couture gowns, and while the band in the entrance hall is warming up for dancing, another inevitable constituent of any Irish social evening has yet to be experienced. My host's friends are prompting each other to sing. Often this is to be enjoyed, sometimes merely endured. After feigning shyness, many are glad to perform. Whether they sing well or tunelessly matters less than the fact that they participate. The men are always more eager than the women to make fools of themselves. Some sing well, with professional ease, practised performers; here the difficulty is not in prompting them to sing, but in persuading them that three songs will suffice. The ex-cabinet minister gives 'The Fields of Athenry', one of the undertakers, 'My Way'. Deirdre, who has a lovely voice, sings 'Don't Cry for Me, Argentina'.

Two women in elaborate bouffant hairdos as contrived as the candyfloss beehives of the court of Marie Antoinette, doubtless the product of an excruciating afternoon in the hairdressing salon, position themselves behind the host, keeping time to unheard music, gyrating slightly. A third woman presents him with a guitar, one of the beehives places a satin high-collared cloak on his shoulders, and while the beehives shimmer behind him (having now become the dooby-do girls from a black-girl backing group of the 1950s), the captain of industry gives impassioned versions of Elvis Presley songs. He strains his facial muscles into a snarl, a sneer, a rictus; his soft voice is tortured into a growl in an attempt to do justice to the renderings of the bard of Memphis. The dooby-do girls sway in the background beneath Jack B. Yeats's vision of Celtic dawns, their beehives vibrating like the cocoons of Pleistocene grubs, about to pupate.

The session is a highlight of the evening, and something everybody except myself had been expecting; no doubt it is a standard element in social gatherings at 'Abaile'. The 1960s appeared to have been a climactic period for all present, excluding their embarrassed teenage children whose musical tastes extended backwards by six months at the most.

The atmosphere of a well-appointed house, well-stocked bookshelves, sumptuous art on the walls and successful people enjoying themselves in a convivial evening is only a partial image of those present. The other side is the corruption and manipulation of the democratic process which seems endemic among people of influence all over Ireland. An inability to perceive the dividing line between public good and personal advantage is usually operative thinking in these circles. My evening's conversations all stem from the perspectives of those with whom I have been talking. They imagine that because I am there, I must be 'one of us'. Not so. The paintings on the walls are merely the superficial evidence of what cultural awareness and an eye to the investment portfolio can achieve. The sentiments and ethics in the air are more related to the exercise of power and political manipulation. In the background, Tammany Hall's greatest hits were being played, again, and again, and again.

Back in Galway, I scrutinise the messages on the hostel's noticeboard: Bill and Doug want a lift to Dublin; Kathy requires a travelling companion for a trip to Bali; Bergit, less ambitiously, wants to get to Armagh. I am going that way, so I leave her a message. The following morning she appears at breakfast, a barefoot, amazonian, Swedish student, terrifyingly healthy-looking. She has been in Ireland for a month.

We leave Galway to travel along the coast, west and then north, a rather circuitous route. The west coast beckons, and I set my back to the central plain and begin to skirt below the mountains, along the meandering and sea-sculpted coastline. Connemara has maintained its harsh and formidable beauty; even now in high season one does not need to divert much from the main roads to shake off the trappings of the twentieth century, and be faced with the untamed grandeur of the landscape.

A few miles before Clifden, the car begins to wobble. I stop and inspect the wheels. One is flat: a puncture, obviously. I remove Bergit's enormous backpack from the boot and retrieve the spare. It is immediately evident that it, too, is punctured. Of this I have no recollection; evidently it happened a long time ago, and I have neglected to have it repaired. Bergit laughs at my problem; people offering lifts are not to be trusted.

With an automatic heave she flings on her backpack, and is out into the road hitching before I have even considered where I am going to find a mechanic. Within ten minutes, a car has taken my passenger away. I am left on the roadside with an immobile car, two dud wheels leaning against the side, and no clear plan of campaign. I can hitch into Clifden and find a garage or set off walking now, with a wheel under my arm. Instead, I sit in the ditch and look at the sea.

A car of similar make to my own pulls up in front; a farmer in his twenties gets out. He has divined the situation without a word being spoken.

'A puncture, spare is flat, you'll have to take mine. Fortunately it's the same size.'

He takes the spare wheel from his car and puts it on mine, despite my protests that I can do so myself. Then, giving me directions to the most efficient garage in the town, and to his house on the far side of Clifden, he drives off. His concern for the problems of a stranger impress me: a sense of responsibility towards a person in need. I drive on to Clifden. The job is quickly attended to. When I return the tyre to his farm, his wife comes to the door, a flock of small children hovering around her, staring in curiosity. I explain; she smiles.

'Ah, Tommy would push the car to Galway for you, if it was needed. And why wouldn't he, he's that sort.'

From Clifden to Killary Harbour the land is both raw and beautiful, yet sparsely populated. Small farms of marginal land are pleasant to look at, difficult to make a living from, and even more difficult to raise a family on, if your expectations are for a decent standard of living. The fjord of Killary is as desolately stunning a landscape as any in Ireland, impressive and dark on a bright day. The deep and narrow waterway penetrates far inland, its hinterland dominated by mountain ranges; the Twelve Bens, the Partry Mountains and Croagh Patrick wrap around its source. The feeling is claustrophobic and there is a sensation on the shores of the harbour of being a long, long way from inhabited places. At Leenane, I pause for the night, then head inland for a long cross-country journey towards Enniskillen.

Periodically, I stop in quiet towns, Claremorris, Boyle and Leitrim, places far from the tourist route where life has the rhythm of other days. In such places, the rural year of agricultural seasons is of far greater relevance than the periods of influx from abroad which now rule the coastline, where farmhouse bed and breakfasts encroach upon even the loveliest of views. In small pubs, male supremacy appears to have maintained its sway. Everything is familiar and local; strangers are not expected. With nothing to do on damp evenings, I spend more time than I would have wished whiling away the hours in small, melancholy village pubs, playing darts (badly) with young local men. The only patrons are from the immediate locality.

The animal world of the Irish male drinker is a gross and unlovely territory, inhabited by men whose lives are often devoid of any human comfort except that of alcohol and pub company. A large man, about forty years old, indistinguishable from the County Cork architectural historian who displayed such an interest in churches with crosses and those without, attracts my attention. He has not removed his cap in the bar – a distinguishing feature. Voices are raised in discourse:

'That team have not won a match since 1936.'

'The British Taoiseach, John Major . . .'

'Cattle prices will never recover; I may as well sell the land to that German fella.'

Closing time approaches and the crowd draws closer to the bar counter, pushing and heaving like heifers at the cattle mart, each determined to squeeze through a gap between those in front. There is a tense atmosphere as serious drinkers under threat of limited time and with unslakable thirsts contemplate doomsday. Although the weather has been fine, all the men in the bar have managed, somehow, to remain outside during a recent downpour. The bright linoleum of the bar floor is a morass of wet and muddy footprints. Last orders have been called and the Cap orders two pints and a short, one pint for now, the other (and the short) for the road. There is hardly time enough to consume the single pint before the local garda will appear outside the pub, and everyone will be flushed, reluctantly, into the street. The publican wants no trouble.

The Cap has a problem: he needs to go to the lavatory, a world away at the far end of the unlit backyard. Drinking time will not allow for the necessary excursion in order to relieve his overly full bladder, as well as finishing the two pints and the short in an appropriately leisured manner. His dress is conventional: a flat tweed cap, never removed except in church, bed or the doctor's surgery, and a dark suit jacket with similar trousers tucked into a pair of outsize green wellingtons. His tieless shirt is clumsily stuck into his belt, and incorrectly buttoned. The conversation has arrived at the point where everybody is talking, nobody listening. Like the pints to be drunk, there are anecdotes to be finished, and points to be made about the Galway and Mayo teams. This is a serious time of day. The Cap has been discoursing on the intellectual prowess of his farm dog, a creature of apparently Einstein-like perception.

'She'uv powerful entellect, powerful razoning ability, powerful . . .'

He talks interminably. Probably nobody is listening to him. The pressure to go out the back increases. The second pint is in danger of being consumed by a rival drinker during his absence. The conclusion of his story about the farm dog has to be reached.

Like passengers on a sinking ferry, the entire population of the bar is now crowded around the gunwale of the counter, shoving and heaving in the last five minutes of indulgence, packed together in a harmony of intestinal strain, alcoholic satisfaction, sound and warmth. A pungent stench arises from the crowd, adding to the cigarette smoke, beer fumes and the smell of damp clothing.

The Cap, dilemma solved, reaches out comfortably for the second pint. His wellingtons, a reliable protection against floodwaters and muddy fields, are also useful containers. First, he urinates into one wellington, then into the other, without moving from the counter. In a vague sense of breached propriety, the drinkers draw back from him. He is still talking:

'The bitch'll be waiting for me back the road. She'uv powerful entellect, she'uv . . .'

A pool is growing around him on the muddy floor. The street doors are opened and a rush of cold air assaults the crowd. When everybody has left, with the mobility of a landlocked diver in leaden boots he will move, waterlogged and slowly, into the lonely night.

CATHARSIS IN DONEGAL

W.B. Yeats, J.M. Synge and many other Irish writers (and artists) – from the 1890s, right up to the 1950s – went west, to the foreshore and islands of the west coast: to Galway, the Aran Islands, Achill, Connemara, Donegal. The range of those who made this journey is wide and interesting. Among writers, the picture is predictable: the Irish participants are well known. Less so are the foreign visitors to the west, who include the American poet Robinson Jeffers and the German Nobel laureate Heinrich Böll, both of whom published revealing accounts of their experiences.

The artists, equally, include many of the most significant Irish painters, from Frederick William Burton in the mid-nineteenth century to Maurice MacGonigal in the mid-twentieth. Also working in the west were important figures from outside Ireland: Robert Henri, of the New York-based 'Ashcan School', William Burra, the English surrealist, and Augustus John, the greatest English draughtsman of his day. Even now, artists and writers looking for inspiration and peace continue to settle on the west coast. The midlands of the country, to some degree, remain a forgotten region on the inspirational map, while the indented rim of the western coastline attracts all manner of souls to its crevices. They seem to thrive here, in the counties of Cork, Kerry, Clare, Galway, Mayo, Sligo and Donegal. Along the Atlantic coast, the sheer anarchy of the weather and drama of the landscape suit the creative spirit. The gales blow straight across hundreds of miles of ocean; nothing ever seems still on the Atlantic seaboard.

An old and childless farmer in the west remarked to me, concerning the decline of the local farming community, 'The blood is wake.' Centuries of inbreeding and emigration do not dispose a community towards vigorous self-renewal. Something was needed to rejuvenate and inspire such a demoralised society.

As though a trumpet-blast from some Celtic mountaintop had been heard simultaneously in Hamburg and Glasgow, Cincinnati and Seattle, couples, individuals, families, groups and extended kith and kin of all ages and capacities in the last 20 years left office and trading floor, university and factory to settle in the west of Ireland. Many came with wealth but little sensitivity to local customs; they either mellowed or departed. Others came with skills, visions, dreams; of these, some failed the tests of isolation, climate and the sheer difficulty of making a living. The more adaptable survived to make a new life in unfamiliar surroundings, to contribute their children to the Irish gene pool.

Never in the country's past has so diverse a group, from such disparate origins, come to take up residence in rural Ireland. Not since the Elizabethan and Cromwellian plantations of the sixteenth and seventeenth centuries have so many people migrated to Ireland, to partially stem the tide of the gradually diminishing native population. In country schools scattered along the western seaboard, between the many Caitrionas and Cliodhnas will be found other Caitrionas whose features suggest Bremen rather than Ballyhaunis, whose family name is probably Müller, Beckmann or Worthington. The motivations vary: Berliners looking for a clean environment, Californians a return to a capitalism-free lifestyle, the English an opportunity to live as in the halcyon years between the two world wars.

The converse of this influx is that many small villages along the west coast can no longer field a football team: too many of their young men are building an autobahn in Germany or serving pints to other Irish emigrés in Cape Cod. The Irish go abroad looking for work, while foreigners come to Ireland seeking a life.

Having an opportunity to abandon the car and travel by more civilised means always attracts me. Almost any means of locomotion can be an improvement on driving. The opposite side of the North from that in which I had travelled during the spring now beckons. Donegal is in both Ulster and the Republic, unlike Antrim, Armagh, Derry, Down, Fermanagh and Tyrone, which are in Ulster yet not in the Republic.

I have come to Enniskillen to join a group of strangers on a cycling tour of the north-west coastline, long held to be the most remote and dramatic in Ireland. Having decided on impulse, I failed to spend any time speculating on those with whom I was destined to spend the next fortnight, and their possible motives for participation. Rather I imagined, in a vague sort of way, that if I fancied such a mode of travel, then, more than likely, the other people would probably reflect my views. This is certainly a fairly dim and egotistical understanding.

Shortly after my arrival at the hotel in Enniskillen, I begin to have qualms. The receptionist directs me to the lounge where some of the other members have gathered, a group of English, Dutch, Canadian, Austrian, American and German individuals who are getting acquainted. They are sharing cycling lore. I quickly gather that I have fallen among enthusiasts.

Chlöe, a retired and elderly English civil servant with a beautifully elfin face and SAS handshake, speaks of having inherited her Sturmey-Archer from her grandfather. He had been a personal friend of John Boyd Dunlop, the inventor of the pneumatic tyre. What is this — vintage champagne, some genetic defect? A vague recollection of the name in John Betjeman's *Summoned by Bells* saves me from revealing my amateur status as a cyclist — a three-speed gear, of course. Ah, saved by poetry!

I merely ride a bicycle; a *cyclist* is a quite different breed, as I am to discover during the following days. My companions swap notes on hand-built bicycles, carbon-steel frames, distances covered and weights of wheels. The Austrian woman, Heidi, has brought her own machine; she does not trust the Irish to know a quality make. She also knows instantly that I am not to be taken seriously as a participant, and ignores me for almost the entire tour, a sentiment which I am quite content to reciprocate. The Dutch family (two adults, two adult children and the boyfriend of one) are equally apprehensive that the bicycles provided by the tour organisation will be less than the full penny-farthing. They expect perfection and spend a lengthy period in conference with Eddie, our guide, as he endeavours to reassure them.

Eddie, an aristocrat of the cycle world, is spending a summer slumming. International racer, winner of various continental trials, three-in-one oil exudes from his pores: he breathes wheels. He is lithe, jolly and enthusiastic, and apparently unflappable. Everything would be attended to, had been attended to, no, nothing is too much trouble. He has an admirable smattering of European languages and chats freely with the group in Dutch, German, French. He seems to have been everywhere and to be on familiar terms with members of cycling organisations from Ullard to Ulan Bator. Despite this *bonhomie*, he clearly regards all the participants as rank amateurs, the also-rans of the cycling world. The first evening ends with too much food and drink being taken, the cyclists retiring in a state of hearty familiarity. I, knowing that in the morning they would regret those whiskeys and pints of Guinness, am more abstemious. It seemed a poor preparation for a health-inducing holiday.

The first day's journey demands an early start: Enniskillen to Donegal town is a longish distance, some 40 miles, even if over unchallenging terrain. At slightly after midday we stagger out to begin on the road towards our night's rest. Before departure, each machine has to be eyed critically, held aloft to assess the weight and balance and ritually cycled in po-faced concentration before anything is declared fit to support an enthusiast's bottom. Heidi decants her foil- and bubble-wrapped cycle from its air-freight package, and looks gloomily at the potholes in the road ahead. The literature had not mentioned this hazard. Because half a day has already been lost, we travel by bus to the adjoining town of Pettigo, a pleasant little village with the border running through it. From here, the journey is to commence. The bicycles follow in, and on top of, the relief van, manned by the team mechanic.

At our new point of departure, the bicycles are allocated. The Dutch family are not happy – it seems clear that this is going to be their permanent state of mind. All the cycles are present except Heidi's. The relief van returns along the road towards Enniskillen, and in a short while Eddie and the bike mechanic reappear shamefacedly. The gold-plated, ivory-embellished super-steed now looks like an expanded Chinese puzzle, its wheels having departed radically from the circular on account of a considerable impact with the public road. This is an inauspicious beginning. Heidi makes a number of remarks, defamatory in tone, then goes to the post office to telephone her insurance broker. The group waits in a pub for another two hours, adding to the damage of the previous night. At three o'clock, Eddie produces a local minibus in order to make up for lost time. With 20 miles left of our proposed 40, we prepare to commence our cycle.

The intended first lap of the journey, along the northern shore of Lough Erne, passes a number of important island antiquity sites – Boa, Lusty Beg and White Islands – at which I had intended to stop. As most of the day's journey has been made by bus to a point beyond them, I am forced to abandon the idea. Boa Island, which I am not prepared to miss, is still within reach. On the island is a strange pre-Christian Janus-headed stone idol. It is an almost unique representation of a Celtic human figure.

Bicycles, rainwear and personal baggage are eventually allotted. We begin on the remainder of the truncated itinerary. At the risk of losing my fellow cyclists, or getting lost myself, I make the reverse journey, a detour to Calderg graveyard on Boa Island where the little man is standing immobile among the old tombstones and long grass. Here one is face to face with the most tangible image of a human person from the Celtic past. Does it represent a god, a king, a captive enemy? So little survives from this period that it is difficult to say.

The figure is enigmatic: two identical heads face in opposite directions, arms stiffly crossed on the chest, a belt (or rope) around the waist, a rudimentary phallus on one side. It is the heads which are so compelling. The hair is pulled back into a pigtail; below is a handsome moustache with pointed ends, and a goatee beard. The eyes stare ahead in a fixed manner; the mouth is pursed with the tip of the tongue showing. On top of the figure is a small depression which I found to be full of leafmould and pennies – good-luck offerings left by visitors to the graveyard. Having made my visit, I set off to follow the crowd, arriving late and weary at our destination.

The second day gets off to a more prompt, less alcohol-fatigued beginning. The team is buoyant with enthusiasm and ready to go; once equipped, they vanish in a matter of minutes. The group is almost entirely composed of couples; the singles are myself, Heidi, and Anna from Berlin. The last is determined to lose four stone in two weeks. Two by two, like the animals out of the ark, the cyclists breeze off into the distance. Heidi, on a replacement bicycle, is already a few miles ahead, Anna close behind but sweating. I establish on the second day what is to become my style: cycling at a leisurely pace irrespective of Continental or North American example, arriving in last each evening. This is effortlessly accomplished, given the company of veteran overachievers. Within individual couples, they have to keep up with each other; each couple then has to keep up with some other with whom an instinctive rivalry has been established. The Dutch family would have continued cycling even if there had been a nuclear explosion; Heidi was determined to improve on her 'personal best'. Anna had miles to go before she shed.

The sight of a hill has a dramatic effect on my companions. To me, a hill of any sort of steepness demands that I dismount and push my bicycle to the top, pausing to look at any passing view, antiquity, wild flower, cow or other distraction. The enthusiasts regard hills as a challenge, the steeper and longer the better. A succession of near-vertical inclines really gets them going.

Whenever there is some formidably steep terrain, I am quickly left behind. I arrive at the top of the fifth long climb 15 minutes after the last one has disappeared over the brow, only to discover them all sprawling on the verges like swatted bluebottles, gasping for air and in an agony of muscle spasms. It is not difficult to opt for an uncompetitive approach, faced with such a panel of experts.

The byroads of Donegal in August are both beautiful and tranquil. We cycle under vast windswept skies over little-used roads which seem to go on for ever, occasionally meeting other empty roads which, in their turn, also go on for ever, heading off into the far distance. On the third day's journey, we wind along the north shore of Donegal Bay, through the Slieve League Mountains, towards the coastal village of Glencolumbkille. Here the high, flat plateaus of bogland, even under a blistering sun, seem dark and gloomy. On the approach to Glencolumbkille I achieve my own personal best: two punctures in a single day; this was to remain the record for the group. At this point in the evening, and approaching the end of my second 40-mile cycle, I do not actually care – one might as well crawl as cycle. I decide that there is no real urgency about arriving anyhow.

The bogland over which the road winds is black and featureless, contained in the near distance by a ridge of dour hills. On one side of the bogland, the sky brightens over invisible sea, and in water-filled bogholes of cut-away turf the sky is reflected in lines and geometric gashes of pale light, dramatic breaks in the almost black landscape. Between the pebbly road and the mountains, little hillocks rise at intervals, turf piles, stacks of sods drying in the wind, dark brown haystack-sized bumps on the flat terrain.

I walk on aimlessly, not thinking of anything beyond my complaining muscles, contemplating the dark hills with scant enthusiasm, wondering if the dinner menu might be, like the previous night's, a choice between petrified crab salad and chicken-à-la-Chernobyl. I come to a fork in the road and consult my map provided by the tour, which, naturally, fails to acknowledge any possibility of choice. Unhesitatingly, I take what turns out to be the incorrect alternative, and continue across the expanse of wasteland. The day has rapidly become colder and the sky clouded in a forbidding manner.

With a putta-putta, wheeze, clank-clank, shhhhhh, Anna rides up beside me and dismounts. Every part of her bicycle which might have become loose without impeding progress altogether has made the movement of a single cycle sound like the manoeuvring of an old-fashioned threshing machine. Anna has also had enough for the day. She no longer cares, even about those excess pounds. She tells me about her job in a publishing house in Berlin, her mother, her fiancé, their apartment. I am too tired to respond. We proceed in silence (both in the wrong direction), too discouraged to bother with further conversation. Suddenly she speaks, and, with a sweeping gesture, points: 'I suppose they use the droppings for fertiliser.'

I look around. There are sheep and goat droppings scattered along the road and on the heathland, hardly worthy of commercial exploitation or comment. Irritated by my failure to respond, she points at the nearest turf stack, composed of large, dark sods of turf. Each sod is almost as big as a concrete block.

'Those droppings, you know, I suppose the locals make a good business in exporting them. Excellent fertiliser, I imagine.'

'Certainly, superb fertiliser. Most of it goes to the Gulf.'

What mammoth beast, I wonder, could be the author of such droppings? We continue our trudging progress without further conversation. I imagine that in the distance I can see a herd of dinosaurs, grazing in the shadow of the mountains, the bull dinosaur belling its shrill cry and leading the herd of females with their young down towards the coast. When they have passed, the Neanderthals will come out from their caves and begin to pile up the droppings for trading with neighbouring tribes. They are small people, the men with their hair in pigtails, their beards and mustachios pointed.

Eventually Anna remounts and putta-putta clank-clanks off along the silvery road. I throw my bicycle on the roadside, lie down on the ground and gaze at the sky. The high clouds race overhead, heavy with rain. An hour later, the relief van appears, with Anna on board. A few drops of warm rain are beginning to fall, as the van takes us on to the evening's destination.

In the hotel I draw the short straw, and am allocated the room over the bar. J.M. Synge developed some of the speech in his plays from conversations overheard in a house in which he was staying in County Wicklow. From his room, he listened through a crack in the boards to the talk below. Had I been contemplating writing a play set in Nashville, I could have followed Synge's example. Long into the night, sound-not-so-alike Dolly Partons and Waylon Jenningses sing a mixture of Irish and American sentimental ballads, as banal as they are monotonous. At an early stage in the proceedings, I go down to the bar, deciding to endure what could not be avoided.

I order a pint and look around. All my friends have apparently taken to their beds, in quieter parts of the building. At the bar counter, men in dark suits drink pints and shorts of spirits, seeking oblivion. Their women sit talking together at separate tables, downing sherries, gins and vodkas. The band belts out country-and-western numbers to which nobody is paying any attention. Everyone drinks as though they had received some unexpectedly bad news, as though there *is* indeed a tomorrow, the music further exacerbating their melancholy. This sad crowd are, I discover, the tail end of a wedding party.

'There's a fool in the mirror, looking back across the bar,' sings the vocalist. I take the message personally and return to my room.

Around Glencolumbkille are a group of early Christian cross slabs. A *turas*, a three-mile ritual walk, takes place there on 9 June, the saint's day. I abandon my Tour-de-France companions to spend half a day in the area. I can catch up with the group later, as they lie gasping in ditches, following their seventh successive Mont Blanc-style ascent of the summit of Errigal. More truthfully, I will phone for the van to return and rescue me in the evening.

In Glencolumbkille, as in many other parts of Ireland where there are early Christian sites, the natural beauty of the location comes almost as a shock. I wander up into the hills above the village, wildflowers in every ditch, lichens mottling the stony walls with shades of green, brown, pink and grey.

The cross slabs are examples of the absolute harmony of art and landscape. In this world of stone, long, thin, naturally-occurring slabs of the local schist (of which the field walls and houses are also constructed) have been erected in fields and by roadsides. Each is carved with a variant of a Greek or Latin cross, spare lines incised in the hard stone. Sometimes they are mere glyphs, visible only when sunlight falls across them at a particular angle. They date from the seventh to the ninth century and, as an art form, suggest a direct continuity across the ages, from the monoliths of the Bronze Age, through these Christian monuments, to sculptural concepts of the present time. In the cross slabs, man has put his mark, identifying these anonymous slabs as the territorial fingers of an early Christian community.

The daily journey passes through some of the loveliest countryside in Ireland, always against a backdrop of high mountains on one side, glistening sea on the other. Precipitous hills, which would scare any but the most demented cyclist, have the effect of charming the enthusiasts. Life is cheap as you hurtle down a 45 degree incline, with three hairpin bends in rapid succession at the bottom, a stratagem contrived by perverse and sadistic road-engineers to send the rider over a sandy bank into the sea.

Days pass. In so far as it is possible when one is descending hills at a giddy speed, time stands still. As I hurtle down an insane incline, my companions lost in a cloud of dust some miles ahead, I come to Loughros Mor Bay, a picturesque set piece from a mythical Ireland. Out in the water, separated from the land by a channel, is a magical island, accessible only at low tide. This oval island is like a pie from a nursery-rhyme illustration, divided by hedgerows into triangular wedges. Following the shore, like piecrust pastry, the hedge defines the boundary of the little fields. On each pie section, a few humpy orange haystacks are scattered on the brown stubble of mown ground. A farmer with a hayfork moves around among the stacks on this Tír-na-nÓg island. Some youngsters play hide-and-seek between the stacks. It is an idyll from another age, a sea-surrounded miniature empire of fairytale fields.

The members of the tour gradually begin to relax. Nobody can remember: is it Tuesday or Saturday; our seventh day or our eighth? The time-trial approach of the keenest has calmed noticeably. People now tend to depart more slowly from the hotel or guesthouse, and arrive later still each evening. Small pubs in the villages through which we pass have to be investigated, advertisements for seafood lunches cannot be bypassed. Getting lost, a fall from grace unthinkable among serious cyclists, begins to become a pattern, as maps are consulted less frequently. Directions which seem more interesting are chosen in preference to those recommended by the itinerary. Days begin to merge into a succession of alternating experiences. Mad freewheeling on coastal hills is followed by calm progress across endless expanses of bogland, nothing to break the silence but the whir of bicycle wheels, no visual intrusion beyond the occasional isolated single-storey farmhouse.

Donegal had begun to work its magic on this group of earnest, determined-to-get-the-most-out-of-their-holiday types. Charles, a broker from Seattle, gets irretrievably lost, and telephones in the evening from some village in an adjoining county. He has to be rescued by the van. Later he remarks how, unaccountably, he had left his map in a pub, and had decided to carry on without it. Away from the trading floor, his sense of direction is evidently poor.

Some rabbinical sage remarked that 'he who has been burned by scalding is careful with lukewarm'. I empathise, even to the point of not being keen on cold either. As a child I nearly drowned when swimming in a river near my home, and have since viewed with a combination of respect and dismay any expanse of water larger than a bathtub. This may be a poor qualification for visiting islands. Alternatively, I can claim to have an appropriate understanding of the hazards of the sea.

Tory Island, off the northern coast of Donegal, is Ireland's most distant corner. Having failed to visit the other islands of Lough Erne, I am determined not to bypass Tory. To forgo a trip to the island would indeed be easy, for it is one of those places sufficiently awkward to get to that an excuse might easily be concocted. It is also far enough away to guarantee a certain allure.

Islands inhabited and islands desolate – the factors by which the former become the latter bear a common thread: disasters of some description. The viability of island life depends on the size and self-reliance of the community; when things begin to slip, there is little chance of recovery. Three-quarters of Ireland's coastal islands were inhabited within living memory. Now only the largest sustain a community, or those where it has been possible to create a physical link with the mainland: a bridge, cable car, air taxi or regular ferry. Fishing tragedies, governments being bureaucratically tidy-minded and removing entire populations to the safety of the mainland 'for their own good', the need for schooling, medical services, jobs for the young to keep them at home – all these are eroding factors in island life. All have conspired to make the islanders a threatened species.

Three thousand people still live on Ireland's offshore islands. On Inishbofin in the Aran Islands, Aran More, Cape Clear, Rathlin, Sherkin and Tory, there is a feeling of inevitability in the passing of a way of life. It is as though the effort were no longer worth while.

The effort is the problem. Whereas in the past the islands were self-sustaining and the population could survive weeks of isolation in bad weather, now almost everything required for daily life must be ferried from the mainland: canisters of gas, fresh milk and butter, even vegetables. If the boat which brings the post-primary schoolchildren to school cannot face threatening seas, they must remain at home or, alternatively, be marooned on the mainland, lodging in other people's houses until the weather improves, which could be a matter of weeks. Expectations also continue to rise; the young do not wish to live the heroic and spartan lives of Synge's Gaelic Idyll, or to succumb to the struggle with the sea which is a preoccupation of all the literature by or about island life. Tragically, the sea usually wins, even today. The mother in Synge's *Riders to the Sea* might be talking for the women of all the fishing communities anywhere along the coast in the desperateness of her lamentation. Invariably, it is the menfolk who are lost, the women left to grieve.

> Maurya: They're all gone now, and there isn't anything more the sea can do to me . . . I'll have no call now to be up crying and praying when the wind breaks from the south, and you can hear the surf is in the east, and the surf

is in the west, making a great stir with the two noises, and they hitting one
on the other. I'll have no call now to be going down and getting Holy Water
in the dark nights after Samhain, and I won't care what way the sea is when
the other women will be keening.

If there is an Ireland of the mind in any popular sense, it must include
islands or even be defined by island life. For an island people, this may seem
rather perverse – to esteem slabs of rock in awkward places, even smaller
than the island itself – but what remains offshore is the only otherness left.
The remarkable ring of islands off the Irish coast represents an entity quite
separate from the mainland which can be experienced without entering
another culture. By any criteria, the islands of Ireland deserve special
consideration, as the westernmost outpost of continental Europe and the
last inhabited land before the New World.

More curiously, the islands have a specific literature of their own, written
both by native islanders and by those outsiders who were attracted to these
grim outposts of western society. Synge came to the Aran Islands in 1898,
Heinrich Böll to Achill in 1956; they represent the outside view. From
within, Tomás Ó Criomhthain, Peig Sayers, Miuris Ó Súileabháin and
others created a written literature out of an oral storytelling tradition,
preserving aspects of what otherwise would have perished.

Visual art and literature, rather than traditional music, have been
instrumental in defining how Irish people perceive their island world and its
peoples. By the 1930s, an indelible visual and literary image of island life had
been distilled from this landscape of *Cois Farraige*, the western seacoast.
Despite island life becoming clichéd in the work of Irish writers and painters
of the post-independence Irish Republic, the reality has endured, and where
communities have survived, some semblance of the old life continues.

No corner of Ireland is as distant and desolate as Tory. Although Rathlin
in County Antrim is the northenmost inhabited island, Tory, off the north-
west coast of Donegal, is the island furthest from the mainland. In January,
I would have borne these factors in mind; in August I expect more
favourable conditions.

Under normal circumstances Falcarragh, directly opposite Tory, is the
point of departure. Because of a sudden change in the weather – stormy
conditions, wind and rough seas – the Falcarragh boat cannot leave the
harbour. This means departing from further down the coast at Bunbeg,
around the corners of a brace of headlands. In the company of families from
the island, some of the cycling group, half a dozen other tourists and a
similar number of Irish-language enthusiasts, we wait on the pier in Bunbeg

for a small fishing boat to get ready for the journey. The island families, mothers and their children, are laden with packages from shopping in Letterkenny. A child's bicycle wrapped in corrugated cardboard brings back images of a similarly packaged cycle which had suffered a mishap; new clothes bulge in department-store bags. Before we go on board, the children are already fractious.

As we sit in the small cabin on bench seats, the captain comes round and chats to the island-folk, cracking jokes in Irish with the language enthusiasts. Later he returns and distributes plastic bags to the passengers. To my mind this is a joke in extremely bad taste, but they are received in good humour. Everybody laughs as the captain blows up a bag to amuse the children.

As soon as the boat emerges from Bunbeg harbour it goes on its ear, a position it retains for the entire journey – when not on its other ear. Within a few minutes the plastic bags are in use and the atmosphere in the cabin becomes fetid. The babies all decide to scream together, the small children wail between throwing up over their parents and the shopping, a few dogs, whom I had not previously noticed, begin to yowl piteously and cower under the seats. As the air becomes intolerable in the cabin, the adults grip their bags more firmly and begin to use them. The robust-looking *gaeilgeoirs* turn green, white or orange as they retch, and hold on to the benches for support. An elderly islander produces her rosary and begins to intone feverishly, others joining in. My intention had not been to join the Tory party at prayer.

At the first heave of my stomach, I flee to the deck and attach myself to some metal brackets on the outside of the cabin. In defiance of the abrupt heaving and plunging of the deck, and the insane manner in which the sides of the boat disappear under the waves and spray, I hold on for dear life. A few of my fellow passengers join me, clinging to any sheltered corner. The old, parents with children, or those more afraid of the waves than cabin-fever, remain below. The journey, advertised as taking three-quarters of an hour, takes two and a half hours of mostly making no progress against the waves, rocking from side to side, just bouncing in the water.

Before reaching the open sea at Bloody Foreland, the boat passes between the coast and a line of islands, Bo and Go and Gola, Inishmeane and Inishsirrer, all previously inhabited, now abandoned. On each little terrace of grassy land rising out of the sea are perched the skeletal remains of cottages, their roofless gables making a jagged saw-blade silhouette against the sky. Adhering like barnacles on a rock, the houses appear stuck to the inhospitable land in defiance of the elements. If there ever were trees on these islands, there are none now; their exposure would not have given growth much of a chance. When Tory comes into view, it is as a black line on the horizon, at a distance as featureless as the uninhabited rocks. The rows of houses, dimly seen, appear roofed, yet hardly more inviting than the roofless ones.

We had thought to stay on the island overnight, miss a section of the cycling tour, and rejoin it at the next stage. On disembarking, the captain announces that if the sea gets worse, he might not sail at all. If conditions are more favourable, he will sail in the late evening. This leaves five or six hours in which to traverse an island two and a half miles long and three-quarters of a mile wide. Before we venture out to look at the landscape, the bar has to be visited and enough hot whiskeys drunk to fortify everybody after the journey. In the newly-built hotel bar, despite the early hour, people are drinking, dancing and singing. All are people staying on Tory in order to improve their Irish. An ancient fisherman, sitting by himself, speaks to me earnestly in Irish. It might as well have been Swahili; his accent makes no concession to my school Irish. His face has the wind-washed look of a megalith, infinitely old and weathered; his eyes are small and bright. A *gaeilgeoir* translates: 'He said that he likes your face.'

With Charles, Anna, Chlöe, Elsa of the Dutch family and her boyfriend, I go on a walk around Tory. The two villages of the island sit in the bleak landscape as though they had been constructed in recent years, like miners' camps in the Yukon. There are no trees on the island; all the turf has been dug out years ago, and livestock or even poultry seems non-existent. Remarkably for any Irish rural village, there is no sense of cohesion in the housing of the villages; they are just there, not organised as a street or anything else. Around the houses there are no boundaries such as walls, fences or gardens; you come out of your front or back door straight on to the side of the hill, or into the meandering path which represents the street. This is the *clachan* principle of Irish village settlement, where the houses are gathered as a community, not as buildings on a route between other places.

We walk east and walk west as the day becomes overcast and starts to rain. This ends the walking and everybody gathers in the pub. Near the time for departure, a boy arrives and says that the boat cannot get into the pier, and is heading for the south harbour instead. We leave and trudge down the island, past the west village, to the little harbour where another panting child informs us that the boat is in fact coming into the other harbour, the pier at which we had originally arrived. Back across the island we go at a gallop, the wind now blowing against us. At the pier there is no sign of our boat. I wander back into the village and look in the shop, a kind of Wild West trading post, with necessities in short supply. Two girls stand behind the counter talking. The room is mostly without stock or furniture; it all looks so temporary. This in fact is the spirit of both settlements, as though the communities are actually only camping.

In winter, at least half the population of the island decamps in inhospitable weather, during which the island can be cut off for extended periods, and takes up residence on the mainland. This seasonal migration may spell the end of permanent settlement on Tory. The island cannot now sustain its population economically or educationally – a short step to extinction, or a survival dependent on seasonal tourism. In August, even during a few days of rough weather, it is busy with visitors, yet, with the exception of the small new hotel, seems to make little visible concession to tourism, or to change.

The boat eventually appears and w · embark, expecting the worst, this time without the babes in arms, dogs or old people. Only the tourists and Irish-language enthusiasts are leaving. The return is as wretched as the outward journey. The thought of having to endure such difficulty in order to go shopping, visit the bank or see a doctor would fill me with dread. For the islanders, it is accepted as the familiar. For those who live from the sea by lobster fishing it is one of the hazards of daily life, and as such is accepted without question.

A powerful image of the relationship of the islanders to their world occurs in the work of the Tory Island painters, a group of mid-twentieth-century naif fishermen-artists. Jimi Dixon is the most interesting of these painters, and his bird's-eye views of Tory maritima are enchanting child-visions of an island nation, seen from within by someone who was an integral part of what he painted. Dixon's painting *An Baile Thiar, Toraigh* captures the sensation of an island-centred world, the necessary facts of life as seen from Tory. The view is taken from above, looking down on the east village with its jumble of houses, early Christian round tower, pier and rocky landscape. The most impressive feature is the sea which surrounds the houses and the island, enveloping everything; the subject of the picture is just sea, with its elemental, primeval, staggering power. In the midst of this turmoil live the people of Tory.

In Irish legend, Balor of the Evil Eye, Cyclops-eyed and capable of incinerating his enemies with a glance, had his fortress on Tory. In the nineteenth century, 'cursing stones' were used to sink a frigate of nosy-parker customs officials. I think of the old man in the pub with the bright eyes. What did he mean by what he said?

By the time we reach the mainland and have retraced our tracks by minibus to meet up with the rest of the group, the weather has resolved itself into a calm, dark night, with promise of sun on the morrow.

From the north-west coast of Donegal our track leads inland, away from the windswept seacoast. The weather changes as abruptly for the good as it had deteriorated in the previous few days, and the skies become calm and unthreatening. From Gweedore, the road approaches and then swings under the slope of Errigal, one of the most distinctive Irish mountains, a volcanic-looking cone, fretted from its summit by loose, white scree. It is to dominate the landscape for many miles.

The social balance of the initial evening of the tour had during the first week remained remarkably intact. I wonder if this is some characteristic of the cycling fraternity, the singles remaining singles, the couples becoming more symbiotic, anxious to preserve their coupledom.

After the Tory interlude, a rift begins to appear among the Dutch phalanx, and I notice Elsa and the boyfriend not heading off *en famille*, but cycling instead with the SAS lady and her brother. It has become apparent that the striving for 'personal bests' is being replaced by a more relaxed tone, as stressed urban overachievers begin slowly to underachieve, talking in the evening not of precipices climbed, but of ditches in which bicycles had lain for an hour while the cyclists investigated a ruin or just sat and looked at an unmoving bog. The fast-forward button is gradually being relaxed to unaccustomed lethargy.

From below Errigal we proceed inland, crossing Donegal on byroads, to emerge on the shores of the inland sea of Lough Swilly. Eddie, the guide, possesses the divine capacity for being in three places at once; superior calf muscles and an intimate knowledge of the terrain enables him to set off in front of even Heidi, take a 30-mile detour, and arrive back behind even the most laggard of the group, myself and the young Dutch couple. By this point I have discovered the boyfriend's name to be Pieter. They are not, now, on speaking terms with the parents.

Eddie has difficulty encouraging the slowcoaches. Our generic bed and breakfast hostesses, Mrs Bridie O'Doherty (Ardara), Mrs Aisling O'Doherty (Dungloe) and Mrs Siobhan O'Doherty (Gweedore), are beginning to complain about late arrivals for dinner.

At Rathmullen, during the evening meal, Anna requests extra helpings and announces that she has abandoned her diet and has phoned her boyfriend to say it was all over between them, that she wouldn't in fact be returning to Berlin. Chlöe gasps at such impetuousness; Eddie smiles benignly. With only a few days left of the journey, members are beginning to lament, to revile Seattle, Toronto, Bremen and any urban centre with a population of more than 150. Donegal has worked its spell and the established barriers of culture and economics are beginning to soften and unravel. 'For sale' signs on abandoned cottages are being discussed, the estate agent's telephone numbers noted.

How can one spend time in the company of a small group of strangers, yet still fail to notice some of them? Only at this point did Jan, the Eastern European man, come directly to my attention, although I had seen him every day, on the road, in the bed and breakfasts. I must have spent hours in his company without actually registering him as a person. He is an academic and political refugee from the former Yugoslavia; the where did not seem to matter so much as the why. He has come from some British city in an attempt to discover if Ireland might represent a more realistic option than Britain, some more acceptable version of what he had lost, a place where he might recreate his life. Suddenly in Rathmelton he breaks down, weeps and says that it is too painful to be in Donegal, it reminds him too much of his home. The parallel may not have been so much between physical landscapes, as something untouched, which sparked his melancholy. Donegal's scars are centuries old and far from the surface. He says that in Birmingham, a place which for him has no particular meaning, he can bear the loss of his former life; in Donegal it is insupportable. He will return to Banja-Luka or Grozny or Sarajevo. I do not remember which he said.

From Letterkenny to Derry City is the last phase of the journey. The roads are now more frequented, traffic building up on the main road. It is still possible to ascend the east shore of Lough Swilly and veer in towards the city, avoiding the modern world for a few more hours. At the Grianan of Aileach, an Iron-Age fortress, we stop and prepare for a last ascent, this time to one of the greatest prehistoric fortifications in the country, a circular stone fort crowning a hill west of Derry. The group has arranged to meet at the base of the hill, to hear a talk on the site above.

Later, I move off up the hill, pushing my bike, relishing what would be a precipitous descent. To my amazement, the amazons, instead of, to a calf muscle, throwing their lusty limbs across the saddle and hurtling up the slope, one by one begin to walk uphill, pushing their bicycles.

The fort from below might just have been a field wall. Close up, it is a formidable circular fortification with a single small entrance passageway to the interior. With walls over 15 feet high and 70 feet in diameter, it must have been impregnable as a defensive outpost. Access to the ramparts is by a series of steps leading to internal walkways. The era from which it dates is among the most elusive in Irish history, but it is probable that the greatest literature of prehistoric Ireland, the *Ulster Cycles*, are of this period, uniting dramatic and ancient sites with the country's heroic literature.

From the summit, the wide sweep of Donegal's west coast is visible: Slieve

Snaght, Errigal, the Derrynaveagh Mountains. Muckish appears in the distance between clouds, the route which we have traversed defined by mountainpeaks. It is possible, like on a contour model of the terrain, to trace in the imagination each ascent and descent, puncture, bed and breakfast, welcoming hostelry and chilly response. From the ramparts of the Grianan, the Iron-Age rulers of Donegal (*Dún na nGall*, 'the fort of the foreigners' — in this instance referring to Norse settlers) looked out at this same view, different then only in that it was more heavily wooded, the now-characteristic pattern of field fences unknown. Yet it is not this pattern which dominates the landscape, but its physical contours, the deep indentation of the waters of Lough Swilly extending inland 50 miles from the coast, cutting right across the view as though the mountains of Donegal were in a different country, entirely cut off by water. The land immediately below the Grianan is a mass of gorse and heather, earth colours. From below, the stone fort merges with its surroundings; above, it is like a place in the clouds.

From the Grianan, it is a relatively short ride to Derry. I had, half-facetiously, imagined that as we passed over the border from the Republic, east of the Grianan, we might exchange the grey and misty clouds of the Republic for the blue skies of Ulster. In Donegal, as in Derry and on all sides, the sun shines joyously, in brave defiance of opinion in Antrim. In Derry, we part under the city walls and go our separate ways: to Berlin, Toronto, Seattle, Banja-Luka, or, remaining behind in the west, reject the blandishments of it all.

PUT MONEY IN THY PURSE

Life, as you know, imitates art. From the north-west, I return reluctantly to Dublin in order to present myself in court. The motorcycle garda who had displayed more interest in my ailing car number plate than in my encounter with the Sledge-hammers-for-Peace assassin is to be my persecutor. The trial is scheduled for a small town in County Dublin.

Internally, the courthouse appears to have been undisturbed by any stylistic change since the 1820s. There is a raised dais for the judge, box pews on either side for the legal team, and a central open space. Behind the bar are the fearful, sweating felons, kept in order by a brace of policeman. I take my place among the accused.

All those nineteenth-century illustrations of Irish political trials might have been set here – abject peasants, about to be transported to Van Diemen's Land for stealing half a loaf of bread; unrepentant revolutionaries, Fenians, Young Irelanders, sent to be hanged or banished to penal colonies. There was always a presiding magistrate, barristers, the crowd of sympathisers, family members and, inevitably, a weeping, aged mother, a young wife carrying a newborn infant, the defiant (or humble) accused.

I stand among the crowd of about thirty people, wondering who they are, of what they are accused. Although 'innocent until proven guilty', some of them look shifty enough. Most are social misfits rather than hardened criminals. A knot of unkempt traveller men in a corner advise a teenage boy in loud, conspiratorial whispers. 'Say you thought the timber had been abandoned.' He looks terrified. Other more subtle individuals lean across the bar to consult with counsel.

First to be heard is a drunken driving case: male, 35-ish, fat and small with puce-coloured eyes, evil-looking in a thousand-pound, silver-grey mohair suit and beige, handmade shoes. I would like to add that he wore a toupee, but his luxuriant auburn hair – the colour surely out of a bottle – appeared to be his own. He had been apprehended by a garda after a chase; he had knocked down an elderly man and had left the scene. I am waiting for the judge to say, 'You shall be taken from this place and hanged by the neck until dead', or some such words; deprived of his licence for life and given five years in jail might just suffice.

The defence, a bright-looking young man, stands up.

'Judge, I request that the serious charges against my client be dismissed.'

'Are you being impertinent, Mr Barrington?'

'I would like to inform the court that the certificate supplied by the garda laboratory which claims to indicate that my client had 0.8 millilitres of alcohol in his blood has the date 1994 on it. The alleged offence took place in 1996.'

Judge Gilhooly displays no interest whatsoever in this surely significant piece of information (the judge looks 75, the barrister 30). His face is getting red with irritation. The evidence, which is fairly damning, is given by witnesses and prosecuting garda. The judge seems to be preoccupied by the barrister's approach.

'Young man, I may represent the State, but I am *not* the State, a distinction which seems to have escaped your fine scrutiny of the documents. Have you anything further to say before I pronounce sentence?'

'Yes, Judge, I would like to read into the court record the Act of George IV, section viii, paragraphs 711 to 932, which bears pertinently upon miscarriages of justice and my client's case.'

'You have my permission.'

A long interval follows, during which the relevant act, as wordy as a Dickens novel, is read.

'Thank you, Mr Barrington. I have been 35 years on the bench. Thank you indeed for that illuminating peroration.'

A lengthy pause follows, while the Judge glares at Mr Barrington.

'One year licence suspended, £100 fine. Next case.'

Puce eyes stares at the judge in disbelief, then turns and gives a broad, conspiratorial grin to his supporters among the felons. He knows that he has had a very narrow escape.

The clerk of the court stands below the dais; her voice sounds as though it has been honed on vodka.

'John and Emily O'Sullivan – disturbing the peace.'

Judge to O'Sullivans (after we have heard an extensive account from a garda of high jinks at 4 a.m., chez O'Sullivan, endless partying, abuse of gardaí, distress of neighbours): 'Go away and behave yourselves.'

Clerk of the court: 'Brian Lalor – digit missing from car number plate, failing to show motor insurance certificate ...'

The list of my crimes proves to be rather more extensive than I had recollected; breaches of the highway code were numerous. Judge Gilhooly, benignly peering over his pince-nez, replies:

'Well, Mr Lalor, have you attended to the errant digit?'

'Yes, Judge.'

'And do you have the insurance certificate now?'

'Yes, your beatitude.'

'Show it to Garda O'Donovan.'

The garda reads my document so slowly, it might have been written in hieroglyphics. His finger pauses under a cartouche.

'This is an out-of-date cert, Judge.'

Judge (smiling at witticism at expense of accused): 'Mr Lalor, if you would search in your purse, perhaps you might locate the correct document and not waste the State's time.' (Laughter in court.)

I fumble in my briefcase and produce various papers, all incorrect, resisting the temptation to remind the Judge that he merely represents the State, but is not the State.

'Case deferred to next sitting. Mr Lalor, you may return the papers to your purse.' (Laughter.)

As it happened, nobody was transported to Botany Bay or given 20 years' hard labour for stealing a pewter thimble or half a loaf of bread. The judge seemed far more involved in a personal battle with the barristers than with any particular concern for the administration of justice. The conflict was between him and legal counsel, the accused merely an excuse for some drama. You might get five years or have your case dismissed, depending on his humour; high blood pressure, a perforated ulcer, disintegrating liver and fatty arteries would be a superficial diagnosis of his medical condition. His face became empurpled whenever Mr Barrington or other counsel rose to speak.

Outside the courthouse, as I approach my car, I notice Garda O'Donovan scrutinising it. I had not, in fact, replaced the missing digit; only when the clerk of the court mentioned it, did I remember this detail. Walking past the garda, I remove a thick felt-pen from my purse, and colour in the missing number. He makes no comment.

I return to town, unimpressed by the morning's display of court procedure. In practically every case to which I had listened, the feeling of the victim and the need for justice to be seen to be done had had little currency. It was a dotty, erratic and comic performance, as though society, the law and people's feelings were no more than a joke. Had the judge or Mr Barrington broken out into Savoyard patter-songs, I would not have been surprised.

The Dublin streets are bathed in sunshine, people dressed in summer clothes. An air of well-being pervades everything in the way that unaccustomed sunshine invigorates those unused to it. The cast-iron railings which enclose College Park, the demesne of Trinity College, are the work of the nineteenth-century Dublin iron master Richard Turner. He was one of those Victorian master-craftsmen who elevated the traditional tinker's trade of tinsmithing to a fine-art form. London's Crystal Palace, Kew and the Botanic Gardens in Belfast and Dublin are among the inspired products of nineteenth-century metalworking. It is from these great spindly cages of sunlight that modern architecture has evolved, a joint product of Victorian idealism and engineering genius.

Trinity's railings are robust and magisterial, still managing to keep Fenians, Whiteboys and Rapparees out of the groves of learning; also winos, beggars, street-hawkers, buskers, arsonists and those loitering with intent. On the broad pavement of Nassau Street, which skirts the south side of College Park, the disinherited offspring of those tinsmiths, honourable distant cousins of the iron masters, are still plying their trade – well, after a fashion.

Where the pavement is wide enough for passers-by to pause, small traveller children have staked out their territory. These are the child street-artists of Dublin, Nassau Street their studio and salon. While conventional children of their age are confined in school desks from nine until four each day, these sprites draw under the open sky. Sprawled on the pavement, bottoms in the air, they colonise the city sidewalks, as much at ease as any suburban child on the living-room carpet. Some are not so much sprites as junior thugs, yet all draw with childish innocence and the ineffable pleasure of defining their own world. These children could be anybody's, more or less. Their art proclaims the universal concerns of childhood – home, parents, siblings, pets, the wonder of the world. The particular is no more so than with the children of any other society, whether in West Africa, South America or Asia, where the symbolic language of a culture will add the appropriate crescent, cross, star or *hamza* (hand against the evil eye, close cousin and spiritual ancestor of Ulster's Red Hand). I scrutinise these bright street-murals each day as I pass, considering what is new, what is missing. Coloured chalks are the favoured medium; wielded by even the smallest hands, they can produce charming results. Always there are pictures of ponies and dogs. Frequently the conventional house image is substituted by that of a caravan or mobile home. Religious imagery is also common, more suggestive of the naif Catholicism of Central America than anything Irish or European.

Today I pause to survey what a small, dirtily-clad girl of about eight is drawing. She has set out her canvas boldly: lots of chevron-framed squares, mandalas and boxes with pictures in them. Good colours and a fine decorative sense lend coherence to the whole arrangement. Unusually, she has also added a text, personalising her work. MY MAM IS ANN is surrounded by a grapevine-like curving line. Next to this, I LOVE GOD is set in a bright blue circle. A cardboard box lid is always there for the public's coins; even the youngest child knows that you do not leave too much money on display, for fear that the enterprise might look less than pathetic. So beautiful are the drawings the traveller children produce that I begin to wonder: is there some latter-day Artful Dodger out in Coolock or Tallagh, giving child-art lessons at halting sites? Preposterous. It was only a thought. Yet something significant is always missing, which anybody who has taught art to settled Western children will recognise as ubiquitous. There are no dinosaurs. Prehistoric creatures are among the most favoured subjects in child art, and a child who might have difficulty cycling a tricycle will be a mine of information on the most improbable creatures such as the Brontosaurus and the Tyrannosaurus Rex. The unlikely anatomy of Pleistocene mammals is known by every child from the Shannon to the Mississippi, yet never appears in the traveller children's bright repertoire.

Perhaps it is a case of having animals more in focus, the presence of hordes of real dogs, horses and ponies diminishing the appeal of prehistory to a traveller child. Possibly, to more practically minded children, it is the sheer implausibility of bringing anything so large into the caravan.

One of the principal appeals of children's drawings is that, irrespective of the child's social status, economics, educational background or culture, they express directly the individual child's personal world, the child's capacity for observation, empathy and sincerity, as well as a certain disdain, an objectivity in stating 'this is what is real to me', which cuts through adult comment.

The adult travellers in the city streets, always women, will be sitting a few shops away from their children. These women have the lowest life-expectancy in Europe. They are squatting on the pavement, seemingly unrelated to the children drawing. The adults are different – shell-shocked, battered by life and by the human fists of their partners, family and neighbours. They have been abused by the slings and arrows of outrageous fortune, yet are still defiant. The older traveller faces have become like relief maps of arid zones, worn and creviced by wind, rain, tears. The women always look the worst: jaunty at 16, childbearing, poverty and poor diet have disfigured them by 30. In old age they take on the mantle of those tragic nineteenth-century photographs of Native American tribeswomen, faces as scarred as the land itself, expressing who knows what indignities.

> I, the old woman of Beare,
> Even in the sun I wear my shawl.

The Dublin Graphic Studio, in the city's docklands, is an artists' co-operative workshop. Here I am engaged in working on a series of woodcuts illustrating Oscar Wilde's *The Ballad of Reading Gaol*. The route to my own studio on the Grand Canal basin is a five-minute walk through a few derelict streets. These are now uninhabited, except for the occasional encampment of an extended traveller family, wedged into some urban space where current landownership is momentarily undisputed.

Sometimes these corners are occupied for a few months by a group of caravans surrounded by the detritus of the scrap metal trade. One of the signs of this community is the perpetuum mobile, to and fro, day and night, to the nearest chip shop. The presence of a fast-food outlet is an obvious advantage to any caravan-bound mother with scores of children. Another sign is the windows smashed overnight by brick-throwing louts, themselves hardly any further up the economic or social ladder, and vastly lower down the ladder culturally.

Suddenly the encampment vanishes; only the litter remains. There will be no forwarding address. The families have either been moved on by the gardaí, departed of their own accord – answering some subconscious urge for change – or, with depressing frequency, been driven out by intimidation from local racists. The entire Irish traveller community represents just one per cent of the Irish population.

It is a warm evening in late September as I walk along the unlit street which leads from the Graphic Studio back to the main road. An encampment has been here for some time. I pass it daily, like most other city-dwellers, seeing, yet not observing, what may be disagreeable, threatening or alien. In the pleasant twilight, nothing could look less threatening than this row of brightly lit mobile homes, each with its small, battery-operated television set. Children play in the dusk outside; adults are inside, talking, having a meal. Altogether it is a very domestic scene, even if the location is unconventional. Everything is visible behind the undrawn curtains, the interiors so close you could reach in and touch the occupants. The glowing caravan windows have the voyeuristic attraction of a television screen, revealing the intimacies of strangers. As I pass an unlit open door, an elderly woman emerges and says, 'Can I speak with you, sir?' – a sure prelude to being dunned for some money. Involuntarily, I stop and she insists that I step into her caravan. Inside, lit by a single candle, it is clean and as cold as the interior of an iceberg. To my dismay the woman instantly bursts into a torrent of tears, rising within moments to a scream of anguish. I am horrified by this outpouring of unconstrained grief, more common now to funerals in the Arab world than to a present-day Irish context. Nonetheless, I am captivated by her distress. Unable to get a word in, and feeling that it would be too cowardly to flee, I stand uncomfortably and wait for the storm to subside. My original supposition of 'elderly' requires qualification. She is ageless, perhaps 35, or maybe twice that age; it is not possible to tell. Life evidently has been hard.

Her story is brief: husband six months dead (I am shown a colour photograph of a good-looking, grinning man), seven children to feed and send (occasionally) to school (I am shown the head-lice shampoo; the children outside in the dusk are indicated), how hard she tries (I am shown the freshly washed dishes in a plastic bowl, the empty gas-cylinder). Periodically she returns to wailing with unbearable intensity, during which she seems to age centuries. She cries, asks for money to buy fish and chips for the children's dinner, cries some more and then returns to her husband's photograph. I hand her a five-pound note, all the money I have on me. She continues to cry wretchedly, and asks me to make it ten. I step back, out into the broken street. Before I have passed the last mobile home in the row, this one with light and music streaming from its door, a pretty young girl with gorgeous foxy frizzed hair, poised in the doorway, speaks to me. With an appraising smile, she says, 'Can I speak with you, sir?'

> I, the old woman of Beare,
> I had headgear bright enough
> When the kings for love went bare.

The matter of the television set broadcasting in the midst of a peripheral culture is an intriguing question. If settled and nomadic families alike spend their evenings watching the same programmes, perhaps they are being inexorably and subconsciously drawn together into a common pool of consciousness? Where the efforts of State, church, social and educational services have signally failed to create a bridge between the settled and the nomad, involvement in the media could provide a more binding medium. I talked about this with a friend who works with groups of traveller women in small towns. Her response was to suggest that any traveller viewing programmes accessible to the community at large would automatically cut out everything which had no personal resonance — that is, that much of what they viewed was either misunderstood or incomprehensible. Not much cause for optimism here.

A few hundred yards from this encampment are the U2 recording studios. Conspicuous wealth and conspicuous poverty, cheek by jowl; the old story of the beggars at the rich man's electronically-controlled gate. I wonder if these high priests of the conscience of youth ever drop by their neighbours' cabins? Maybe they do.

Along the Liffey quays, a cold wind is blowing up from the bay, a breath of the approaching autumn. The streets are almost deserted. A few people are eddying into Adam and Eve's church, old men and women. I huddle into my coat, facing the wind as I head towards the city centre. Walking in front of me is a small old man, clad in what appears to be a silver space suit. He walks unsteadily and I assume that he is someone with a drink problem: the Simon Community refuge is nearby. Also close is a low-life flat complex, behind which are some traveller encampments. He is probably not far from home. As I get closer, the details of the space suit become clearer and I see that he is in fact wearing a donkey-jacket and jeans, liberally splattered with silver paint. Could he be a rather incompetent house-painter? The grey hair of the elderly, at closer quarters, becomes ordinary hair, sprayed silver. The spaceman is walking slowly, and in a weaving pattern. Before long, he and I are walking together. I glance around to look at him. Face to face, I see into the dead eyes of a boy of ten or eleven. Even his face is covered with silver paint. His young lips are beautifully smooth crescents of aluminium, a picture from the lower depths of human misery.

Aghast at this spectacle – he looks not at all like an extraterrestrial, but a very human torture victim; he would have ignited instantly if a match had been struck – I seek an explanation. In one hand he holds a plastic sack, in the other an aerosol of silver paint. This is a child glue-sniffer in an advanced state of addiction, his movements that of an automaton: spray – sniff – stagger. The appearance at close quarters of his silvery skin and bloodshot eyes is so appalling that I look for help of some kind. Approaching from town are two tall young gardaí, strong backs braced against the icy wind. I stop them, indicate the silver space-child and ask what should be done.

'He belongs to them shagging knackers at the back of Usher's Island,' one replies, giving me an encouraging Kerry shove in the opposite direction. 'Mind your own shagging business, will you; feck off, now, like a good man.'

The garda's iron fingers on my shoulder indicate that neither discussion nor argument is required.

For a people with such an enormous diaspora (in the region of 60 million, worldwide) and a hospitable attitude to individual outsiders, particularly if they are affluent and white, Irish people display a pronounced unwillingness to accommodate their own aberrant or inconvenient minorities. The contradiction of this position is in the freedom with which the Irish go abroad. They take it for granted that they have an inalienable right to do so, to settle anywhere in the world which appeals to them.

Antagonism between settled people and the caravan-dwelling or council-house-occupying travelling community is a continuing saga. Each depressing incident comes from a different area of the country; most involve violent behaviour against traveller families, often those with large numbers of children. The flashpoint is almost always the same issue: attempts by the local authority to house these nomadic people, and a determination by local residents that they should be housed elsewhere. Many travellers spend their lives on motorway lay-bys, at roadsides, anywhere that they can park their caravans. People are united in a desire not to live next door to travellers, who are not Romany but merely dislodged and landless Irish wanderers of some earlier epoch.

But if one is seeking Irishness, some flavour of Celtic spirit, some individual look of distinction, then one need go no further. Travellers have the virtue or curse of carrying a classic Irish face as their badge of identity: round faces, an abundance of freckles, unkempt carrot-red curly hair. It is socially their undoing — that and untidiness, a reputation for dishonesty (whether merited or not) and for heavy drinking, feuding and fighting, which seems more based on fact.

The most disturbing aspect of traveller life is the sight of small children sitting on wet city pavements begging, attempting to imitate the calls of their mothers down the street, the women crying incantations on the passers-by: 'Givus yer change and I'll pray for you, sir — any change for a bit of food for the childer — any change, mister, for a cup'a tay?'

Child beggars are one of the sights which severely jolt visitors, who expect that care of the young might be part of the high moral tone in which the Irish people like to bathe themselves. That particular concern is more willingly expressed for Chinese or Romanian orphans than for the Third-World-on-the-doorstep.

Grafton Street is thronged with hurrying crowds of shoppers. Above the general noise level rises the sharp twittering of a flock of birds. I pass through the people, heading for a meeting in Bewley's Oriental Café. At the base of the lampposts and bollards which line the street are sitting a group of small, close-shaven and tough-looking traveller boys, each with a tin-whistle, playing in among the knees of the crowd. They sound like a congress of blackbirds, these outcast children, Ireland's untouchables, creating the music of angels. One little boy without a whistle raises his bony cheeks to the sky and, eyes closed, emits a series of notes, words perhaps, like some tragic ancestral lament. He appears oblivious to the grimy street and the indifferent crowd, transported by his singing to an imaginary world. Around the boys, prosperous matrons carrying loaded shopping bags sail into the safe haven of Brown Thomas where all is ordered, respectful, expensive.

After my meeting, I wander down through the milling shoppers of Grafton Street, passing from the sound zone of one busker to another. As happens with performers in separate auditoria, the abundant bodies of the crowd absorb the music, and different modes do not intrude upon each other. A string quartet of healthy-looking college students is delivering Mozart with aplomb; a large audience listens appreciatively. In the next sound bay, a solitary man is singing blues, with mouth-organ accompaniment. Further down the street, a ballad group perform loud renderings of Dublin street-songs. They do not appear to be enjoying themselves.

I have time to kill, so a glass of stout in Davy Byrne's seems like a good idea. I rest my feet and contemplate the frothy surface of the drink. The barman had poured it with skill, twisting the glass so the froth settled with a shamrock indentation, an unsolicited decoration. Across the bar I spot the face of an acquaintance, a writer of some reputation, a drinker of rather greater renown. He approaches the bar counter and sits on the next stool.

'Brian, me old mate [a lie], how're y'doing? Y'know [loud laugh], I heard [guffaw] you were dead, ha ha!' This witticism is, curiously, a prelude to being asked to pay for his drink. I decline and, unabashed, he asks me to buy him a packet of cigarettes. I reply, callously, that I do not smoke. Hurriedly I leave, and go around the corner into Kildare Street. The Grafton Lounge, a subterranean speakeasy, is sure to be deserted. Another glass appears, no shamrock this time. I settle back into a dim corner and consider the state of the world. Life among strangers is surely preferable to death among one's alleged friends.

From my vantage point on the studio balcony, I observe activity on the floor below. Artists come here to make etchings, lithographs, woodcuts; the studio's wide-open spaces are usually a hive of creative activity. The artists work in many styles, as varied as current practice will allow. A small number are highly successful, but most live mundane lives with mortgages and teaching jobs. Some are unemployed, although not in the pejorative sense of being without work or prospects; rather the opposite. All are hard-working and productive, lacking only an adequate market for their art. Some disdain the attractions of teaching or a night job in a bar or waitressing, preferring to do without and concentrate on their work. The studio is a serious place, a Renaissance studio in embryo, missing only a Master. Here all are *petits maîtres*, each pursuing a private vision.

Ages range from those recently out of college to septuagenarians of long-established reputation. Styles of work vary from the academic to the bizarre. At one etching press, flower studies of an eighteenth-century formalism are being printed; at another, a child's teddy bear is about to be run under the rollers of a press, the image of its murdered body a metaphor for the artist's personal grief or forming the basis of some comment upon childhood lost or innocence defiled.

The doorbell rings. A tall figure arrives into the midst of those brooding over etching plate or lithographic stone, studying the arcane practices which lie between the artist's intention and the finished work. The new arrival is clearly an artist of superior species, with a jaunty – if unsteady – walk and scarf slung over the shoulder in debonair style. Surely this is the Master missing from the Renaissance workshop? All are greeted by the new arrival somewhat fulsomely.

'How *are* you? Are you *well*?'

The Master places a small case on the worktable, among the work-in-progress of others. He opens it, and a pile of worn socks and soiled clothing tumbles out. From this disagreeable heap he extracts a bottle of wine and a glass. In response to gasps of disgust at the inundation of freshly minted lithographs by soiled socks, he returns his unwashed laundry to the case, then turns to the nearest person.

'I believe you might know where there is a corkscrew?'

The necessary equipment is produced.

'Very sweet and *kind* of you, so, so kind.'

Edwardian courtesies. He sits at the communal table, uncorks the bottle, pours and drinks. The flood of pleasantries continues: 'How *are* you?' again and again. A garrulous discourse of observations, prejudices and bigotry follows. This is the artist as 'free spirit', uninhibited, drunk. Then he begins his daily rant: an anti-clerical jibe to a seriously religious artist; another artist, not present, is referred to as 'Protestant Dick'. Sexist remarks follow, directed at the many gifted young women artists who form a substantial part of the studio membership. Predictably, next is an anti-semitic anecdote, followed by other remarks directed towards Protestants. The last are delivered to the winds, on the (generally correct) assumption that there will be one or more among the working artists. No one responds to these provocations. The artists concentrate on their work. They hope that he will shut up – or go away.

Who is this unclubbable man, an anomaly among a creative community, usually courteous, respectful and sensitive? The answer is interesting, a late-flowering example of the Joyce syndrome, the Irish genius living abroad, the voluntary exile – preserving, unlike Joyce, the small pieties and larger prejudices of the Irish intellectual of a generation before. Here is an example in aspic of the professional Irishman, a 'roaring boy', moulded on the Behan or Kavanagh image of drunken boorishness. These individuals are so preoccupied with their own genius and despair that the infantile manner of their behaviour is never revealed to them.

The Master is, however, more than just another tedious pub philosopher. An artist of considerable talent, he busies himself between the remarks and the wine bottles. Day by day the bottles accumulate in the corner where he works. There is always a full one among his underpants and vests. A second glass is added to his own, and fellow geniuses are invited to drink. None do. As he works, he punctuates the air with anecdotes and endearments:

'My old friend, how *are* you, are you *well*?'

Then follows an anecdote about a gallery director (among artists, the nadir of the human species), his greed and duplicity. The story builds up over some ten minutes until he has attracted everyone's reluctant attention. There is a strategic pause. Is the story finished? The speaker stands, turns around, delivers his final line: 'Jewish, of course.'

Silence. Nobody wishes to be drawn into an argument with such a loquacious bigot, who is mouthing the prejudicial sentiments of the Irish of the mid-century and before, now served on a plate, half a century later, by a returned emigré.

Most exiles should never return. Progress at home makes fools of them; their presence becomes an embarrassment. This is what we were – an unpalatable thought. This is the mirror image of the citizens of the Irish Free State and later Republic of not so long ago: bigoted, parochial, half-sober. After a sojourn, the Master returns abroad, his sentiments undimmed. The fact that a more generous-spirited and civilised generation has followed his remains unnoticed by him.

The only problem with islands is that they are surrounded by water. Getting to them or returning demands the involvement of some other person, the one with the boat. Dalkey Island in Dublin Bay is ruled by goats and inhabited by rabbits and sea-birds, and is a summer refuge for occasional visitors from the city. From a small harbour on the mainland, small boats powered by an outboard motor ferry visitors across the troubled waters of Dalkey Sound.

I wait with half a dozen others in order to make the five-minute journey in an open boat. This is captained by a tanned fisherman, one of a clan of local people who tend lobster pots and fish in this beautiful area of the south Dublin coastline. The passengers are mostly a group of settled traveller women on a skite, escaping for a day from the dominance of their menfolk and the demands of their children. Laden with bags of provisions, rugs and packages, they are in high spirits, prepared for a day of freedom among the long grasses and rocky shores of the island. On the far side we disembark and separate.

There is really nothing to do on Dalkey Island other than inspect the early Christian and Napoleonic ruins, ramble around trying to find the goats, or fall asleep in the sun. I rigorously pursue this itinerary. The normal tranquillity of the island is upset by a gang of offensive young men hunting rabbits with wretched little Jack Russell terriers. Each lout carries a bundle of small corpses in a sack. Visitors come and go throughout the afternoon, the small boats crossing and recrossing the Sound. Yachts and motor launches put in close to the island and more day-trippers cross over in dinghies. By mid-afternoon, the island has become busy with a few dozen people.

Late in the evening, having satisfactorily frittered away a long day in utter laziness, reading and sleeping in the sun, I approach the island pier. This is not a pier in any strict sense of the word, but a strip of slippery rock, painted white for visibility. When enough passengers have assembled, a boat will set out from the harbour – when somebody there has noticed the gathering. There is no schedule. The island now appears deserted; no boat comes to collect me. I have heard of people being marooned here, and do not look forward to a night spent with the goats.

In a gabble of voices, the traveller women appear over a rise and come down to the landing stage. They are considerably louder than when we set out in the morning, much happier, in fact, and, evidently, quite inebriated; the baskets must have contained more bottles than food. This happy group joins me, the women not at all perturbed by being left behind. Insulated by alcohol, they laugh and joke while we wait. As we sit on the white-painted shoreline, I notice something which had escaped my attention on the outward journey. They are all rather large; heavy, in fact.

Over an hour later, somebody on land notices our small group still on the island, and a boat sets out. A speck becomes the familiar form of prow, captain, wash from the stern. The boat approaches rapidly, yet does not seem to get any larger. The water in the Sound is now quite choppy and a stiff wind has arisen. As our rescuer draws in to the rocks it becames obvious to me that not only is the boat actually smaller than the one in which we had arrived, so too is the captain – about nine years old, in fact.

In the boat, the by-now-ecstatically-jolly women expand to occupy all the available space. The captain, a thin child in a navy blue fisherman's sweater and faded shorts, is clearly not impressed. He sits silent and unsmiling at the tiller, I am at the prow, the women everywhere else, floundering in the bilge, passing around a bottle of Jameson as we sail out into the channel. Perhaps dimly conscious of the increasing swell and diminished crew, the women begin to sing to keep up their spirits, launching into 'We all Live in a Yellow Submarine', while swinging from side to side. I would have preferred some less aquatic image for the moment. It is clear which of us are going to experience a happy death. The whiskey bottle is passed to the little captain, who puts it to his pale, pinched face and drinks, his frightened expression indicating a true understanding of the dangers of the channel and the imminent risk of the deep. The singing has moved into 'Amazing Grace', as the boat reaches mid-channel. The image of St Brendan sailing across the market square in

Bantry comes to my mind, the saint standing in the prow, arms outstretched. I hope that none of my sturdy companions has the same idea.

Somehow, this ship of fools reaches harbour without floundering. With difficulty the women haul themselves up the wet steps to the pier and I follow. The little captain remains behind in his boat, throwing up over the side.

ABOUT TO WRITE A LETTER

In 1935, Jack B. Yeats painted a portrait of a solitary, formally dressed man, standing in a heavily furnished room. The walls are closely hung with paintings in gilded frames; against the wall is a grand piano, covered with porcelain ornaments. The curtains are partly drawn, and in the foreground a rich red mahogany table separates the viewer from the figure. The painting, called *About to Write a Letter*, suggests a sense of unease or hesitation in the stance of the man as he confronts the paper, pen and inkwell on the table. Both the immediacy and the ambiguities of communication by letter are implicit in the scene.

Cork City is the epitome of the nineteenth-century towns and villages of Ireland, expanded to city-size to encompass the essence of them all. It began to come into its glory as a mercantile port during the American War of Independence; since then, it has reclined in faded grandeur on the banks of the Lee. The sprawling modern suburbs which crowd the Mahon Peninsula on the south-west of the harbour are another country, flat as a flounder, while the core of Cork is its steep river-valley and hills stacked with Victorian terraces, the solidity of the houses balanced by the spires of umpteen churches.

Cork is a place of strange contradictions: it is the second city of the Republic, yet has no medieval buildings or any significant architectural quarters. It is the only Irish city of Viking foundation which is almost totally devoid of ancient buildings: the crossing-tower of a small friary, a few medieval carved heads and a Romanesque doorway at St Finbarr's Cathedral are all that survive. Likewise, there are no Georgian squares, yet the ambience, location, and multiplicity of bridges on the twin channels of the river give it a distinctive character. Its charm depends on not having too much that is charming, yet exploiting the natural features of the landscape and the built environment to make it one of the most handsome places in Ireland. The individual buildings of significant architectural merit are too scattered to make any cohesive impression.

The emotional antennae of the citizens of Cork are being stirred by an exhibition in the Public Museum of the love letters of Michael Collins, commander-in-chief of the Free State army, and his girlfriend, Kitty Kiernan. These letters represent 12 months' correspondence, abruptly terminated by Collins's death in a Civil War ambush at Béal na mBláth in West Cork in 1922. The site of the ambush is some 25 miles outside the city. Many people in Cork 'know' what happened there – Collins was set up/shot by his own men/it was an accident/he consciously went to his death/he knew that his name was on a bullet that day, and so on. Much ink has been spilled on the subject. More old IRA men have confessed on their deathbeds to having fired the fatal shot than were possibly present at the ambush.

I went to see the exhibition and found two rooms full of well-dressed, silent and respectful women reading Collins's clear civil-servant's hand and Kiernan's emotional scrawl. Irish people, so voluble in conversation, are in many respects intensely secretive. The publication and exhibition of a personal correspondence such as this is indeed a phenomenon. Little has come into the public arena concerning the personal lives of the founders of the Free State, assuming that they had private lives at all – hence the fascination of the letters. The self-same leaders liked to give the impression that they were, to a man, solid and respectable citizens, leading exemplary domestic lives. The very idea of 'the love letters of Patrick Pearse' seems improbable. Naturally, the fathers of the State did have a personal and emotional existence, but, like the human body, this was better not mentioned.

The letters are a sequence of brief daily communications between the most charismatic leader of the Irish War of Independence and his fiancée; they are platonic, and sometimes almost anonymous – more like the correspondence of fond siblings than lovers. The banality of the fact that love, passion, personal thoughts and humour are here constrained by discretion and the need for secrecy makes even this archive of personal correspondence singular by how much it conceals. Everything, effectively, is between the lines, or not alluded to.

Collins probably had his lover, Hazel Lavery, on his knee while he penned some of these notes. The apolitical Kitty, alas, was on hers.

Collins was a guerrilla leader, a 'terrorist' in today's parlance, a freedom fighter, the IRA head of intelligence, the person who ordered the execution of British agents in Dublin. He was a cool customer, who became as resolute in his opposition to the Irregulars during the Civil War as he had been to the British during the War of Independence.

Some years ago I stumbled on a secret that will upset all serious historians of the period; this revelation concerns Collins's death. The events are not at all as is generally believed. The assassination was an occult one, the ambush in Béal na mBláth merely a manifestation of malign forces elsewhere. Perhaps the letters need to be reread in this light.

My informant was a very old man, a retired soldier, living in the Magazine Fort in Dublin's Phoenix Park. I had come to study the decayed early-eighteenth-century fortress. The soldier was full of old-fashioned hospitality. Tea was proffered in a large mug, the brew black as tar and almost as thick. Clearly campaign conditions had marked his culinary style – after such tea you could have survived the siege of Stalingrad. I parked my gallon-mug on a convenient windowsill and moved off to look at the buildings. I forgot about the soldier, who disappeared into his quarters and probably spent the morning blanco-ing his puttees. He belonged to an ancient military tradition, dedicated to order.

I finished my work and went back to the soldier's house. More asphalt tea was poured. While I drank, he handed me a fragment of broken glass and watched closely as I examined it. Considering the environment and realising that some intelligent response was required, I asked: 'Is it bulletproof?'

The glass was thick enough to grace the windows of an armoured car, and smoky green in colour. My question was ignored.

'Did you ever hear of Mick Collins, the "Big Fella"?'

I said that indeed I had. Nothing further was required to start him on his tale about Collins and the glass.

'It happened during the night. A Crossley Tender arrived with this massive framed photograph of Mick Collins in the back of it; he was the C-in-C of the Army at that time. They took it down from the Tender and stood it over there against the wall, where I showed you the glass.'

I glanced over towards his quarters, basking in the midday sunshine. The shards of glass on the windowsill refracted the light.

'They shot at it with their pistols, smashed the heavy glass and riddled the photograph. I thought little of it at the time, that night. Those were violent years we lived through and I was a mere private on sentry duty. To the officers I was only a cipher, another half-literate soldier from Louth. The following morning we heard the news. Collins had died in an ambush in Cork. It wasn't them ambushing Irregulars at all what done it. The murder was here in the Magazine Fort in the Phoenix Park. It was the men with the picture what done the murder. He was killed right here in Dublin, by his own, not in West Cork at all. He would have come through the ambush unharmed but for the malice they bore agin him.'

Like Coleridge's Ancient Mariner, having concluded his tale, he fixed me with his glittering eye, and paused while I absorbed the significance of his extraordinary story. Then he collected the tea mugs and moved slowly towards the door. Later he returned and handed me a fragment of the violated glass, thick and greenish, with sharp edges.

'I can tell that you understand. The day that they murdered Mick Collins was a black, black day. *Béal na mBláth*, the mouth of flowers.'

Was he mad? Did I imagine it? Neither, I think. The secret of Béal na mBláth had been revealed: 'Great hatred, little room.' And then, of course, there *is* the glass.

I returned on a number of occasions to the exhibition of Collins's and Kiernan's letters in Cork. On each occasion the atmosphere was the same, the audience predominantly women, mostly of a certain age, intense and absorbed. Collins's status as the only untarnished hero of the War of Independence remains, enhanced by the discretion of his correspondence.

Later that month, at the Hugh Lane Gallery in Dublin, the actual papers found on Collins's body after his death are on display in conjunction with an exhibition of Sir John Lavery's portraits of the participants in the treaty negotiations. A small envelope is inscribed, in Collins's hand, 'Hazel Dearest'; the suggestion is not platonic. At the Dublin exhibition, identical women of an identical age hovered so long over the vitrine containing these talismans that I had to review the entire exhibition before they eventually moved on.

Outside the Cork Museum is a gargantuan bronze bust of Collins by the Cork sculptor Seamus Murphy. The marble original presides over the foyer of the Hugh Lane Gallery. These heads represent Collins in his best Fascist hero-of-the-people manner; to stand face to face with a three-times-life-size representation of any human figure is to be confronted with an image of the superhuman. The enormous marble head of the Emperor Constantine in the Palazzo dei Conservatori in Rome has exactly the same sense of cold and imperial indifference to human needs. This is the image of Collins which the Free State wished to perpetuate, the 'Big Fella' as a hero of mythological proportions. The marble head was carved in 1948, the year that the Free State became the Irish Republic. No other Irish political leader, North or South, has been thus commemorated. Collins was safely dead, his very human love life and liaisons erased from the record.

Simultaneously with the showing of Collins's letters in Cork and the tattered remnants from Béal na mBláth in Dublin, another exhibition is being hosted in Dublin by Trinity College's Douglas Hyde Gallery, entitled *Fragments sur les institutions républicaines IV*. More letters, although not the actual documents in this case, are the subject. These are the 'comms', or communications, written on cigarette papers by the 1981 IRA hunger strikers in Northern Ireland. They were smuggled out of the prison wrapped in cellophane and concealed in body orifices, during the weeks preceding the death of the hunger strikers.

Installation artist Shane Cullen has used the texts of the 'comms' to fill the walls of the Douglas Hyde Gallery with a display which transforms the language of desperate, ironic and furtive communication into the monumentalism of classical Roman public inscriptions. The programme accompanying this exhibition of republican dialogue masquerades as an official document published by the Government Press Office. It carries on its cover the Irish harp, exclusive symbol of Irish State documents (and – reversed – Guinness's Brewery – an institution which predates the Irish State by almost 200 years). On the catalogue, the manipulation of symbols has been taken a step further. Here the use of the official harp appears to validate the actions of the dying terrorists, inviting the ten dead men to join the sixteen executed in 1916 and the seven against Thebes among the immortals.

In the same month, and under the imprint of the self-same harp, *The Irish Times* carries a Department of the Taoiseach announcement concerning a ceremony to commemorate the Easter Rising. Northern observers of political language in the South, from either side of the divide, might be forgiven for coming to appropriate conclusions. Fortunately, few IRA men or stalwarts of the Combined Loyalist Military Command are likely to frequent art galleries, preferring to destroy art rather than respect it.

31-1-81 To Army Council

Comrade, we received your comm (dated 30-1-81). We have listened carefully to what you have said and we recognise and accept the spirit in which it was wrote. Likewise in view of the situation we do not deny you or criticise your extreme cautiousness. But however distressing it may be we regret that our decision to hunger strike remains the same and we reconfirm this decision now with the same vigour and determination. We fully accept and in full knowledge of what it 'may' entail, the right of the army to carry on unlimited operations in persuance of the Liberation struggle, and without handicap or hindrance. We accept the tragic consequences that must certainly await us and the overshadowing fact that death may not secure a principled settlement.

The IRA's postal system appears to have been more prompt than that of the Royal Mail. In the era of performance art, the intensely political act of the dead republicans is used in the exhibition to transmute the hunger strikers themselves into performance artists. Their self-sacrifice is seen in the light of the self-mutilation process common to performance art (head-banging, flesh mutilation and other abuses of the human body are among the 'media' being practised at the moment). The tendency in the early years of the State to recreate the dead revolutionaries as saints has been replaced here by an urge to see them as artists, the drama of their deaths endowed with mythic proportions, the causes and consequences conveniently avoided.

The strikers were at the beginning ordinary men: mechanic, draper's assistant, milkman. In Crossmaglen the bronze cenotaph implies that they were titans. *Fragments sur les institutions républicaines IV* makes art of their violent and tragic lives, and attempts to promote the hunger-strike participants into the guise of being artists themselves. If poets are the true legislators of the people, artists — and, by inference, those drafted into their ranks — acquire formidable status.

I am interested in the issue of the government harp being used to validate the hunger strike and phone the Douglas Hyde Gallery to see what they think about the matter. The staff member I discuss it with says that the use of the harp is intentional on the part of the artist, in order to parody official publications in the South. Nobody had objected (or noticed, perhaps) that the exhibition had been shown in Belfast and Leeds before coming to Dublin.

Then for the other side. I phone the Government Press Office in order to get the official view on the use of the harp in compromising circumstances. After being transferred from Eileen to Michael and then to Sineád, it is clear that they know nothing. Sineád says:

'This is really a problem for the Department of Enterprise and Employment; they are in charge of copyright law. I will transfer you.'

Miriam, a very pleasant and loquacious woman from the west, comes on the line. She interests herself in the matter, telling me that she comes from a nationalist background and has firm views on the use of the harp. I discover that I have been transferred to a Telecom switchboard, and that we were just having a nice chat.

From Telecom I am put through to the Department of Enterprise and Employment. Eamon in the solicitor's office says it is a matter for Government Publications, and gives me another number. This turns out to be the Office of Public Works, who also know nothing, but put me through to the publications office. Here, Donnchadha reveals to me that 'they are not obliged to be informed of the relevance or content of the publications which they handle'. He thinks that I should be talking to the Government Press Office, where I had begun this quest. I explain to him my problem and he offers to call them for me; on my end of the line I hear him, on another line, ask Eileen, Michael and then Sineád the question which I had originally put to them and receive the identical answers. After another ten minutes of waiting on the phone, during which I hear sounds from deep space, dolphins singing and a vacuum cleaner, some other woman comes on the line, informs me that Donnchadha had spoken to X, Y and Z (all of which I know), and that Phyllis is looking into my problem and will call me back.

An hour later Sile Ní Flahertaigh of the Taoiseach's Office phones to say that I should direct my enquiry to the Department of Enterprise and Employment, giving me a name there. I phone but my contact is out of the country for a week. This is going to be a lengthy business; the government harp does not seem to be a very hot or sought-after property at the moment. Do I really care? I phone again when my contact, Seán Og Ó Baoil, has returned, but he is 'unavailable'. His secretary takes exhaustive notes regarding my enquiry, and promises a response. Nothing follows.

The following week I try again. The Minister of Enterprise and Employment had resigned over the weekend in curious circumstances; the receptionists are wary of awkward questions from strangers. Eventually I speak with Seán Og Ó Baoil, who confirms my understanding that the harp (and also, apparently, the shamrock) is an internationally protected national mark. Its use within or outside the State, other than on State documents (and Guinness bottles), can take place only with official permission, rarely granted. He refuses to be drawn on what response there might be to any particular instance of infringement.

The 'comms' and their validating harp will probably continue on their world tour, unmolested by official scrutiny. 'Representing the State but not being the State,' as Judge Gilhooly might have said.

The quality which Cork people seem to most admire in their fellow citizens is an assured smugness. Cork may have much to be smug about; being the second city of the Republic, it can rejoice in the fact that it is not the first.

I have been speaking to an elderly woman with whom I became acquainted in Cork, an intellectual and academic, now retired. She belongs to a world in which it was possible to be, simultaneously, dottily religious and intellectually progressive. With the kindest of motives, she demonstrates the insane logic of imagining one's own group to be innately superior to all others. Her perspective on humanity is as seen from within the ranks of the chosen ones.

Somehow, in a roundabout way in conversation, she understands that I do not have religious beliefs, and that I have numerous daughters. The latter information causes her serious anxiety. Another day she confesses herself to be resigned. She has had a dream. This nocturnal ramble has relieved her mind.

'I was concerned about your children,' she said. 'About their decease, in fact.'

This struck me as being patently absurd. The prospect of my lusty daughters' imminent demise did not strike me as plausible.

'I had a dream,' she continued. 'It was following my death. I was in Heaven and your girls came to the gates but were not let in. I was tremendously upset; it troubled me greatly. Then I had an idea. I got some chairs and took them outside the gates to your girls. That way, they would not have to stand for eternity.'

To assert belief in a three-dimensional Heaven, complete with furniture, is an interesting concept. I had heard of the throne of Heaven, but not the ironing-board.

The chairs stuck in my mind. What kind of chairs? Black oak Gothic Revival, like in a convent parlour, or Louis XVI, with brocade upholstery and rococo ornamentation, appropriate to a bishop's palace? I rather prefer the idea of small gilded bamboo hall chairs, as in the foyer of a brothel or a smart ladies' hairdresser's. Heaven, I suppose, must also have its anterooms, sculleries and attics. A heavenly car boot sale could be worth attending.

The Long Valley in Winthrop Street is one of those rare pubs unaffected by the wind of change. It is a pleasant, dark place in which to meet people, or while away an afternoon reading the newspaper. Some of the furniture is from a sunken merchant ship, a comforting consideration. I am installed in a quiet corner, a cup of coffee and a plate of bulging ham sandwiches on the marble-topped table, the elderly, aproned bar staff eternally polishing glasses. In mid-morning there are few customers. A youngish man at an adjoining table is studying some book intently, making notes; a student, I assume. Half-way through my sandwich I am conscious that the young man has spoken, perhaps not for the first time. He has been attempting to attract my attention.

'Would you know at all what is a hair shirt?'

I explain. No doubt, he is a novice religious maniac, studying a manual on mortification. I seriously doubt that any of Cork's drapery stores will be stocking this unfashionable item. Perhaps he might try in Shandon Street. He continues to read, then asks: 'What is a mitre?' Again I explain and am taken aback when he begins to write my replies into the margin of his book: self-mortification has never been my forte. I ask what he is reading.

It is *Becket* by Jean Anouilh. He is a drama student, preparing for a performance. More questions follow. I end by explaining a play which I have never read, to a person whom I have not previously encountered, including defining words which anybody of sufficient education to be involved in performance could be presumed to understand. How is it possible to grow up in an overly bishoped country (twice as many bishops as there are counties), and be unfamiliar with a mitre? My interrogator is from a small country town where bishop-reverence reaches Hollywood levels of delirium. I can provide no explanation. Perhaps there is less danger of receiving a belt of a crosier if you fail to recognise the weapon.

Any modern institutional building, if it wishes to project a human face, must have an atrium, an internal glazed courtyard space where indoor palms and rubber plants may flourish while the public wilt in an airless and overheated space. Cork's new Garda station is thus endowed. The circular atrium has ceramic murals and a small and sinister-looking section of rain forest. There is no whiff here of the cells or solitary confinement. Around the public space are small counter windows where business is engaged with those paying traffic fines or reporting a stolen car. I have come (successfully, as it turns out) to dispute a traffic fine.

As I wait at my counter, a largish garda from inside the counter asks me to move, and leaps over the counter into the atrium, evidently in a hurry. I discover that I am at the wrong counter, and move to another where there is nobody in attendance. After a while I get a tap on the shoulder from another garda, who climbs over the counter from the outside, this time with some difficulty, because he is holding a paper bag containing his lunch. The person dealing with my case has gone back and forth to the inner office. While I wait, another garda, at the opposite side of the atrium, leaps out from his office through the window, like a uniformed cuckoo in a Swiss clock.

Clearly something is wrong here – a serious design flaw leading to doors in the wrong place? – or is it some kind of compulsory window aerobics, designed to limber up the more sedentary members of the force? I consider the commercial possibilities of the latter: a garda video promoting this new form of exercise; the obligatory government health warning might mention the hazard to occupants of high-rise flats.

High on the northern hills of Cork is the Shandon quarter, a warren of small streets, lanes and near-perpendicular flights of steps, alleyways, courts and culs-de-sac. Shandon church dominates the area; below its steeple is an undulating succession of small open spaces, each different. The architectural cohesion of this intriguing quarter is Italianate in the manner in which the public spaces and the buildings, all different in form and scale, unconsciously complement each other. A classical portico faces a village street; the curious rotunda of the Firkin Crane building, like a mini-Colosseum, is surrounded by pubs and houses which could be in Clonakilty or Sneem. The Firkin Crane was originally a butter market, then a margarine factory; later it became the headquarters of the now-defunct Irish National Ballet. It is now a small theatre complex, with auditoria and studios packed inside its circular walls.

A crowd of teenage youths are kicking a football around the street. They look the types who might collect hubcaps – mine, preferably – or car tyres.

I attend a modern-dance performance at the Firkin Crane, in which choreographer and dancer Tara Brandel presents a solo programme. The major section of her performance is concerned with a response to suicide, the most submerged issue in the personal lives of Irish people. As a young woman whose father took his life two years earlier, she delves into the pain and rejection implicit in the suicide of any friend or family member. This requires enormous personal courage and honesty: the subject is both personally traumatic and publicly taboo. With an understated artistry, the dancer becomes both the victim and the bereaved, involving the audience in the discomfort and tragedy of her theme.

People seem to feel so comfortable and relaxed in their familiar pubs that they become less than discreet. Listening to other people's conversations in the quietness of a Shandon bar, I eavesdrop on two couples in a corner who are discussing the establishment of a joint business, combining the skills of running a small nursing home, which is in the possession of one couple, with that of an undertaker, which is the other's profession. Their plans seem neither nice nor ethical. They talk conspiratorially, ignored by the other customers and by the bar staff. They might have been the Popish Plotters, four individuals bent over a table in a dark bar, conspiring against the elderly of the nation.

The woman of the nursing home is clearly the promoter of the scheme. Her face is in shadow, yet I can hear her voice and observe the earnestness of her gestures. The undertaker is a quiet man, as bland of face as any of his trade. He is less sure. His replies are murmured. She attempts to attract him by the limitless potential for his business.

'It's like this,' she explains with conviction. 'I will have the caring of them, and you will have the coffining.'

The symmetry is undeniably attractive, a tidy arrangement. Had I been the elderly couple chatting in another corner, I would have experienced a frisson of unease, a sudden chilling of my drink.

Conversations in the Long Valley can be fraught. Finbarr has led a difficult life; now unemployed, he was hardly much busier when he had a job, as this tended to interfere with his other activities. Spells in prison further complicated his life.

'Do you realise, Brian, that I am not in the Nile anymore?'

I think of all those phrases — 'down in the dumps', 'up the creek' — which describe unsatisfactory locations in which people can find themselves, but 'the Nile' is a new one for me.

'When I was in the Nile, I behaved without restraint. I was violent, abusive, unreasonable, bigoted. I have to admit it: I hated other people for no more reason than they were who they were — fecking gobdaws. Of course, I took it for granted that they hated me. When I was in the Nile, spiritually I was a dead man.'

I feared what was to follow: 'a personal relationship with Jesus' or espousal of a macrobiotic diet?

'The Nile is a long way from where I am now.'

I think of the seediness of Cairo: 'Welcome, welcome, I give you good price', the dirt and the pollution, the frenetic traffic and the smells. Oliver Plunkett's head — in another golden casket and wearing the insignia of upper and lower Egypt — is displayed, mislabelled, in the Cairo Museum. More plausibly, perhaps it is that of Captain Charles Scarborough Cottingham, dead at Abu Haras on the Blue Nile. I consider the merits of assassinating tourists in order to promote an Islamic second coming. The Long Valley might be twinned with the Valley of the Kings: Welcome. Welcome.

'The Nile is the lowest point a human being can reach.'

This seems to be going a bit far: Cairo is not *that* bad. Nor is Cork so glorious that its citizens should be too critical of other places. At night, the second city of the Republic does resemble the Valley of the Dead. A further round of pints brings me no nearer to the source of Finbarr's Egyptophobia. I make some excuse and drift into Oliver Plunkett Street, where the normality of daily life continues undisturbed.

Local Cork pronunciation tends to substitute d for t, and word-endings become elongated. Finbarr was in *denial!* As soon as the enigma had been solved, the Nile Valley became crowded with the denial crocodile-procession of Irish pilgrims, all in desperate need of its purging waters. With Lambeg drums resonantly beating, the Orange Order in their papyrus sashes lead a phalanx of green and orange terrorists, regiments of the British Army, Catholic and Protestant clergy, cardinals and bishops, deacons and rural deans, archimandrites and vergers, followed by patriots of all persuasions, collectively examining their ventricle muscles and finding different truths, all in near-catatonic states of denial, about themselves and the world they live in.

Welcome, Welcome.

REBIRTH OF THE EMPTY QUARTER

The anatomy of a many-times-vanished, and even still disappearing, quarter or community is intangible and elusive. So much can remain in part that every relic of the past seems to have a predecessor, each ruin made youthful by an older neighbour.

The Iveragh Peninsula in south Kerry begins inland with the justly celebrated mountain landscape of Killarney – now endangered by a surfeit of tourist traffic, which travels as sensitively on the roads of Kerry as Hell's Angels negotiating at speed the balconies of the Leaning Tower of Pisa – and ends beyond Bolus Head with the equally spectacular Skellig Rocks. Fortunately, the latter are well protected from the attentions of tour buses by an inhospitable sea and a challenging landscape.

In so far as we can catch glimpses of it in its hidden places, the physical landscape of prehistoric Ireland was breathtakingly beautiful. Where it survives it remains so. The uniting of extraordinary locations with an architecture to which classical order was unknown invests all early sites with an organic quality. The buildings grew out of the land. This is true over a vast span of time, from the burial mounds of the Boyne Valley necropolis, dating from 3000 BC, down to the beehive huts of the Skelligs of the seventh or eighth century AD.

The Skelligs are three jagged triangles of rock protruding from the waves, seven miles offshore: the Great and Little Skelligs – a mile apart – and Lemon Rock. The last is no more than a rock, giving counterpoint to the other two. The Little Skellig, nearer the shore, is an important bird sanctuary, home to some 20,000 pairs of gannets, as well as guillemots, razorbills and kittiwakes. The entire upper surface of the rock looks like the summit of K2, white with guano. From the Little Skellig the birds rise and fall throughout daylight hours, clamouring and squawking. Its further neighbour, the Great Skellig, is among the wonders of antiquity and the westernmost outpost of Europe; up to the fifteenth century it was the absolute and utter end of the known world.

From the brow of Bolus Head, the Skelligs appear shipwrecked in the mists, shards of inhospitable rock. I attempt to draw them whenever I pass though St Finan's Bay. Sometimes they project from the waves; on other occasions they seem attached to the sky. In the mists they often vanish. Once, at twilight, while I sat gazing at the horizon, a shaft of heavenly light struck the Great Skellig, making it appear to hover in mid-air, illumined by a supernatural glow.

The Great Skellig, *Sceilig Mhichil* or Skellig Michael, is the site of the most famous and least accessible early Christian monastic settlement in Europe. Everything about the Great Skellig is a triumph – of the human spirit, the imagination and the power of belief.

Only those excessively world-weary could have been motivated to build a hermitage on the bird's-nest-sized areas of habitable space on the Skellig. Steps were cut into solid rock, rising from sea level to where settlement was possible. Platforms and retaining walls were created to support stone beehive huts for dwelling and oratories for prayer. The monastic community, which could have been cut off from the mainland for lengthy periods, had to be self-sufficient. Their diet was fish, birds and their eggs, seaweeds and pulses. Only goats and perhaps poultry might have survived the terrain. Yet, in calm weather, the Great Skellig could have been an inspiring place from which to view the world.

The monastery was founded around the seventh century AD by St Finan, and nearly 1,500 years later it survives substantially intact. It is poised on a platform between two peaks of the rock, and is accessible only after a giddy climb. Here, the main monastic site consists of six beehive cells, two oratories, a graveyard, a garden and a ruined medieval church. All are enclosed in a series of small terraces of flat land maintained by retaining walls. There is a subsidiary site at the south peak with a second ruined oratory. The little space between the stone huts and the tiny oratory is the ultimate refuge from the world. From here the Irish mainland becomes a distant outline.

In the early ninth century, two Viking raids began the gradual dislodging of the monks from their spiritual eyrie. A medieval manuscript records that in 824,

> Scelec was plundered by the heathens and Etgal was carried into captivity, and he died of hunger on their hands.

In the twelfth or thirteenth century, the community decamped for the mainland, following hundreds of years of isolation and communing with the seas. Another half-millennium was to pass before the Great Skellig would be reinhabited. Two lighthouses were built on the rock in the nineteenth century. One has long been abandoned, the other has recently become automatic. The lighthouse keepers and their families were the last humans ever likely to live on the Great Skellig. Puffins, fulmars and shearwaters now share its hummocky slopes with the rabbits.

Terra firma is represented by Bolus Head, a protecting hump of land crowned by a Napoleonic fort and a tiny World War II observation post. Its wind-wracked bleakness, even in October, makes it hard to contemplate as a residence during worse weather. A local proverb, 'No one went ever to Bolus but in hope of getting something there', may refer to adepts of force-eight gales, although sustenance from the seas, fish and sea wrack is a more plausible explanation. The name Bolus derives from an Old Norse topographical description, tangible evidence of Viking-Age presence in the area.

From the Head the land drops towards the sea, upland bog giving way to a field pattern of small, rectangular patches of walled land. The fields tumble down to the water's edge, moulding their shapes to the awkward contours of the hillside; rooks hover and plummet above the waves. High up on the side of Bolus Hill, a single triangular green field seems to have taken leave of the others below, and to be flying like a kite against the orange background of the hill. Beneath it, a smaller russet one floats in tandem. On a saddle of hillside behind the head is a Bronze-Age stone alignment of four standing stones which, according to local legend, is the burial place of Erannan, a mythical Milesian invader who made landfall in Ballinskelligs Bay.

Below the summit, three houses are still occupied, two by elderly bachelors, a third by a widow; these three are the last survivors of the entire community of Bolus Head. The jagged gables of long-abandoned dwellings appear among the ferns, visible only when the eye begins to distinguish them from the pervasive stone of the hillsides. The walls here have the quality of macramé, built of small stones which give an almost fabric-like texture. They are quite different from the openwork stone walls of Clare and Galway, constructed as though to let the wind pass through. The russet of decaying ferns envelops many of the field walls, and the field patterns are everywhere being encroached upon by the briars and bracken of unworked land. No human presence moves on the headland; a few cows graze in the crazy fields, sheep clamber on more challenging terrain.

The road from Bolus Head runs east towards Ballinskelligs, hugging the slope of the peninsula, dipping and rising with the landscape. Beside the road is a nineteenth-century primary school building, now a holiday home. In a twist of black comedy, which would have been comic if it had not been motivated by contempt for the indigenous culture, the language of instruction in the school was English. The children, unfortunately, spoke only Irish.

From 1879, Irish was permitted as an extra subject, but instruction had to be outside school hours! Bilingual education was eventually introduced here in 1909. Pádraig Ó Siochfhradha, 'An Seabhac', author of the much-loved (or, by schoolchildren, much-hated) Irish-language children's book *Jimín Mháire Thaidhg*, was one of the part-time teachers of Irish at this little school during the period when he was employed as an organiser for the Gaelic League in Munster. Even in 1926, Irish speakers in the adjoining townlands numbered 100 per cent in Canuig, and 99.6 per cent in Ballinskelligs, despite the benefits of instruction through English. The children might as well have been taught through Urdu or Afrikaans.

Around a bend from the school, on the seaward side of the road, is another early Christian hermitage, *Cill Oirbhealaigh*, a cashel or stone ringfort. This is a monastic enclave from the same period as Skellig Michael. Here, as with the abandoned farms, the circular stone wall is difficult to see among the long grass and brambles. It effectively merges with the field boundaries and boulders. Within the wall is a roofless oratory and a few small cells, also roofless.

I sit in the oratory to draw its cramped interior. It seems an inescapable fact that the seventh-century inhabitants of Iveragh must have been very small indeed – four feet and a few inches high, narrow of shoulder. All the buildings of the little settlement are similarly diminutive, capable of accommodating only a few, short, individuals.

From the cashel, the view over Ballinskelligs Bay is superb. Under ever-changing skies, the waters are alternately the most translucent of turquoise and deep, deep green, then blackening with overcast clouds, then lightening again to a cobalt blueness, all the time ruffled by small, white waves. Behind, the Macgillacuddy Reeks, the hills of the Kenmare Peninsula, are soft and distant. A shift of cloud lets sunlight fall on a few small green fields, which just as rapidly disappear. West of the monastic enclosure is *Tobar na mBráithre* (the Friars' Well), once a holy well, perhaps even the water source for the hermit's settlement. It is no longer venerated.

Immediately beyond *Cill Oirbhealaigh* is the abandoned village of old Cill Rialaig (the church of the Cannons Regular). It was deserted during appalling weather conditions in the 1790s, when the downdraft winds from the mountain encouraged the villagers to seek a less windswept location. These roofless ruins continue to decline with the passage of time. From here the replacement settlement is visible, half a mile further along the narrow, winding road. Under the brow of *An Pheic* (the Peak) is Cill Rialaig, where I am now staying. This is this empty quarter.

The rise, fall and rebirth of Cill Rialaig has in its story all the essential elements of the decline and resurgence of post-medieval Ireland, as seen through the fate of a single small community. Sometime in the latter years of the eighteenth century, the monoglot Irish-speaking fisherfolk-farmers of the earlier village constructed this one, further east, and less in the maw of the Atlantic gales. The new position for the village was carefully chosen. The community of Cill Rialaig lived here until, through death, emigration and population movement, the village ceased to be inhabited during the 1950s, 150 years later. A photograph from the 1930s shows a row of perhaps ten small thatched buildings, cottages and outhouses, arranged like parked cars, parallel to one another, their gable ends up against the overhanging hill, their backs to the prevailing wind. Each house was sheltered by the one behind.

During that century and a half, the villagers lived mainly from the sea, the waters of which rush madly at the cliffs directly below. Life in Cill Rialaig was a case of living with the elements, even in this preferred location. Each house had a small farm of rough grazing – precipitous hills covered with boulders – and some small arable fields, capable of providing grazing for a few cows. The effects of the Great Famine were less severe here, on account of the community's knowledge of the sea and all that it can provide.

By the 1980s Cill Rialaig had become, like the earlier village, the monastic cashel, the ruins on Bolus Head and the hermitage of Skellig Michael another series of decapitated ruins. The withdrawal of all human life from the western seaboard, the people defeated by the rigours of spartan living and motivated by a desire for some improved standard of existence, slowly moved the centre of gravity further and further inland.

Although it expired as a community, Cill Rialaig did not pass without trace. What has been recorded of its culture is as remarkable as anything from better-known areas of the western seaboard. Seán Dhónuil Mhuiris Ó Conaill, fisherman and farmer, was born there in 1853. Although he could neither read nor write, his knowledge of the Gaelic oral tradition was extensive. As a *seanachi*, or traditional storyteller, he represented the end of a tradition going back to prehistoric Ireland; his stories and lore were handed down from one generation to the next. Seán Ó Conaill, who died in 1931, spoke no English. His stories were written down by Seamus Ó Duilearga (Delargy), a folklorist from University College Dublin, during the last years of the storyteller's life.

Ó Conaill and his wife, Cáit Ní Chorráin, had ten children in their tiny cabin in Cill Rialaig. One could hardly live in such a magical environment and in such a traditional society without having a healthy respect for the mysterious and the unexplained. Seán Ó Conaill's repertoire abounded in tales of magical and improbable happenings, of the Fianna, of spirits and of wondrous events. That so much might have emerged from such a minute corner of the world, six houses on a cliff overlooking the wild Atlantic, is a testimony to the imaginative richness and humour of the people who created these stories. Although the tales had remained unchanged for centuries, Ó Conaill's listeners were always happy to hear them recounted again and again by a master storyteller, speaking from what W.B. Yeats called 'the book of the people'.

As though it were a precursor to Beckett's Vladimir and Estragon, this short anecdote from Ó Conaill's collection gives a suggestion of the extraordinary sense of surreal timelessness which surrounded the listeners at the firesides of Cill Rialaig.

The Three Brothers on the Lonely Island

Three brothers they were who went to sea in a ship. They spent a long time at sea without meeting land, and they feared they would not meet any, but finally came to an island which was wooded to the shore. They tied their ship to a tree, and they went inland. They saw no one and met no one. They set to work then, and worked for seven years, and at the end of seven years one of them said:

'I hear the lowing of a cow!'

No one answered that speech.

Seven more years passed. The second man spoke then, and said:

'Where?'

It went on like that for another seven years.

'If you don't keep quiet,' said the third man, 'we will be put out of this place!'

Seán Ó Conaill's stories were mostly remembered from when he had heard them as a boy; they had been told by old men of the area and occasionally travelling storytellers. His voice in the 1920s represented the authentic speech of the remote past.

The Old Woman of Dingle

There was an old woman in Dingle long ago. The name given her was the Old Woman of Dingle. She lived to a great age – 300 years and more. Her fame spread through the nation because of her great age, and many came to visit her from faraway places to find out what had given her so long a life.

She said she could not tell anyone what had given her so long a life, but the top of her head had never seen the air, and she had never put the sole of her foot to the ground, and she had never stayed in bed longer than she slept.

A few feet from my front door is the rear wall of a roofless ruin, the derelict remains of a cottage and cowshed, in decline among the nettles and gorse. A sheep is grazing on top of one of the broken walls. The lintel of the front door is gone, the rear one teetering dangerously near collapse; the chimney and gable have fallen or the stone has been stolen.

This was the home of another fisherman-farmer, Pats Ó Conaill. His ruined house and its interiors can be reconstructed from the fact that a Swedish ethnologist, Åke Campbell, took this farm and dwelling as a case study in 1934, and illustrated them in a paper studying the farming methods and housing of South Kerry. In that year there were six inhabited houses in Cill Rialaig. A century earlier, in 1834, in a census commissioned by Daniel Ó Connell, whose estate at Derrynane is on the southern lobe of the peninsula, there were eight houses with a population of 50 souls. The population decline over 100-year period is insignificant. This was to come a generation later.

Campbell's publication shows the inverse of an archaeological recon-struction of an excavated medieval dwelling: a small, whitewashed, thatched cottage, its roof held on by a fishing net which is pegged to the outer wall.

Two tiny windows flank the door; a drystone cow byre is attached on one end. Internally the 13 foot by 25 foot space is divided into kitchen and bedroom. All life concentrated on the fireplace, the hearth and cooking place and the position from which a storyteller would recount his tales. There was a sleeping loft under the eaves.

In 1934 the plough was still not in use in Cill Rialaig. The predominantly cattle-grazing aspect of local agriculture did not require extensive ploughing, and all cultivation was done with a spade – soil cultivation was required only for potatoes and rye. Pats Ó Conaill cultivated half an acre of potatoes, sufficient for a single household. Isaac Weld, writing in the 1790s about agricultural practice in Reen, West Cork, south of the Iveragh Peninsula, relates that the plough was then introduced on Lord Bantry's estate, yet the local farmers eventually returned to cultivation by spade: 'The people had been reminded that their forefathers dug the ground; that the plough was an innovation. A unanimous resolution was instantly made to follow in the steps of their ancestors.' Yes, but 1934 is surely modern times, with the collapse of the Weimar Republic and the establishment of the Third Reich – commencement of World War II was a mere five years away. In Galway, the Corporation demolished the cottages of the Claddagh fishing village in 1934. Time was clearly running out for such communities. In Seán Ó Conaill's words, Cill Rialaig was 'a poor, wild, cold and wet spot'.

This much is the record, what Seamus Ó Duilearga and Åke Campbell saved. Twenty years later the village lay abandoned. Time, weather and the frugal quest for reusable materials, timber and stone, has done the rest. The final indignity would be removal of the ruins by county-council bulldozers, widening the road to facilitate tourist access to Bolus Head. This last option has been emphatically rejected, and on the partially demolished end wall of Pats Ó Conaill's house is a plaque, dated 1991, recording the beginning of Cill Rialaig's resurgence.

The Burning Ember

Not long ago, about 50 years or so, Donal Ó Murchu of Ceannuig came to Cill Rialaig to visit an old friend of his, Donal Deas by name, whom he thought he would find at home but who was not there. He stayed within to wait for him for part of the night and it was late when he came. He wanted to go with him to Ceannuig. He agreed, and they set out, and they did not forget to take a couple of embers from the fire with them. There was a good breeze of south-west wind to blow up the light, and as they went along the road they had a good blaze of light. They noticed nothing strange until another light lit up before them on the green verge of the road.

'Throw away the fire!' said Donal very quietly, as in a whisper, to the other man.

'Wisha, I will not,' said the other man boldly. 'I will certainly keep my own light.'

No sooner had he said the word than the other light went out.

That is a story without a lie, you may be sure!

A photograph of the *seanachi*, standing outside the door of his cottage, decorates the frontispiece of the collected stories. Although taken in the late 1920s when Ó Conaill was in his seventies, it might be a photograph taken by Fox Talbot in the 1840s. It shows a vigorous elderly man with a face of great strength of character. His features are as firm and weathered as the stonework behind him. He is dressed in a heavy homespun frieze coat, jacket and vest, with a high neckerchief. The image is an archetypal one from the Irish collective past: some about-to-be-transported Fenian revolutionary, or perhaps an Ulster Presbyterian ancestor of an American president. Åke Campbell refers to the agricultural 'culture-landscape' of Cill Rialaig; men like Ó Conaill represent the human culture-landscape from which has emerged the best of imaginative modern Ireland.

The storyteller's house is gone, but the ruins of Pats Ó Conaill's house will be restored as a community house, where the storytelling tradition of the region can be maintained into another century.

In the morning, I go out to look at the sea. A giant puffball has appeared on the edge of a little field beside the road. It had not been there the previous evening. I pluck it; it is as large as a football, heavier, and creamy white in colour, its surface soft yet not exactly smooth. It smells strongly of that indefinable mushroomy scent, slightly pungent and loamy. In the kitchen it falls like a loaf into thick, pale white slices. I fry a few of them for breakfast, each as large as an omelette, light and faintly sweet to taste. With fresh coffee it makes a most agreeable meal. Puffballs are among the delights of nature's 'food for free', not scattered widely but rare manifestations. Although October is late for fungi, the weather has been so mild that it should not be a surprise to find some types of field mushrooms still putting in an appearance.

A wispy mist has descended on the headland and my view from the tiny rear window is obscured for a while. The clouds lift; I glance out and am dumbstruck by a transformation in the grid of small fields. The empty landscape has become populated by a veritable forest of puffballs, large, white and round. They are scattered across the ferny land, moon shapes among the boulders and wet ground. Surely this is a record: what one might occasionally find alone, more rarely in pairs, has here appeared in abundance. I am astonished. While I marvel at nature's profligate behaviour, all the puffballs levitate slightly and then resume their positions to the right. This leads to an alarming thought – hallucinogenic mushrooms. What if I had mistaken the puffball for some magic mushroom? Am I suffering from drug-induced delusions? I return to the window. The puffballs have not moved. Then faintly, in the distance, I hear a dog bark. Again they rise into the air and then resume their position. Sheep – round and creamy-looking, fat as puffballs. An hour later they appear not to have moved.

This little thatched cabin is one of the group tucked in under the side of the hill, gable ends facing the road, backs towards the prevailing wind. For the view you must go outside. Through the front door little can be seen but the ruins of the cabin in front. The houses are close together; some have a few small outbuildings. I am reminded of those little shelves of rock, small islands off the Donegal coast, each with a saw-blade outline of roofless ruins, silhouetted against the sky. Here in Cill Rialaig, on the extreme western end of the Iveragh Peninsula, the phenomenon is the same. The skyline is gashed by the characteristic outline of the gable ends of clustering long-abandoned homesteads. This, however, is the mainland, where communities were not threatened daily by the perils of sea-passage in tarred canvas boats.

The road which runs past the house, out to Bolus Head or back towards Cahirciveen, winds and turns according to the whims of the landscape. Uninhabited ruins far outnumber occupied dwellings on the peninsula; the population must have dropped like an ever-sinking graph, generation after generation, since the beginning of the twentieth century. Now there is little to sustain life: a few cattle, sheep, farmers' welfare, tourism. Out walking, I meet an elderly man pushing a bicycle which is laden with shopping; he must be one of the bachelors. His face is open and untroubled; poverty and isolation appear to have been philosophically accepted by him as the norms of life. Time for him has a different dimension than for myself.

Attracted by the extraordinary beauty of the area, Dublin magazine publisher Noelle Campbell-Sharpe came to live in Ballinskelligs in the 1980s, where she bought and restored a row of ruined farm buildings on Ceanuig Hill, a mile or so across the land from Cill Rialaig. Aware of the inexorable tide of emigration from the area, and the historic connection between the village and its famous *seanachi*, she evolved the idea of saving the village from destruction or tourist development by restoring it for some purpose which would be life-enhancing, creating employment in Ballinskelligs through the project. In 1991 a locally-based trust, the Cill

Rialaig Project, guided by Campbell-Sharpe, began a long-term development to restore the settlement as an international centre for artists and writers. So far two cottages have been completed; two others are almost ready for occupation. My neighbours in the other cottage are a Canadian novelist and her painter husband.

The location of the village can hardly be surpassed anywhere in Ireland for inspirational scenery. A stroke of genius would be required to transform and recover the sense of a living community without succumbing to the creation of holiday homes, tourist facilities or commercial outlets of some kind. That this has been, to a large degree, already achieved, with the scheme only at its beginning, is proof of the dynamic power of the idea. Implicit in the concept is the conviction that the Ballinskelligs area could again become a beacon of light, like the Skelligs were in another age. To come to Cill Rialaig is certainly to retreat from the world and to be as the early Christian monks were, surrounded only by overpowering and ineffable natural beauty, food of the spirit in a difficult world.

Just to go out the door of the little cottage in which I am staying is to experience views so rapidly changing that it becomes difficult to remember what you previously saw, so utterly transformed are the islands, the contours of the hills and the distant mountains. The landscape and the exterior of the cottages are an entity, that classical west-of-Ireland look of great hills and diminutive thatched dwellings. Inside, the transformation is total. Seán and Pats Ó Conaill, 'An Seabhac', Åke Campbell, all intimates of Cill Rialaig, would be confounded. Inside is a modern studio-apartment, anybody's ideal 'away from it all' refuge. The new dwellings are enclosed in a skin of vernacular architecture, contrived to look as though nothing much had changed, Seán Ó Conaill having just gone down to his fields, where he is telling his tales to the winds, for fear he should ever forget a single word – 'One of the fragrant trees of Paradise is the cow.'

In time, the Cill Rialaig Project, driven by the energy and vision of Campbell-Sharpe and with the support of local people, can ensure that Cill Rialaig becomes a living village once again. Some of the works produced there will be sold in the already-completed Cill Rialaig Centre in the village of Dun Gaegan. Here the assured architectural idiom has come adrift somewhat, and the centre, a complex of round, thatched and stone-built buildings, resembles more the thatched palace of the Kabaka of Buganda than any satisfactory reinterpretation of local vernacular styles. Stanley and Livingstone in pith helmets, posing with the Kabaka, would not look out of place outside it. Nonetheless, the eccentric building is both a potential showcase for the genius of Cill Rialaig and a focus for the whole community, establishing something generative within the region, on a higher plane than interventions normal in the regeneration of disadvantaged regions – small factories and EU handouts.

On Saturday morning I drive to Killarney to collect my daughter Allegra from the Dublin train. The weather is not promising, yet in so photogenic a quarter, something should always be possible. I wait on the platform as the passengers disembark. Shortly, the train shunts off, to resume its journey. No Allegra. On the train, the sleeping photographer is heading for Tralee, the next and final stop. It takes some hours to re-establish communication. When I return to the ticket office in time for the following train from Dublin, the clerk, whose microphone does not appear to be working, gesticulates from behind her plate-glass screen with elaborate semaphore: 'Your passenger – Tralee – next train.'

The rest of the weekend is spent crouching on hillsides, sheltering behind boulders and broken walls, attempting to capture the essence of the scenery without being either blown into the churning seas or soaked to the skin. So fierce is the wind on Bolus Head that it is impossible to remain upright. After an energetic and gusty weekend, Allegra returns to the city, I to reading Seán Ó Conaill's tales of his neighbour's encounters with the *Pooka*, malign spirits whom one would not wish to meet on a dark road.

The following day breaks brightly, with clouds flying high up in the distant reaches of the sky. Later it darkens, begins to rain, then blows seriously. By midnight it has become a storm.

I awake at 4 a.m. The house is in the grip of a tremendous wind which tears at the thatch. Every beam of the roof structure heaves and groans. Extraordinarily shrill and high-pitched winds seem to come from far away, up above the house. Swiftly they descend on the roof with wild and eerie screeches, attempting to reduce the thatch to tatters. At this moment I remember the *Pooka*, dark forces abroad at night, and wish that I had not done so. These terrifying sounds are just the ones which blew across Cill Rialaig when the families had gathered on wild nights around the warm fireside to listen to folktales of signs and wonders. With such supernatural sounds filling the night, one could reasonably believe in almost anything. While I am contemplating the *Pooka*, there is a tremendous tearing sound, followed by a loud bang. I spring out of bed and go down the stairs to investigate. All appears normal. There are no further explosions, so I return to bed.

In the morning I venture out on the road to survey my world, which is as benign and tranquil as before, the light from the east casting the islands into dramatic relief. Up the road I find that the outside rear storm door has been torn from its frame by the force of the gale. A windborne stone has smashed one of the windows of my car. Had the latter happened in Dublin, I would be fulminating against thugs and vandals, writing letters to *The Irish Times*, calling for the reintroduction of transportation to Van Diemen's Land. On the tip of the Iveragh Peninsula I can only wonder at nature's capacity to undergo such extraordinary, non-drug- or alcohol-induced mood swings, terrors in the night transforming into sun-filled mornings of limpid light. All the dread *pookas* of the darkness have now vanished. A new pair of jeans, which had been on the clothes line the previous night, is now probably providing warm nesting material for puffin burrows on the Great Skelligs.

The thick warm thatch and solid drystone walls of the original cottages provide secure protection against the Atlantic winds. Only in winter storms far more severe than the winds which I have just experienced would there have been any serious threat. In *Oiche an Gaoth Mor*, 'the night of the big wind', in 1839, hardly a house in Ballinskelligs was left with its roof intact.

I go to a mechanic in Ballinskelligs, inquiring after a replacement window for my car. This proved to be more complicated than I had anticipated. South Kerry was not in a position to provide a rear side window for a Japanese car of the particular make and year; it would have to be ordered from Cork or Dublin. I make do with a sheet of bubble-wrap, attached with masking tape to the exterior of the car. A week later I wondered why bubble-wrap had not previously been considered as a medium for car windows. It has the inestimable advantage of sufficiently distorting the driver's vision to make any driving experience more challenging.

A few days later, as I return by car to my house late at night, a gilded crescent moon hovers above the diagonal outline of Bolus Hill, dimly illumining the landscape. I decide to walk west towards the Head in the dark. As soon as my eyes are more used to the sooty blackness, it is just possible to discern the silvery-grey roadway. From far below comes the noise of the waves rushing on the rocks, pounding and swelling. Along the sides of the road, streams of rainwater run noisily. Above on the hillsides small cascades gush down to flow on the road – a world of water, mist, darkness and rock. The farther I walk, the more I am able to make out in the still moonlight: soft, deep shadows of stone walls, the familiar rugged outline of the earlier village, the cross slabs of the monastic site rising above the brambled walls. A break appears in the clouds and a pool of light falls along the road. Into this spot a large hare soundlessly bounds, its furry silhouette like a child's black felt animal. I pause to stare at the motionless hare. There seem to be many on the peninsula; this is one of a number which I have met on the roads. An old belief of the area was that hares were really bewitched old women. Seán Ó Conaill was ready for this emergency with a word of protective advice: 'If you have a hazel stick in your hand when you are out at night, you are in no danger from spirits or *Pooka*.'

Here we are not very far from Yeats's world of the mysterious and magical – hazel woods and hazel wands with their curative and protective powers.

With a windy 'whooooo', an airy demon sails across the sky, and the clouds gather before the moon. Abruptly, the moon drops below the outline of Bolus Hill and I am plunged into darkness. I turn and slowly retrace my steps to the house. Halfway back, a final shaft of light brightens the road again, and catches a small square of card: a sign on the roadside. I clamber into the wet grass to see what it says, then remember that I have already noticed it in daylight. It is a planning permission application for a bungalow, in a commanding position on the side of the hill. Please no, may the *Pooka* haunt the planner's dreams if they grant it. With the bungalow will come bungalow taste, the final conquest of Ireland by the visual anaemia of British suburbia. The Celts had a verse form, triads, trinities of matters to be praised or condemned. I here contribute another stone to this pile:

Three things which afflict all the kingdoms of Ireland:

Garden centres

Funerary masons

Blindness

As I travelled around Ballinskelligs, Valentia and Cahirciveen, I noticed everywhere, apparently synonymous with progress, the two cutesy plastic lions on the gateposts, the lepre-gnomes in front gardens, box-hedging which would do justice to the tidy minds of Croydon. It seems that the wild anarchy of the Irish landscape must at all costs be kept at bay. This is a pity, for the wildness is the main part of what there is to distinguish Ireland from any other country – its singular natural richness and untrammelled quality, the fuchsia drunk on air, the thorntrees crazed with delight.

On another occasion, close to Bolus Head, I have serious need of that hazel stick. As I am retracing my steps towards the village, a small furry creature darts across the road and disappears into the undergrowth of mosses and heather. A stoat, perhaps. Then it appears on top of a wall, paws on the stone, its head alert and staring at me aggressively. A wild mink – a non-indigenous species which has become naturalised, having escaped from mink farms in various parts of the country. The mink may, like diamonds, be a girl's best friend, but alive it is not anybody's companion. As an ardent carnivore, it has seriously diminished the bird and wild animal species of the countryside, and it has no natural predators in Ireland. We regard each other, the mink and I. It smiles its rodent's teeth and I decide not to pursue further acquaintance.

Dun Gaegan is the village nearest to Cill Rialaig, consisting of a church, a community hall, shops and a pub. Although this region is officially a Gaeltacht, I hear no Irish spoken except by the primary schoolchildren and their teacher.

In the pub the evening scene is lively. In most respects this is a conventional village pub except that it has a dance floor in one corner, large enough for perhaps a dozen couples to perform. The drinkers continue to talk at the bar counter or around the floor, not involved in the dancing. Music is provided by a two-piece electronic band: electric guitar, synthesiser and an accordion. The musicians are middle-aged and jolly. A hard core of dancers remain on the floor for all the dances. Reels such as 'The Walls of Limerick', 'The Stack of Barley' and 'The Bucks of Oranmore' are named in the curiously abstract manner of traditional Irish music, the title having no conceptual connection with the tune; it is more a label than anything more descriptive. Children are present in some numbers, but never more than would tip the balance which defines the pub as adult rather than family territory. As in many Irish country pubs – and neighbourhood ones in towns and cities – children are welcome and at home in the convivial environment. Some of the children dance with the adults. A ten-year-old boy is evidently master of the most complicated steps as he effortlessly moves with his partner, an older sister, or possibly his mother. A tall and well-built elderly man dances every number, changing partners at the end of each dance. He has his pint snugly placed on a convenient little ledge above the dance floor. Between dances he takes a deep draught of Guinness, laughs good-humouredly and continues with gusto. He looks like a character from a black-and-white movie of the 1940s: ruggedly charming, the Clark Gable of the western world.

A car pulls up as I stand on the road to Brow Head. The day is cloudless and I have been out hill-walking. The driver is a youngish man wearing a woollen hat and a suit jacket with prominent evidence of his own erratic sewing technique. He wishes to find out my business. We discuss the problem of my car window for far longer than I would have believed possible; I assume that either he has a cousin with the appropriate replacement or he may be just passing the time. I cannot decide. While we talk, he remains seated in his car with the window open, never looking at my face. He then speaks of other matters; the sea preoccupies him. I find his observation melancholy:

'There is a lot of water down there.'

'Yes, indeed.'

'I suppose it has no bottom at all.'

'Mmmm.'

'Can you swim?'

'Mmmm.'

'You would drown quickly in all that water, I suppose.'

'Mmmm.'

'Do you know the name of that island?'

'No, I am not long around here.'

'You wouldn't dig cement in your Sunday suit.'

'Indeed, no.'

He drives off. I continue on my way, conscious of the fact that although Ireland is a small island and has the appearance of being culturally cohesive, within it are many separate cultures. This man is probably closer in spirit to aboriginal dreamtime than Greenwich mean. The reference to cement bothers me.

It being Friday, I go down in the evening to another more local pub, not in Dun Gaegan but in the middle of nowhere. Disconcertingly, the middle of nowhere is actually the centre of Ballinskelligs, which is not a village but a region. Cill Rialaig is on its perimeter. The clientele are mostly young men and women drinking and playing pool; there are a few older men, but no older women. My friends are prepared for a serious night's drinking. One of the young men, who has drunk more than the others, is already becoming belligerent and wrongly identifies me as an Englishman. Ancestral scores have to be settled and ancient wrongs righted. At the pool table the women concentrate on their game, their pints resting on the counter. A man is stretched out, dead to the world, on a bench inside the door. Apparently nobody minds. Some considerate soul has put a blanket over him. This makes the bar resemble an Irish sea ferry of the 1950s, with morose passengers attempting to sleep uncomfortably in every corner. In an alcove sits a venerable old man with a craggy face under a broad-brimmed straw hat. He is dressed entirely in shades of off-white – not exactly October gear in Ballinskelligs. I ask a girl at the bar, 'Who is the man in the hat?'

'Oh, that's just "Jack the Hat".'

Need I have asked?

On the north side of Bolus Head is St Finan's Bay, accessible from Cill Rialaig on this side, or Valentia Island on the other by roads which rise up over the brinks of hills and plummet madly down the other side. The Skelligs sit on the horizon of the Bay, a pair of submerged mountain peaks. Below the hills is a small medieval church, decaying and neglected, with an abandoned nineteenth-century Catholic chapel built against it. The latter is filled with modern burials like beds in an overcrowded hospital ward, all the patients dead. It distresses me to find in many historic sites throughout the island the practice of using the interiors of early churches for present-day burial.

In the past poverty preserved, in Ireland as in Greece. When local communities were too poor to afford more than a suitable fieldstone to act as a marker for their family plot, little damage was inflicted on historic remains. An improved economic climate has led to a deteriorating aesthetic one. Few early Christian sites, medieval chapels or abbeys have, in the last 20 years, escaped the scourge of modern funerary monuments, as shiny and as lacking in dignity as *pissoirs*. Funerary masons prosper in reciprocal proportion to the desecration of historic sites. I cannot see that people's right to bury their dead in the family plot can supersede that of preserving the cultural heritage of the island; this in fact is what is happening. A sanctified site should not be interpreted by any community as granting a licence for collective vandalism.

Down the road from these two ecclesiastical ruins is the modern parish church; inside it is as bright and spiritual as a ball-bearing factory. Perhaps some future swing in ecclesiastical taste or worship might lead to the abandonment of this industrial eyesore, and the restoration of its predecessors.

Over Kilkeaveragh Mountain and down a great slope of orange-brown bog, the road descends towards the coast; it is one of the finest walks in the region. I stop halfway down at a little lay-by, opposite a holy well and modern shrine. In the archaeological survey of the region, this site is described as an antiquity. Between the actual survey and its publication in 1996, the site has become a folly, complete with virgin and garden-centre planting. At the current rate of progress, very little of interest or simplicity from the past is going to survive the new broom of the anodyne.

Below on the coast is the pretty fishing village of Portmagee, from where I cross to Valentia Island. Wise islanders: in a post-Chernobyl age they have constructed a compellingly grim yet handy nuclear shelter on the foreshore of the island. Built of featureless stone and roofed in grass-covered concrete vaults, the buildings will not be visible to an enemy overflying in helicopter-gunships. In the search for appropriate interpretations of vernacular style in which to create new institutions, this must represent the nadir of achievement. The building is actually a heritage centre, constructed supposedly to celebrate the history and natural wonders of the region. It is just sad. I doubt that even Bord Fáilte, the tourist authority, which discusses tourism in the language of crude oil futures, could love it. My reservations regarding the somewhat frivolous appearance of the Cill Rialaig Centre's thatched beehives fade completely. At least they are joyous and colourful buildings. By comparison, the Valentia bunkers have nothing to say to the landscape or to the human presence.

In mid-October, Knightstown, the metropolis of Valentia, is deathly quiet. In the bar I have soup and a ham sandwich (railway buffet-car standard circa 1950, bread curling away from the ham in dismay). A monstrous colour television screen plays to two men at the bar counter. They ignore it and talk about fishing and Mad Cow Disease. A melancholy young customer informs me that he hates scenery, and can't wait to get out of Valentia and go just anywhere, Dublin, New York – as long as there are some people and pavements. He says that he is tired of being poor and unemployed. If he remains in Valentia he will never get work, other than digging the roads with the council or FAS training courses which lead to nothing, just more unemployment.

'I spent my childhood in a tea-chest, my parents were that poor. Now I live in a slum. If I had children, I couldn't even afford a tea-chest.'

He orders another pint. He will get smashed before the evening is over. We sit in silence for a while, then he says: 'Anybody who has not lived penniless through an Irish winter should shut their fucking faces about the scenery. It makes me feel like hitting them.'

The air outside is unbelievably warm, despite the fact that I have walked through a cloud of impenetrable mist in order to cross the hill from St Finan's Bay. The main street of Knightstown dips down the hill, seeming to disappear under water and re-emerge on the far shore, to vanish into the far distance. In summer a ferry plies from one bank to the other.

Towards the end of October, another fierce storm hits the south-west coast, with winds gusting to 88 miles per hour, strong enough to do considerable damage. Throughout the day the treeless peninsula is wreathed in spray whipped up from the angry seas. Rashly, I decide to go to Cahirciveen. It is a bank holiday and there is supposed to be a street market in the town. Half-way from Ballinskelligs I see a woman hitching, bent double by the gale. She has difficulty in remaining standing on the roadside as her clothes are pulled and torn by the wind. Large gorse bushes sail around in the air and the wind howls across the flat bogland. I assume that she must be on some desperate life-saving errand – a doctor needed for an ill child, the telephone lines down – to venture out on foot in these conditions. I ask her where she is going.

'Ah, Cahirciveen. I just needed a few things. I am parched for a cup of tea!'

As I prepare to leave Bolus Head with its three elderly and solitary inhabitants, its village of Cill Rialaig long abandoned and now symbolically reborn, the category of Gaeltacht for the area of Ballinskelligs seems doubtful. I heard almost no Irish spoken anywhere in the area. Possibly, the viability of small 'reservations' of Irish speakers is no longer realistic in a media-conscious world of which the lingua franca is English.

Each time I returned to Cill Rialaig, the moment I saw the outline of the little houses of the village, I was struck by the absolute otherness of the place, the quite out-of-the-world quality which the original tiny settlement must have possessed. In its resurrected state, it still maintains this unique sense of separateness from the world, as distant from the fleshpots of Amsterdam or Bangkok as a stylite's pillar or an anchorite's cell. The small cabins poised on the brow of the cliff between mountain and sea appear wrapped in a snood of light.

From the sleeping-loft in the mornings, sunlight enters through a tiny window in the gable end, four small panes of glass through which the immensity of sea and sky appears. Seán Ó Conaill's stories of the folklore of the area do not directly refer to the character of the landscape. Doubtless it never struck the community as being anything other than what it was to them – their own place. Yet the magic which infuses the folklore is everywhere in this environment. It is the land of the possible.

THE COURT OF LIGHTS

During September, a combination of events had diverted me on my journey to Cork. I eventually arrive there by a circuitous route, coming down from Dublin to the south-east of the country. I travel through the bustling towns of Carlow, Clonmel and Carrick-on-Suir, and then by way of the Comeraghs towards the coast.

South of Carlow, I pass the well-manicured countryside of smooth farms and large distant houses hidden among trees, everything abundant under an autumn sky. Outside the town, I take a byroad into an unfamiliar landscape. The wild hedgerows have here been trimmed by a county-council hedging-machine, the verges cut to a neat border of thick, lush grass. Small farmhouses sit behind flower-gardens, tidy and prosperous-looking in an old-world manner. Everything has the air of conservative well-being; nothing out of the ordinary might be expected.

In Oldleighlin I stop to visit the cathedral, which I find locked. When in doubt, ask in the nearest house or shop. I chat with the owner of the grocery shop which, other than the single pub, is the village's only business. The interior of the shop is barricaded with ceiling-high boxes and packages of everything conceivable – the supermarket principle in embryo, reduced to the floor space of a bedroom. The grocer directs me to a farm, a mile outside the village. Before I have opportunity to knock on the door, a child appears with a key in his hand – strange cars stop for only one purpose. The toddler says something unintelligible which only unsnarls itself in my mind as I return towards the cathedral: 'Me-mam-said-bring-it-back-I-am-Dennis-I-am-four,' delivered in the music of the local accent.

The tiny cathedral at Oldleighlin is architecturally eccentric; for its size, it has very few windows, and there are two early medieval fonts. As one of the least-known cathedrals in the country, it has been lucky to survive the enthusiasms of both prelates and architects. The combination of oddness and charm makes it a building of great interest; its presence in such a tiny village seems accidental.

In the afternoon I continue my journey along the well-ordered roadways. Suddenly, I pass what appears to be a free-range fragment of Birnam Wood on its journey to Dunsinane – moving out to occupy the topiary avenue of roadside. I stop at a convenient gate and return to investigate. The initial impression had been correct: a large and wild thorn-bush growing in the hedgerow has been permitted to wander and weave its branches at will, untrimmed by the municipal attendant. It sticks boldly out into the road, its thorns decked with all sorts of bits of tattered fabric and small objects, like a beggar's Christmas tree. It is yet another holy tree, sacred to the memory of Brigid, or some more local saint. I poke around at its base and locate the well. This is no more than a small trickle of water between stones, but pure and brimming in a little cup of rock, a *bullán* stone.

The most substantial decorations on the tree are a sun-bleached babygro and a bra. Other bits have been torn from clothes – the lining of a coat or the hem of a dress, some socks, a child's glove. They appear as flags and sails of cloth, blowing in the wind. There are bits of jewellery: an earring, a bangle. Thorntrees are invested in Irish folklore with mysterious and malign powers; they must never be cut, or brought in to the house. Here that power has been inverted and the 'fairy tree' has become the habitation of a benign spirit, capable of granting wishes.

Around the Mediterranean basin are numerous shrines to Asclepius, the Graeco-Roman god of healing. They date from the fourth century BC to well into the late Roman era. Many of the sites have been excavated, and the ex-votos left in antiquity by those who visited the shrines bear an uncanny resemblance to the artefacts on Irish holy trees. In the shrines, clay models of limbs perform the same function as portions of garments, organs and other objects representative of the injured parts – a breast instead of a bra, a ceramic foot instead of a sock. There is no gulf between these shrines of the pagan classical world of the centuries before Christ and the holy trees of Irish Christianity, more than 2,000 years later. Epidaurus, one of the principal shrines to Asclepius, has been described by the classical scholar Betty Radice as 'the Lourdes of the Greek world'.

When I visited the ruined sanctuary of Epidaurus, the toy limbs in the museum struck me as representing some parallel to the folk-wisdom aspects of Irish religious belief. I don't think that I was too far off the mark.

While in Clonmel I stop to look at the Main Guard, a mutilated seventeenth-century courthouse built by the duke of Ormond, whose manor house is in Carrick-on-Suir. As I am studying the building, I encounter Timmy Bourke, self-proclaimed intellectual and patriot. He invites me into the snug of a local hostelry. In the course of conversation, I mention that I am interested in regional dialects and the odd and archaic Norman French, English or Scots usages which survive in different parts of the country.

'English is it? The finest English spoken in Ireland, or anywhere else, for that matter, in the English-speaking world, is spoken in the South Riding of Tipperary. We speak Spenser's English.'

I nod appreciatively, and say that I am sure it is so. I mention the 'slypes' in Kilkenny, a locally-surviving Norman French word for the alleyways of the town. He is not at all interested; Kilkenny, after all, is a separate county. He continues:

'Add to our Spenserian heritage the rich and melodious vocabulary of the high-born Gael and the precise terminology of the Norman squire – *then* you have language. Scholars come from Oxford colleges to study the local speech.'

I did not doubt the Oxford scholars. Perhaps their motivation was other than he imagined. Outside Clonmel, on the Carrick road, I passed a little cottage with a prominently displayed sign: RUBARD PLINTS FOR SALE. Spenser's orthography, perhaps, or Chaucer's?

In Carrick-on-Suir I stay in a former convent, now a cheap hotel. The nuns may have departed, but the whiff of wimples hovers around the dark, pine-panelled corridors and heavy mahogany furniture. On the walls, windowsills and sideboards, relics of the previous regime survive. Gloomy Victorian parlour pictures and heavy religious statuary are everywhere. In a bookcase in the back hall I find the 12 volumes of *The Complete Plumber and Sanitary Engineer*, circa 1911, and imagine Mother Eucaria on her knees under the sink with volume six, trying to release a blockage, her coif entangled in an S-bend.

The glory of Carrick is the Ormond Castle, the duke of Ormond's Elizabethan manor house, which has the only significant interiors of the period to survive in Ireland. Many other fine but gutted Elizabethan houses remain. Like empty tea-chests, they represent absence rather than presence. The young guide does his best to share some inadequately absorbed historical facts with the visitors. This one had opted for a nationalist interpretation of events in Carrick, at variance with the excellent Office of Public Works guidebook to the house. The bilingual Anglo-Norman Ormonds had by the sixteenth century been in Ireland for 400 years. The guide presents them as Englishmen in disguise, aristocratic highway-robbers. I am beginning to be irritated, yet know that if I challenge the guide, he will be embarrassed (I have made this mistake before). The other people on the tour (Irish, English and French) will also be annoyed; they would much prefer the guide's pleasantries to my own more critical observations. I bite my tongue.

The seventeenth-century Gaelic poet Flann MacCraith's description of the manor house suggests an atmosphere of opulence and hospitality:

> Court without grief, the court of lights,
> A court of wax-tapered glitter,
> A palace food-filled, stuccoed, monstered,
> Gabled, sunny, wall-adorned.

The house today is as cold as modern tastes in restoration dictate. Although the gables and the stucco remain, much has to be imagined. Years before, the first time I ever came to Carrick and asked a passer-by for directions, I received a discouraging response. Two women and a child were standing on the pavement in New Street, around the corner from the manor house, which was then neither visible nor signposted. I explained my quest.

'Is it th'oul ruin you are looking for? Tis just down there in them trees.'

The manor house is the most elegant ruin in Ireland – not a ruin at all, in fact. It only needs more oak furniture, tapestries, wax-tapered glitter and firelight to make it again the court of lights.

At the end of the tour, as we inspect the Ormond charters, the guide pauses before the small portrait of an obese Queen Anne which decorates one of the manuscripts. In my eyes he entirely redeems himself by adding: 'She was so fat when she died that her coffin was square in circumference.'

One of the joys of travel in Ireland is people's capacity to speak English with a fine and inventive disregard for conventional rules. The image is perfect and worthy of Sir Boyle Roche, the most bumbling member of Dublin's eighteenth-century parliament. Among Roche's bulls is the wish that he 'would have the two sisters embrace like one brother'. Britain and Ireland are the siblings in question, still pulling each other's pigtails. The Oxford scholars with their notebooks were nowhere in sight.

The contrast between the east and the west coasts of the country could not be more evident than in the hinterland of Carrick-on-Suir. The land is better – some of it is among the finest farmland in the country. With better land comes a greater social stability, less emigration and significantly less dependence on tourism as a focal point of the local economy.

In Galway, Kerry, Mayo and Cork there are as many signs for bed and breakfasts as blackthorns in the hedgerows. If you threw a stone in ancient Ireland you would hit a king; in the west of Ireland today it would smash the plate-glass window of a bed and breakfast: *Ard na Greine, Dun an Rí, Ard Muire, Teach Pio, Naomh Padraig,* and disturbingly, family names reversed, such as *Navillus* (Sullivan) and *Ekruob* (Bourke). Any suggestion that the last-mentioned are the homes of Romanian or Turkish emigrés is misleading. These spiders' webs are laid in every hedgerow of the west to trap the weary passers-by. The bed and breakfasts will swaddle the tourists in nylon sheets, stuff them with cholesterol and send them on their way, satiated and half-blinded.

'Was that place really dreadful? Do the owners not appreciate that seven different styles of wallpaper in the breakfast room and 103 Waterford glass knick-knacks on the sideboard induce premature blindness before midday?'

It would greatly grieve the collective Mrs O'Donnells of the Irish bed-and-breakfast world that the only thing their front rooms truly resemble are fairground trinket-stands. While having my breakfasts, I often contemplated flinging the salt-cellar at one of the glass displays in the hope that I might win a teddy bear. In the south-east, ignored by coachloads of tourists, the damage is slight.

The beautiful green byroads of Counties Kilkenny, Carlow and Waterford have an air of sedate and prosperous well-being. The fine ample fields are surrounded by substantial tree-planting on their borders. The nationwide epidemic of bungalows is less necessary in an area where the housing stock has always been of a better quality than that of the west coast. These differences create an atmosphere which has none of the desolateness of certain present-day images of rural Ireland. Missing also is that sense of desperation induced by communities prostrating and prostituting themselves before the tourist industry.

A drive through the Comeraghs to the south coast passes through countryside as unlike the west as it could be. This is not the Ireland of the Bord Fáilte advertisement, the media image of dramatic sea cliffs or, pints before them, fiddling fiddlers. This territory has a far greater claim to being the 'real Ireland' than all the places which, for economic benefit, have claimed the title.

In Waterford, as I walk down Lady Lane with a friend who is a specialist in eighteenth-century architecture, we pass the St Vincent de Paul Hostel for Men. This is an impressive early-eighteenth-century town house, distinct in style from Dublin's Georgian architecture. Abruptly, my friend disappears; when I notice that he has vanished, I see that he has entered the hostel. I follow.

Inside, a large, gap-toothed 60-year-old man with a truly amazing head of inky-black tousled hair blocks our way. We say that we are interested in the architecture, and the man – the cook – takes us through the rooms of the ground floor. Under the splendour of a baroque ceiling, aged derelicts and young homeless men passively watch a violent boxing match on television with the sound turned off; all are half-stupefied by the intense central heating of the darkened cave. In another even more extravagant room with an elegant bowed Venetian window, a formica-topped table is laden with loaves of white sliced bread and aluminium cutlery which looks as if it has been cast from a World War II aeroplane fuselage. The extraordinary hair smiles benignly over his catering stove as we leave. A slim young man in jeans with an alert and intelligent expression stares at us quizzically in the hallway – he might have liked to discuss the plasterwork.

In November, having drifted up the west coast and then sojourned in south Kerry, I return to Carrick-on-Suir. A cold and silvery mist hangs in the air of the river valley, suspended halfway between the roofs of the town and the hills which overlook it. *Gleann an Óir*, the Glen of Gold, its summer persona, now hides under fields whitened by frost and puddles glazed with ice. At midday the mist has not lifted. The low winter sun is slow to penetrate into the streets of the town, and the crispness of the light makes the outlines of the streets hard and sharp.

Carrick sits with its back to the Suir, its fourteenth-century bridge (for centuries, the only crossing-point on the river above the estuary) linking the main town on the north bank with Carrickbeg, the site of a vanished medieval monastery and now a huddle of houses with two church towers still giving it a medieval look. A newer bridge to the east takes the modern traffic. Carrick is as historic, pretty and well-sited as any town in Ireland. Its features are both typical and unique.

Above the new bridge stands a granite male figure wrapped in a bathrobe, with an enigmatic granite ball at his feet. This is a recently-erected monument to Irish-language pioneer Michael O'Hickey, who, on account of his ardent enthusiasm for the revival of Irish, was ejected from his professorship in Maynooth. He spent six years in Rome, unsuccessfully petitioning the Vatican for redress – Carrick seems to attract such unfulfilled souls. Seán O'Casey dedicated one volume of his autobiography, *Drums Under the Windows*, to O'Hickey, describing him in 1945 as 'forgotten, unhonoured, unsung'. In Carrick he has been remembered.

More recent archaeological strata of the town are clearly revealed by remains on the main street – Victorian lettering in high relief on the upper floors of business premises gives way to painted information on the fascia below. The Grocery Hall becomes the Europa Takeway, the Cloth Hall the Direct Bargain Centre: Factory Prices. John Hearn, Ironmonger, has widened his trade to deal now in Hardwear. Pubs offer the choice of The Comeragh Lounge, The Harp Bar, Just Gerry's and, a rare breed even given the spelling, J. Lawlor. The Tholsel, a medieval remnant capped by an eighteenth-century cupola and weather vane with gilded salmon, stands at the north end of Main Street where it constricts access out of the town. This leads to the rather decrepit Sean Kelly Square, named in honour of the European champion cyclist and local man. In the square are Owen Darmody, Racing Office and, papadums embracing cod fillets, the Taj Mahal Indian Takeaway and Ella's Fish and Chips. P. Kirby, Poulterer, with fine stained-glass hens strutting on the window, has ceased to trade, the shop now a private house.

Carrick's mid-nineteenth-century Catholic church is pure Florentine Romanesque, complete with free-standing campanile – Santa Maria Maggiore on the banks of the Suir. This opulence is relegated to tawdry William Street where it remains unnoticed. Its façade demands a piazza, fountains, street cafés, pigeons in flight, blistering sunlight. All it gets by way of attendant grandeur is Lupita Walsh, Chiropodist. I pause outside Dilly's, which is offering Fancy Gifts, Sweets, Ices and Wreaths, but feel it is far too cold for an ice cream, although the children of the town clearly do not agree.

I have lunch in a restaurant which serves a meal to be found (and apparently loved, although not by myself) in all parts of Ireland. My plate swims with thick chocolate-brown gravy, from which emerge the upper portions of scoops of mashed potato, like the exposed sections of icebergs. A landmass of frog-green boiled cabbage forms an island in the gravy. I probe beneath the surface and locate the meat – lamb or beef, I cannot tell.

Forty per cent of Ireland's population is under 25 years of age. Travelling around the country, one could reasonably come to the conclusion that nine-tenths of the entire population of the island are school-going teenagers. At specific times of day they throng the streets, occupy the pavements, inundate the shops and loudly state their presence, enlivening the torpor of small-town life.

In Carrick the midweek lunchtime blocking of the pavements has begun. The streets are overcome with teenagers in school uniform, chatting, exchanging banter, promenading, appraising each other, exploding in hilarity at the latest school gossip, celebrating the inanities of their teachers. On corners and in shop doorways, the gauche, acned young men vie for the attention of the passing bevies of girls. Each girl has attempted somehow to subjugate the uniformity of the school outfit in order to emphasise some sense of individuality. Shoes seem the principal area for daring. Many wear square-toed, broad-heeled, shiny black shoes like ladies at the court of Charles II. The boys, with a tie under the ear, can hardly compete: an extreme haircut is the best they can muster. The more forward of the youngsters are meeting girlfriend or boyfriend in shop doorways, and walking two by two in sweet oblivion.

These teenagers may well be among the first generations of Irish young people who have more of a future than a past. They embrace the mental freedom to work abroad without regarding leaving Ireland as a receipt for lifetime emigration. They can have the education and confidence to achieve more than their parents could have contemplated. The negative side is that some of them, in Carrick and in other similar towns of high local unemployment, will not be going anywhere, even to work. Suicide among young men is abnormally high in small-town Ireland. More often than not, the tragedy is recorded as 'death by misadventure'. Despair is usually the reason.

At the far end of Main Street I make some purchases in a small grocery shop. As I am paying, the middle-aged woman behind the counter says to me, as though I were Dennis aged four, 'Santy won't be long in coming now, pet.' I repeatedly encounter this form of salutation between adults. The teenagers are far too mature to mention such an archaic figure as Father Christmas. In a little bar where I idled away a rainy hour, a very old man remarked to me, 'I suppose Santy will be coming to you soon.'

I acknowledged the likelihood of a visit. He responded by giving a verse of 'Away in a Manger' in an ancient, windy voice, straight from a wind-up gramophone. The barwoman cut him short by a reminder: 'Santy has a while to wait yet.'

Down by the old bridge on the Suir, three ten-year-olds are fishing, oblivious to the bitingly cold wind which has made their fingers blue. Their neat haircuts and short trousers make them look like 1960s' children, innocent and full of fun. The most cheeky of them nudges his pal and says to me, 'He's a great fisherman, catches loads.'

I inspect the catch laid out in newspaper on the parapet of the quay wall: three plump fish of unknown denomination. I ask what they are; the boy names them. The third time he says it, I still cannot understand him. I ask what he intends to do with the fish.

'Bringem home t'me mam for the dinner.'

He begins to giggle at the banality of my questions. *Anybody* would have known that. Whatever I say, they collapse in laughter, amused that a stranger should talk to them. The river quay in Carrick, now at the back of the town, was originally an area of thriving warehouses when the navigable river was the main communication route to the coast. Now commerce and life have deserted the area, leaving it to ruminating old fishermen contemplating the waterlogged boats moored on the opposite bank, and boys fishing.

Over the period of a year, I have been in Carrick-on-Suir three times. On each occasion I call to the Heritage Centre, located in the former Church of Ireland church, behind the main street. In the graveyard lies Dorothea Herbert, but she may as well have been buried in Haworth for all the personnel of the Heritage Centre know about her. The girls in attendance, bored but probably otherwise among the unemployed, say they have never heard of her, neither knowing nor caring where she might be buried. On my third attempt, in November, I am more successful. A charming and interested young woman – although not from the town – is leading an FAS course for the unemployed. She knows about the writer, and feels that her neglect should be rectified. She makes a few phone calls for me and later that day I am shown the burial plot by a committee member.

A rector's daughter, Dorothea developed a passion for a neighbouring landowner during the period when her father was incumbent at Knockgraffon, a rural parish half-way between Cahir and Cashel on the Dublin road. The young man, John Roe, rejected Dorothea and faithlessly married another. Dorothea entitled her memoirs, written years later, *A Help to Memory, or Retrospections of an Outcast,* by Dorothea Roe. She persisted (to the dismay of her family) in regarding herself as Roe's true wife.

Dorothea now lies without an inscription, not with the bodies but with the memorial stones of Major James Kelly and John Carshore MD, respectable members of the 'Carrick Set'. Either of these gentlemen might, in life, have been a suitable husband. In the tidying-up process which accompanied the establishment of the Heritage Centre, tombstones were moved in such a cavalier manner that any relationship between stone and plot has been lost. The Catholic stones in the foreground of the church remain undisturbed; the Protestant ones were afforded less courtesy.

Dorothea, rejected by her real or imagined lover, seems to have become seriously disturbed. Those of her writings which survived her death in 1829 were not published until a century later. This publication was unsuccessful, and a recent reprint brought this passionate and neglected writer no more recognition. In life and in death the fates have conspired against her.

> Ungratefull John Roe! – How terrible was the moment that joined us! and how terrible were we both to each Other at that black Instant when you Infamously resolved to forsake me and I as desperately Abandon'd Myself to Despair! I swear by the great God of Heaven I think that Hour united us in Bonds that were indissoluble – In an eternal Union sacred and sure – That Bolt of Heaven or Hell struck him a determined Villain but all its Terrors lighted on me and left me as stiffened Corpse – Blasted! – Undone for Ever!
>
> Sure No Woman had ever such strong Claims to any Man's Love as I had to John Roe's for No Woman was ever so wrap'd up in One Man or so much ruin'd by him.
>
> Well might I that Night have cried to my Destroyer, How are thou fallen! Oh Lucifer! Son of the Morning! – No other Idea could be so applicable to his Conduct and Phisiognomy at that decissive Moment.

Nearly 200 years after her death, the sad and unlucky Dorothea Herbert might envy the town's teenage girls. Notwithstanding the petty-minded restrictions of small-town life with still-squinting windows, they have the freedom to love and be loved for which she so desperately yearned. Dorothea Herbert deserves more than to have her grave unmarked, and then violated by the well-intentioned.

Some miles to the north of Carrick, and not far from each other, are the monastic sites of Ahenny and Kilkieran. Between them they contain a remarkable collection of six High Crosses of possibly the eighth or ninth century. Both these beautiful and hallowed spots are under direct threat from grotesque and ill-mannered modern monuments and grave goods.

In 50 years, unless early Christian sites are protected as antiquities, the monuments will be lost among forests of brashness and sentimentality, such as the teddy-bear-shaped brown granite polished tombstone for a dead child. Italian-style monuments complete with large framed photographs of loved ones crowding round unique and vulnerable antiquities are becoming commonplace. The vast majority of antiquity sites could be removed in an afternoon with a bulldozer. The early Christian monuments like High Crosses will within two or three generations be mere curiosities in an ocean of contemptible dross unless action is taken to keep the Irish dead at bay.

Outside Carrick on the Waterford road is the Sean Kelly Sports Centre, a multi-gabled facility of swimming pools and fitness studios. Here, the local boy made good has returned to share both his fame and his dedication to physical achievement with his community. From the foyer the main pool is visible. Lithe and eager toddlers are dabbling in the water. Around the entrance the schoolgirls from the street have been transformed into Hans Christian Andersen's little mermaid from Copenhagen harbour, their long, wet hair draped over their shoulders, their bodies as gracefully disposed as any mermaid's.

Buildings like this hold the key to unlocking one of the nation's ills: confronting the physical body and banishing the ingrained Victorian prudery which has been such a destructive inheritance. Sexual prudery became so much an integral part of Irish nineteenth-century Christianity of all denominations that it acquired the status of a central tenet of faith, as though it were an eleventh commandment: 'Thou shalt not have a physical body.' This inheritance, and the whole baggage of accompanying prurience, has made personal relations between the sexes so difficult. As much as political unrest, the difficulty of the male orientation of a great deal of Irish life needs to be abolished if the island's potential is ever to be achieved.

Instead of remaining in the town, I am now staying at a restored farmhouse some miles outside Carrick-on-Suir, not far from Ahenny. A friend had remarked earlier in the year, 'Please do not write about going around Ireland in the rain; it's just too depressing.' He was right, yet rain in Ireland is hard to avoid or ignore.

The weather rapidly deteriorates, becoming extremely cold, with storms of searing iciness. I had intended to walk a portion of the South Leinster Way which runs north-east from Carrick towards County Wicklow. However, I am confined indoors by a lack of enthusiasm to accompany

Captain Oates on his heroic journey. Snow covers the Comeraghs and Sliabh na mBan, the roads become hazardous and mud in the fields is as hard as steel. I remain indoors and work on the set of woodcuts for this book.

Throughout the year, I carried with me sketchpads in which I drew, in a not very consistent manner, whatever seemed appropriate at the moment: ideas, landscapes, incidents, anything which was either pictorial in its own right or which might serve as an *aide-mémoire* to things seen or experienced.

In a small case I have a collection of woodblocks and a set of woodcarving chisels. This is all the equipment one requires in order to work in the oldest known form of printmaking, a method of creating images which has remained unchanged since the fourteenth century. While branches are being torn off trees and blown across the fields by the Arctic winds, I cut and chisel on the small woodblocks, extracting material from my sketchpads to fit individual chapters. In Donegal I had been conscious of the open sky, in Derry and south Armagh political tension, in south Kerry the power of the sea, in Dublin literary legends and poverty; each place has its own particular character and importance.

How do you refine down so many images to a few little cuts in the surface of a block of wood? It is a question of attempting to define some essence, to use solid and void, black and white to suggest colour and form, place and mood. Representing any aspect of life in black and white is not an attempt to present it in such terms. Rather, it is an effort to distil some central idea in a number of small images, all derived from a wealth of possibilities, as well as a rich range of colours.

The harshness of the woodcut derives its language from the plane of memory and the silence of dreams. Black, the colour of night and jet and the interior of caves, contrasts with the whiteness of paper and light. In the dream Portavogie merges with Sliabh na mBan, Swanlinbar with Errigal; Orange marchers elide into Bolus Head, and the gannets of the Little Skellig rise around the topers of the Long Valley. A stroke of the woodcutter's chisel can create or annihilate. This is where the worlds of the artist and the bomber, the musician and the politician meet, united by a common impulse and opportunity – to create or to destroy.

AFTERWORD

Early in December, on a bitterly cold and clear Sunday afternoon, Allegra and I attend a race meeting at Fairyhouse in north County Dublin. This is a man's world. While there certainly are women present, particularly at the more moneyed end of the business in the form of trainers and owners, the punters are predominantly men, all keen followers of the turf. Passionately knowledgeable on form and pedigree, they are shrewd and gullible by turns, loyal to a fault when a favourite is concerned, and always ready to put their money where their heart is. Race meetings are an aspect of life that, given a change of clothing, might be taking place any time in the past. Touts and tick-tack men, jockeys and punters, owners, trainers, gamblers and men in the know all jostle together in a timeless involvement with horses.

Fairyhouse is a place for connoisseurs of great outdoor complexions: there are men with faces the colour of Burgundy, port, old brick and Tuscan red; men who look like they might have been with Mao Tse-tung on the 'Long March', seven years before the mast, with Shackleton to Antarctica.

Hats and coats range from the style of the highwayman to that of the belted earl.

Between races, the stands empty and there is a rush towards the parade ring. A large number of the crowd career past the jockeys leading their mounts among admiring intimates, and head for the refreshment stand. Here a beef company, mindful of the low status of red meat following repeated scandals in the trade, has spent the period during races charcoal-grilling hamburgers. Even the most fastidious are tempted: hot and savoury-smelling food restores life to perished limbs. Nearby, a small crowd of seedy-looking individuals clusters around a red-hot brazier, warming blue hands. They are straight from Hogarth's *Four Times of Day* engravings, miscreants of Covent Garden, inhabitants of another world.

In the third race, Danoli is the firm favourite. Churlishly, the odds suggest that Doran's Pride, with Richard Dunwoody in the saddle, is tipped to win. Anticipation mounts before the off. The stands are humming with excitement and tension. Suddenly, a vast and deep-throated 'Aaaaaaaaaahhhhhhhhh' goes up from the crowd, a spontaneous gasp of anguish and disbelief. Danoli, the bravest of horses, has fallen at the first fence, again sinking hopes all over the country. Defeat falls like a cold shower on Fairyhouse, drenching Carlow and sending cold gusts across the North Riding of Tipperary, distorting Spenser's English into the unprintable.

Periodically during the year, as I pass through Dublin, I pause on O'Connell Bridge and gaze over the parapet in order to see how the millennium clock is managing its countdown towards the end of days. The bridge, whether hectically thronged by day or deserted at night, always appears to have a few disconsolate individuals staring down into the murky waters, seeking something. They are not at all sure what they should be looking for, or if in fact there is anything there. I had shiveringly attended the launching of the clock in mid-March, doubtful of its relevance and not enamoured of its appearance. The passing of multitudes of seconds has not improved matters. Neither Leopold nor Molly but algal bloom in the river waters has caused what had originally been indistinct to become invisible.

Dubliners, always eager to puncture savagely what they regard as the pretensions of others, dubbed the timepiece, with more venom than accuracy, 'The Chime in the Slime', a title under which a work of much greater genius might have succumbed. It did little to enhance the dignity of the grandiosely-named Countdown Millennium 2000 Timer. In August, the millennium clock was raised from beneath the waters to facilitate the annual

Liffey Swim. In December, Dublin Corporation announced that the clock would not be returned to the river. No doubt there are simpler methods of counting the seconds towards the year 2001, the advent of which is inexorable, timepiece or no. A man on the bridge ominously observed: 'The tock is clicking.'

In his memorial poem written after the death of W.B. Yeats, W.H. Auden wrote, 'Now Ireland has her madness and her weather still.' I can vouch for the continued and all-embracing presence of both.

North of the border the real millennium timepiece continues its tick-tocking towards a doomsday scenario, without any prospect of timely immersion in the cooling waters of the Lagan or the Foyle. Sectarian bigotry is as vigorous in the winter as it had been in the spring. The confrontations of the marching season began the long slide through boycotts, intimidation and rioting towards the 'Bosniasation' of the region, violence being answered by reciprocal behaviour.

> Intellectual disgrace
> Stares from every human face,
> And the seas of pity lie
> Locked and frozen in each eye.

Sledge-hammers for Peace, in a surge of creative activity, has held a year-long festival of their art form, smashing the limbs of countless young men and women, even teenagers, so that Ireland might be united, or, if you prefer, Ulster might remain British. Trinity College's Douglas Hyde Gallery may yet, to critical acclaim, mount an exhibition of the X-rays.

As I return from a foray into Christmas shopping on Nassau Street, my arms laden with packages, I walk over the rain-washed ghost of a traveller child-artist's drawing of Santa Claus, made visible on the pavement by the light streaming from gaily decorated shop windows. Further along, in the comparative darkness of Clare Street, a pale hand reaches out from the shadowy surrounds of a telephone kiosk. Crouched in the wet and dark is a traveller woman with a sleeping infant in her arms.

'Givus some change, sir, and a happy Christmas to you, and may you and your childer have health and good luck.'

Hard-hearted, I walk on.

In the gathering dusk of a winter's evening, with crowds thronging the pavements and the street glutted with traffic, I cycle in heavy rain from the city centre, home towards Ballsbridge. In a wash of water a double-decker bus speeds·past me, too close for comfort. In the slipstream my bicycle wobbles into a spin, finally falling into the street, myself and my packages strewn in the wet. As though cast for a slapstick comedy, four kilted and soaked Scotsmen, in Dublin for some unknown purpose, raise me from the tarmac. They restore my packages and bicycle to my hands.

'Are y'injured? That wee bus could have near killed you.'

Never has the diminutive been less appropriately used. I cycle on, but the downpour increases. In desperation I abandon the bicycle and shelter in a small grocery shop. A crowd has gathered between the counter and the shelves of produce, glad to escape from the punishing rain. A lively discussion is taking place among the drenched shoppers, concerning the prospect of terrorist atrocities in Dublin at Christmas; they must be in an apocalyptic mood, induced by the floodwaters outside, or by paying too much attention to television sages.

The shop owner, arms folded in a magisterial manner on her apron, leans across her counter and pronounces upon each topic mentioned. She is a big woman, used to commanding her small empire. She monitors the ensuing conversation, commenting with authority on the probable behaviour of the private armies of the North. She seems to regard the leaders of this and an adjoining island as recalcitrant children who, periodically, need to be confined to their bedrooms. She is firm in denouncing everybody mentioned in the conversation: politicians, assassins, peace workers – all must be cast aside.

'Women are the answer. Only when the women have taken over the leadership will anything be solved. I tell you this now and it's a true fact. This whole fecking island, and all the fecking people in it, they just have to wait to be born. You can't hurry something like that.'

Tell it not in Gath, publish it not in the streets of Askelon; lest the daughters of the Philistines rejoice, lest the daughters of the uncircumcised triumph.